SIGN, IMAGE AND SYMBOL

VISION + VALUE SERIES

SIGN
IMAGE
SYMBOL

EDITED BY GYORGY KEPES

George Braziller, New York

A Theory of Pictorial Perception by James J. Gibson is reprinted
from AUDIO-VISUAL COMMUNICATION REVIEW, I:1, Winter, 1954.

The Painter's Handwriting by J. P. Hodin is reprinted from
THE JOURNAL OF AESTHETICS & ART CRITICISM, VII:3, March, 1949.

CONTENTS

LAWRENCE K. FRANK

THE WORLD AS A COMMUNICATION NETWORK

The world, as Norbert Wiener once remarked, may be viewed as a myriad of To Whom It May Concern messages. The significance of this statement becomes apparent when we recognize that everything that exists and happens in the world, every object and event, every plant and animal organism, almost continuously emits its characteristic identifying signal. Thus, the world resounds with these many diverse messages, the cosmic noise, generated by the energy transformation and transmission from each existent and event.

While every thing and event contributes to this cosmic noise, each emits its identifying message and also has a highly selective receptivity for only a selection of these multiple messages, while indifferent or insensitive to all others.

Through evolution, each organism has developed a concern for those messages which are essential to its living functions and survival as a species, while ignoring what is not biologically relevant or useful. Accordingly, in any one geographical area, many different species, bacteria in the soil, worms, insects, fish, reptiles, birds, amphibians, and the array of mammals, carry on their life careers, selectively receiving and responding to the signals that are of concern to each species, while unaware of the many other messages that are being concurrently transmitted.

These basic biological signals are received, filtered, and amplified or reduced by the sensory apparatus of each species, selecting from the spectrum of messages to which it is exposed, what it has learned, through evolutionary development, to expect and to utilize for guiding its behavior and organic functioning. It is as if each species, even when exposed to other species, sometimes in lethal conflict, lives as if in a separate world of its own—the only world it is aware of and with which it can cope, through the exercise of its inherited capacities and what it may learn from experience. The truly amazing sensory capacities of different species enables each to maintain this selective awareness and utilize that range of signals which are essential for its survival, many of which are not recognized by other species and some of which far exceed the limited sensory abilities of man. These different sensory capacities have been well described in the recent book, *The Senses of Animals and Men*, by Lorus and Margery Milne.[1]

Relying upon these inborn capacities, often sharpened by learning, to alert them to the world with its varied opportunities and also its dangers, each species that has survived the rigorous testing of "natural selection" lives and reproduces its kind, carrying on the endless succession of generations until it is wiped out, often by man.

But organisms are not limited to these basic biological signals to which they respond with their inherited capacities. Even the lower organisms, like worms, can and do learn to recognize not only these basic signals, but also other signals which initially are not biologically evocative but may become operational when they have been experienced concomitantly with biologically active signals. These concomitants of biological signals, which may be initially ignored by the organism, but can be recognized as significant, operate as *signs* when, as Pavlov showed, a biological signal such as food is presented along with another signal, the sound of a bell; after a number of such combined presentations, the bell alone evoked the response of salivation which had previously been limited to the biological signal of food. Thus, the bell became a *sign* to alert the dog and to stimulate its physiological response in preparation for eating.

1

Conditioning, as it is called, may take place naturally in an organism's normal environment as it learns to recognize as signs those signal messages which occur concomitantly, or just preceding or following the appearance of a biological signal. Becoming responsive to these surrogate signals or signs orients and prepares the organism for seeking food or a mate or the approach of an enemy, indeed, for a variety of activities which are instrumental or preparatory to its normal life. The many experiments on animals compelled to run through mazes, to open puzzle boxes, and to respond to various signs have shown that most organisms have latent potentialities for behavior not ordinarily exhibited in their normal life zone.

More recently animals have been conditioned to exhibit patterned actions by being rewarded or reinforced when they perform the required action in response to selected signals, as in operant conditioning. By this conditioning an animal may learn a sequence of motor activities that is goal-directed or purposefully oriented, in the sense that it learns to perform the patterned activities which an experimenter has set as a task to be achieved. Here the selected signals become signs by the intervention of the experimenter who selectively evokes the behavior he reinforces and concomitantly eliminates the nonsequential actions, thereby focusing the animal's sequential behavior in a controlled experimental situation. The human voice may be learned as a sign indicating what an organism is being ordered to do or not to do.

Obviously this capacity for learning to recognize signs as precursors of biological situations is of great advantage to organisms, enabling them to devise strategies for exhibiting some degree of flexibility for purposive behavior and also for play.

This term, "sign," may be confusing because it has long been used for advertisements and other displays intended to attract the attention of individuals and also as travel indicators on roads. These advertising displays are not signs according to this classification but are publicly displayed symbols using written symbols, the meaning of which is discovered, not by individual learning as in the case of biologically derived signs, but through instruction by more experienced persons who teach individuals to recognize and respond according to the symbolic meanings that have been defined and accepted by people generally.

Thus, red, green, and yellow lights are signals which have become symbols for regulating traffic with a precise meaning of "stop," "go," and "slow down"; when used on roads they have been so established and legally sanctioned in our society, although these same colored lights may have other meanings in other contexts, as, for example, on boats. Moreover, arrows pointing vertically up in road signs are symbols, since the observer must recognize their meaning as symbols and respond with the appropriate behavior of continuing straight ahead horizontally, not vertically, as the arrow actually points.

Man has a wide but limited range of signal recognition, and he can and does learn to recognize a variety of signs for orienting himself to the world by those signs that have become not only substitutes for biological signals, but precursors of many events and situations by which he can deal purposively. His existence and functioning as an organism depends upon recognition and response not only to biological signals, but also to this wide array of signs, which he learns to perceive and interpret. To use a contemporary expression, man learns to recognize and to utilize signs as "feedbacks" for orienting and directing much of his patterned conduct, evoking these signs for his guidance.

But, man, with his large brain and capacity for speech, has been able to achieve what no other organism has found possible, namely: to create symbols which he perceives as patterns or configurations of signals in nature and so has identified and named or labeled them. Man has developed the unique capacity for "information processing," as it is now called, whereby the input of signals is transformed into symbols and interpreted as meaningful messages. Equally important, he has also fabricated designs, painted, articulated combinations and permutations of visual, auditory, and tactile signals as symbols which he invests with meanings to which he responds with purposeful goal-seeking conduct.

There is an enormous literature dealing with symbols, and the word "symbol" has been used with many different meanings and in different contexts. Over the centuries there has been prolonged and intensive controversy over symbols, especially by those who have reified symbols, attributing to them a reality superior to the actual world of our sensory awareness. More recently, the role and functioning of symbols have been examined and illuminated by Alfred North Whitehead,[2] by Ernst Cassirer,[3] and by Suzanne Langer[4] who, along with Cassirer, has asserted that the urgent problems of philosophy are primarily those of symbol use and recognition. Earlier, Hans Vaihinger, a German philosopher, proposed recognition of the "Als ob" or "As if" world in which human living takes place.

The terms "signals" and "signs," like the word "symbol," have been used by different writers with different meanings. Some writers limit their discussion to signals and signs, others to signs and symbols, so that there is no established uniform usage for these terms.

In his lecture on symbolism, Alfred North Whitehead asserted a distinction between "pure instinctive action, reflex action and symbolically conditioned action," thereby recognizing three kinds of responses to messages, such as signals, signs, and symbols.

Further support for a threefold classification of messages as signals, signs, and symbols is found in the words of Cassirer:

> Symbols—in the proper sense of this term—cannot be reduced to mere signs. Signals and symbols belong to two different universes of discourse: a signal is a part of the physical world of being; a symbol is a part of the human world of meaning. Signals are operators; symbols are designators.[5]

Arthur F. Bentley accepted three kinds of messages, which he described in his paper, "Kennetic Inquiry":

> Within the range of sign, the word *signal* was chosen to name the underlying sensori-perceptive level; the word *designation* for the next higher evolutionary level, namely that of linguistic sign operation; and the word *symboling* for a still higher range in the evolutionary sense. . .
>
> The word signal was adapted for the lowest stratum of behaviors largely because of Pavlov's increasing employment of it as his skill and breadth of vision increased. . .
>
> The word designation is used as the name for the next higher level of behavior . . . designations are subdivided into cue, characterization, and specifications as stages in evolutionary growths. . .

Symbolings evolve out of designatings and operate to increase the efficiency of signalings . . . the surviving logics of their past and their reconstructions of today, including most of symbolic logic, still operate under a confusion of symbolings with designatings, and with signaling as well.[6]

Because of these many confusions and the often conflicting definition of symbols, it may be permissible, therefore, to use these three terms as identifying different kinds of messages from, and responses to, the world. Thus we find the basic signals emitted by whatever exists or occurs embracing the wide range of what we call physical, chemical, and biological messages and also varied radiations and vibrations to which all organisms are exposed. To these we must then add the many different signs which have been learned from experience and have become signifiers or designators. Finally, we must recognize the almost unlimited array of man-made symbols, emphasizing that symbols are human creations by which man has established and maintained his varied cultural worlds, transforming the geographical and biological world of signals and signs into a world of meanings and values which he himself has imposed or projected upon the world and thereby has been able to create and maintain a human way of living. Symbols, of which there are many varieties to be described later, are genuinely human creations that never existed in the world before men invented them, like tools which man invented for manipulating materials so that they could be used as instruments for specific purposes.

The absence of values in nature has been deplored by theologians, humanists, and poets, who fail to realize that the absence of values has made it possible for man to create and continually revise and refine the symbolic goal values by which he has advanced his humanity. If nature had built-in unchanging values, like its basic processes, man would have been restricted to the elementary and archaic patterns of organic existence.

Thus a value-free nature has not only permitted but has fostered the creation of symbols for imputing meanings and values and fostering sensibilities for the many different cultural worlds which man has established. Likewise, a value-free nature, of almost infinite potentialities, awaiting evocation by man, has made possible human choices and decisions, purposive goal-seeking, striving toward that which the human imagination has symbolized. Man's vision and his values testify both to the plasticity of nature and the creativity of man as exhibited in his varied symbol systems, his diverse social orders, and in his idiosyncratic personalities.

What took place ages ago and probably can never be definitely known, but may be inferred, is that, at some time in man's human career, he began to create symbols for communicating with the world and the larger universe, with other human beings and with himself, according to his beliefs and feelings about and toward those foci of his concerns. These early communications were probably nonverbal, using a variety of nonverbal messages such as chants, dances, change in gait or stance, postures, including bowing and kneeling and other forms of obeisance, gestures of arms and hands, facial expressions, and varied tones of voice (which apparently gave rise later to articulated language). These were used in the early rituals and ceremonies, the choral dances and dramatic performances by which a people attempted to communicate, to propitiate and to invoke favors or protection and, at the same time, to exhibit their group solidarity.

4

Early in this development each of the different human groups created a variety of symbols, more especially the linguistic symbols of language, for transforming the world around them into a symbolic cultural world of meanings and of patterned conduct for group living.

When we examine how signals, signs, and symbols operate and how they have been variously used, sometimes singly, and sometimes in combinations, we find that they are often subject to confusion and conflicts because the human being was not limited by inheritance to a single mode of reception and response to biological messages as in other organisms.

As noted earlier, every organism, including man, is aware of and responsive to some biological signals. Thus, most organisms, with different degrees of sensitivity, are aware of light, of sound, of touch, of odors, and of tastes, and respond to these messages, either by functioning, or grossly as over-all reactions, or as stimuli for specific overt behavior. For example, most organisms orient themselves by light and sound, although some are blind or have no eyes, and some apparently have no ears. Those with eyes and ears scan the world, reacting to changes in light intensity by which they may perceive the form and pattern of what they see and also to changes in sound, especially loud noise, as in the startle reaction.

All organisms are responsive in varying degrees to tactile messages, relying upon feelers and tactile probing of objects and situations to evoke signals for identifying them as safe, useful, or to be avoided; many seem to require some close contacts, at least when young, and they may communicate with each other by touching or tactile messages.[7] Some of the so-called lower organisms exhibit what are called tropisms; their behavior is governed by changing intensity of light, or temperature, or by direct contact with substances or objects of different texture or temperature.

Many organisms rely upon odors to guide their behavior, and they sniff the air for olfactory signals of food and especially for mating. Most organisms, likewise, rely upon taste to orient their eating and other functioning such as maternal licking of cubs, kittens, foals, and calves. Humans are also oriented by odors and tastes which they may train and cultivate to enhance the enjoyment of living.

The sensory apparatus serves to collect a variety of biological signals by which organisms are oriented and to which they respond in characteristic inherited patterns of functioning and behavior.

In addition to these sensory signals, however, organisms are also guided by a variety of non-sensory signals, such as those by which they resist gravity and maintain their postural balance through the delicate internal "gyroscope" of the inner ear. They also seem to have what has been called a body sense, or a capacity to recognize the position of their limbs and to respond to various kinds of pressures or tensions of so-called kinesthetic stimuli. Moreover, organisms also are responsive, often without awareness, to the changing pressure of the air, also to heat and to cold, to pain, and to a wide range of radiations, both natural emanations and man-made radiations. Thus we can say that organisms are continually exposed to a wide spectrum of signals, only some of which they are aware of but to all of which they are responsive physiologically, either by overt behavior, or by some alteration in attention. Also, we should recognize that some of these various biological signals are satisfying, soothing, as we say, pleasurable, and are sought by organisms, including humans, while others of these signals are, if possible, avoided or repelled, through flight, bodily coverings, shelters, and the like.

All organic behavior may be said to be predetermined in the sense that the evolutionary development of each organism has given it a susceptibility to various kinds of signals with an inherited pattern of functioning and response. But, the actual behavior and functioning of an individual organism at any one time is not determinate, since what it will be aware of and how it will respond is governed largely by its physiological state at that time and by the context in which the signals are met. For example, the most enticing food will not evoke a response from a fully fed organism and, except for the *human* female, female organisms seek and accept copulation only when they are in heat, ovulating and ready to be impregnated.

However numerous, intense, and compelling are these external signals, organisms are also engaged in continual internal communications: each cell, tissue, liquid, and organ system emits its characteristic signals that are transmitted to adjacent components within the organism or are communicated through the nervous system, the blood, the lymph, and other channels for transmission of messages to other locations in the body, or for elimination as breath, urine, feces, sweat, and heat.

As individual organisms have a special concern for those messages upon which they are dependent, so each component of an organism also has a concern for those internal signals upon which it depends for its functional operations. Likewise, each emits its characteristic signals to other components, sometimes as a response to an incoming message, but also at different times to evoke a response it requires from another component in order to fully function in its ever changing cycle of operations. Some of these internal messages, physiological signals such as hunger, thirst, pain, pressure in the rectum, bladder, or the stomach, are recognized and interpreted by the individual as indications of disease or of urgent need for action.

It is difficult to grasp the immense significance of these varied organic communications: some from the geographical world of nature, especially from other organisms, and including the intakes of food and liquid and air; and also the varied and highly specific messages that are continually being sent and received within an organism, governed to a considerable extent by the messages from outside, but which may also be selectively accepted depending upon the organism's ever changing physiological states. Here we need a larger conception of communication than that given by the formula of stimulus and response, or of sensations, or Information Theory. It is indeed remarkable how these varied external and internal signals operate, usually without confusion or conflict, as they are mingled, amplified, buffered, and reduced, and sometimes filtered and reinforced,[8] as when a nervous signal and a hormone or endocrine signal together alter and energize an organism, as in emotional reactions and in sexual functioning.

No less significant is the variety of signs which become established as substitutes or precursors of biological signals. Since there are innumerable signals being sent at one time, almost any concomitant signal may become the sign for a biological signal and once learned it will evoke, from the organism thus conditioned, preparatory or appetitive behavior. This was repeatedly demonstrated by Pavlov's dogs and by what was a once familiar sight, when a horse shied whenever he came to the place where he had once been startled, recognizing the signs exhibited by that location as occasion for again reacting as he did when originally startled by a biological signal. Frequently man has accepted some concomitant signal as a sign of a desired or feared event, only later discovering that it was not a reliable indicator, as witnessed by many surviving superstitions.

A world of relevant biological signals and of learned signs is a world in which organic existence and survival are possible for many species over long periods of time, interrupted by large-scale environmental alterations as shown by the successive geological periods that marked the end of some species and gave rise to new species or at least provided more favorable circumstances for the evolution and further development of certain species.

But organic existence governed by signals and signs, however biologically fruitful, was not adequate for the human species which created a human way of living by transforming the geographical natural world into a symbolic world. The gifted members of each culture—prophets, poets, dramatists, and artists—created the patterns for perceiving and interpreting the world, created the linguistic and other symbols by which meanings were imputed to or projected into the world. Thereby the world became meaningful and subject to evaluation and purposeful goal-seeking conduct, as distinguished from the naïve, impulsive behavior and direct biological responses exhibited by other organisms.

Symbolic performance arises when, beginning in early childhood, the individual is inducted into the use of symbols; he learns to recognize the human voice and language symbols and to project meanings into those verbal symbols as defined by more experienced persons; he learns to speak and to use language to communicate the meanings which he himself has imputed to these verbally labeled persons, objects, and events. Thus the child establishes this circular, reflexive transactional relation for the use of verbal and other symbols by which his conduct is increasingly oriented, if not directed, and by which he develops the process of human *knowing* and the exercise of what we call reason and intelligence as essentially symbolic operations.

While the human child receives varied biological signals and experiences many internal physiological messages, his orientation and his conduct are governed by what he learns to recognize as a symbolic meaning of those signals. One of the primary tasks of childhood is to recognize and identify the symbols, especially the verbal symbols, and then to respond to them in terms of their meaning as interpreted and expected by more experienced individuals. This is often a very difficult lesson to learn because it requires the child to disregard, or to repress, his naïve response to a biological signal or a physiological impulse, and to act instead according to group-defined symbolic meanings of these signals and impulses in the patterned conduct expected of each member of his cultural group. It is, therefore, not unwarranted to say that a child must learn to transform the world of actual things and events, of signals and signs, into a symbolic world of meanings and purposive striving in accordance with the symbolic patterns which have been devised to make human living more orderly and goal-seeking. The current focus on cognitive processes is concerned with symbolic learning and responses by linguistic symbols, especially written symbols, although many of these studies fail to recognize them as symbolic operations.

Only those who have learned to recognize and interpret the meanings of symbols can and do respond to them according to the requirements and expectations of their group. Children who are handicapped and unable to see or hear, and children whose learning has been stunted or distorted, as

7

in autistic and schizophrenic children, may be unable to master these subtle processes of symbol learning and use. But a more familiar example of the necessity for indoctrination in the use of symbols is shown by the perplexity and often bewilderment of a visitor to another cultural group where the language, both spoken and written, and the graphic and plastic symbols, are strange and unknown and hence he is unable to communicate, to orient himself, or to perform what is expected in the varied life situations he encounters.

This symbolic cultural world arises and is perpetuated in and through the individuals who constitute the cultural group and use their familiar culturally derived symbols for maintaining their social order and for patterning their behavior into the required conduct and relationships. The written records and other graphic symbols, the monuments and buildings, all the artifacts by which symbolic meanings are maintained through time, are dependent upon human observers and interpreters for their operation as symbols. All over the world people have left symbols which cannot be deciphered or interpreted because there are no living persons to provide the meaning for those symbols when they were in use.[9]

Symbols, as here interpreted, are not to be considered as surrogates because surrogates have the power and capacity of agents that can operate in place of and with the authority of that for which they are surrogates or substitutes. Symbols do not, and cannot, operate as such, because the symbol has no power and becomes meaningful and evokes human responses when, and only when, a perceiver of that symbol projects meaning into it and responds to it in terms of the meaning which he has learned as appropriate for that symbol.

While some symbols, such as glyphs and other graphic symbols, may appear as visual designs, symbols should be distinguished from the images which ordinarily serve as visual replicas, judged by their verisimilitude and carrying little or no meaning. Unlike images, symbols need have no resemblance to that which they symbolize since their meaning is derived from what the observer imputes to them, and only occasionally from their physical properties or likeness to what is symbolized.

Symbols, it must be emphasized, cannot and do not alter the world, but operate in and through the human actors who perceptually have learned to transform the world according to the meanings of the symbols by which they pattern their perceptions of the world and evaluate its possibilities. By symbolizing the world, man acts like a Maxwellian demon, selectively establishing and maintaining a more or less orderly, meaningful world as he imaginatively conceives and perceives it, amid the seemingly random flux of events.

These distinctions may help to resolve some of the widespread confusion about the meaning of the term "symbol," which is sometimes used for any kind of visual or auditory image, especially of the fantasy or hallucinations of individuals and also to indicate the highly idiosyncratic visual and auditory images encountered by those who study these individuals and privately developed images and representations that are often difficult to interpret. The word "symbol," in this discussion, refers to those group-recognized and commonly used symbols which have been established and defined by tradition or may be newly created and then generally accepted for this process of transforming the world —the actual biological, physical, chemical environment—into a meaningful universe for human living.

8

Symbols of all kinds may be highly ambiguous because each individual has learned to recognize and to use these symbols in his own idiomatic way, imputing meanings and coloring these symbols with feelings and sometimes with strong emotional reactions which may warp and distort them and seriously interfere with communication, as in the use of verbal and written symbols. This ambiguity as well as the highly diversified use of symbols have been increased by the entrance into one cultural group of individuals deriving from another ethnic-cultural group, who may learn to use the language of their adopted country and to interpret its varied symbols sufficiently to participate in the group life, but who in turn infuse these symbols with meanings and feelings that may vary widely from the originally established patterns for the use of these symbols.

Another source of confusion over symbolic recognition and use comes from the multiplicity of communication to which we are now exposed. In addition to the many person-to-person confrontations involving individuals of many different kinds, backgrounds, skills, and offices, we are increasingly receiving replicas and reconstructed images and synthetic representations of speech and actual persons and events. Thus we are daily exposed to the synthetic communications coming to us by telephone, radio, TV, phonographs and tape recorders, moving pictures, and the flood of pictures and cartoons in newspapers and magazines, to which we may respond as to actual events and persons. Much as symbols have superseded actuality for human living, so these images and replicas are likewise becoming the major focus of visual and auditory perception as we increasingly accept them and find them often equal, if not superior, to experience of actual persons and events, especially if artistically contrived and sometimes deliberately distorted.

For centuries we have been concerned with symbolic expressions, especially language, and have spoken of many of the linguistic symbols as knowledge, viewed as some kind of intangible substance that can be transmitted, stored, and acquired. Some years ago John Dewey and Arthur F. Bentley[10] proposed that we give up this highly improbable conception of knowledge which has given rise to prolonged controversy and widespread confusion. To replace the concept of knowledge, they proposed that we think and speak of *knowing* as an active cognitive relation of the knower to the known or the to be known. This reflects the contemporary shift in thinking from reliance upon nouns and abstractions to the use of verbs and the concept of processes, especially the acceptance of a transactional process as the crux of *knowing*, viewed as essentially a symbolic process.

Knowing may be seen as essentially the recognition, interpretation, and response to the symbols by which the world is identified and made meaningful and understandable in terms of the basic concepts and assumptions of each culture. Knowing is therefore an active transactional process established by a knower with the known or the to be known. Much of what we consider as evidence of intelligence is the capacity for symbol recognition and response, although many nonsymbolic performances may be highly intelligent and exceedingly skillful.

Thus we may say that the child begins, through the use of language symbols, to perceive the world and to interpret whatever he experiences in terms of the linguistic symbols by which he names, labels, and identifies and understands things and events, animals and persons, imputing to them their symbolic meanings and responding to the meanings which he himself has projected into them.

Thereby he enters into a cognitive, knowing relationship as a circular reciprocal process, a transaction whereby the knower establishes, from what he perceives and symbolizes, the meanings which it has for him. Therefore, knowing, or more precisely, cognitive experience, operates through symbols and is limited to symbolic use and recognition. Thus a cognitive relation to the world is distinguished from the many other relatings in which biological signals and signs evoke from the individual a variety of responses—aesthetic, motor, physiological, and emotional. Recent studies are showing that there are different cognitive styles or modes of knowing: thus some individuals rely chiefly upon visual recognition, others upon auditory recognition, and some upon actual handling and responding kinesthetically to the world. Accordingly, each child, while using all three, may be able to learn more effectively by his exercise of his individual cognitive style or mode of learning.

The conception of a knowing process has the great advantage of recognizing that the actual world of nature may be symbolized and known in many different ways. This is clearly exhibited in the history of Western European culture, with its successive climates of opinion, each with new and sometimes radical revisions of its basic conceptions and established symbols which have brought cumulative alterations in the interpretation of events. This diversity of symbolizations is also shown by the many different cultural groups all over the world, and especially by the highly idiosyncratic personalities, each of whom develops his own way of knowing the symbolic world and of dealing with what he individually recognizes and interprets as meaningful.

The foregoing does not imply any vitalistic or dualistic assumptions. Cognitive experience, the entering into a knowing relation with the world through the use of symbols, is to be seen as the uniquely human way of dealing with the actual world of signals to which all organisms are selectively responsive. But man has imaginatively invested these signals with the meanings which each cultural group has established for ordering and interpreting the flux of experience and giving meaning and significance to human living.

By this knowing, symbolic process, each group of people has created an "As if" world of its own, transforming the actual world into a "virtual world," as Suzanne Langer has described works of art, which do not represent actuality but present a humanly created set of images or symbols.[11] Just because these symbolic worlds are human creations which can persist only insofar as members of a cultured group recognize and use these common symbols and perform what those symbols require, almost all groups are greatly concerned with the early indoctrination of their children into their symbolic worlds, and have sometimes established rigid constraints upon deviations and penalties for neglect of the prescribed patterns of thinking, speaking, and acting. Individuals in each culture, if they are to communicate and enter into various activities and relations with others, find it not only necessary to utilize the group-sanctioned symbol systems, but they may also find themselves, as personalities, confused, distracted, and distorted when their culturally patterned use of symbols and their expectations of responses and conduct of others are not realized.

While linguistic symbols are the major mode of human communication, either through spoken or written speech, there are many other kinds of symbols. Thus every culture has historic symbols, symbolic narratives such as myths and legends about its past; since human living is governed primarily by memory and expectations, these are expressed in terms of a variety of beliefs and theories and interpretations, or explanations of what has or is happening or about to occur, as formulated linguistically. Every culture also has a variety of graphic and plastic symbols as shown by its arts and by its varied designs, maps, and charts, and by modern plans and blueprints. It also has symbols that are represented both graphically and plastically such as the Christian cross, the Jewish star, the Communist hammer and sickle, the Nazi swastika, and the many other symbols into which meanings are invested. In the modern world of science and technology there is an immense variety of linguistic symbols and also many graphic symbols for physical, chemical, and biological communication, plus the symbols used in mathematics and symbolic logic.

Of major importance in human development was man's eagerness and increasing capacity to become aware of messages from nature which he had previously ignored or overlooked, but which required systematic observation and recording and symbolic interpretation as science has developed. More recently, a variety of ingenious instruments and subtle techniques have been invented to evoke signals from otherwise occult and unobservable events, making it possible to penetrate, as by X rays, magnetic resonance, and similar procedures, into the interior of substances, or to discover internal processes by making them reveal the orderliness and patterning of their "perishing" events. The so-called Secrets of Nature are not mysterious, concealed events, but rather the most frequently repeated and unequivocally transmitted messages waiting to be received and encoded symbolically into scientific formulation.

Every culture also has a variety of aesthetic symbols which members of that culture find enjoyable, since they can and do respond to these symbols according to their aesthetic significance. Included here are the ways of symbolically presenting nature through graphic and plastic arts. The sensibilities of each cultural group are created and communicated in and through their arts, which provide the selective awareness and the patterned perceptions with the feelings by which members of the group relate to and communicate with the world and other persons as they have been artistically defined. Likewise, every culture has various discursive symbols exhibited in literary creations, in philosophy and law, in theology, and by narrators who as speakers or writers may employ a variety of so-called figures of speech, metaphors, similes, and so forth, for communicating symbolically.

Every cultural group has developed a variety of symbols and symbolic transactions for the operation of its social order and the carrying on of the varied functioning and performances of its established institutions. These include a variety of monetary symbols which we call money or credit and find circulating in a variety of sizes, shapes, and materials, with usually some quantitative designation. There are also a variety of political symbols as in voting or legislation, as well as legal symbols for deciding disputes and administering organizations. In addition, there is a truly amazing variety of symbols and symbolic rituals and ceremonies for the many kinds of human communications and relations such as betrothal and marriage, kinship, small group associations. These varied symbols may be widely current and generally used or limited to a specified group of people or an organization. These socially sanctioned symbols order and pattern human conduct and relationships and thereby contribute to the maintenance of social order.

Language is probably the most widely and most frequently used symbol. Through its daily use each member of a cultural group continually reasserts and reaffirms its symbolic world and communicates with others. Every language has a vocabulary of words for every thing and event, animal and person of which it is aware, and usually has some kind of grammar and frequently a syntax for the orderly use of these words in communication. This syntax, which governs the order of words, such as our Western pattern of a noun or subject preceding a verb and followed by a predicate, with various modifying adjectives and adverbs, and prepositional phrases attached, reflects basic concepts of the world of the people using that language. Thus, Benjamin Whorf has remarked:

> The categories and types that we isolate from the world of phenomena we do not find there because they stare every observer in the face; on the contrary, the world is presented to us in a kaleidoscopic flux of impressions which has to be organized by our minds. . . . We cut nature up, organize it into concepts, ascribe significances as we do, largely because we are parties to an agreement to do it in this way.[12]

Each of the many different languages throughout the world may be viewed as a symbol system that conceives the world according to the basic beliefs and assumptions of the cultural group using that language, each defining, punctuating, and relating events according to the way it perceives the world and interprets whatever happens. Each language presents another way of "codifying reality," as Dorothy Lee has shown in her studies of language systems.[13] She has pointed out how each culture has developed its own ways of perceiving, thinking, and speaking about the world and human affairs, as well as its own symbolic scheme of evaluating and interpreting events and relations, many of which cannot be adequately translated into our Western European languages.

We in the West have long viewed the world in terms of a serial order of events, of some antecedent cause, stimulus, or creator, operating upon some portion of the world to bring about an effect. Moreover, Western culture has, for more than two thousand years, viewed events in terms of the behavior of individual atoms or particles, as L. L. Whyte has so well described in his *Essay on Atomism*.[14]

This pattern of thinking of the world in terms of particles and of a serial lineal order has governed our use of linguistic symbols and has very much shaped our thinking and our attempts to understand nature, since we think, reflect, and discuss primarily in terms of our language and the syntactical patterning it provides. We are beginning to realize that these long-established ways of perceiving the world are only one way, and a very limited way, of thinking. They may be regarded as what the scientists and mathematicians call a "special case" that does not contradict, but must be accepted as part of a more generalized pattern of thinking, which we are now trying to develop through a new conception of communication, both symbolic and nonsymbolic, and through a new set of assumptions about events that are not limited to traditional cause and effect sequences or to discrete atoms and particles and linear relations.

In his study of Chinese science, Joseph Needham has contrasted the Chinese pattern of associative or relational thinking in terms of wholes, with our Western analytic procedures for dissecting and fractionating wholes to smaller units or variables, and reducing whatever is organized to its smallest components. Needham suggests that this associative thinking of the Chinese may be the more fruitful for some of the problems of contemporary science involving organized complexities and dynamic processes.[15]

Increasingly efforts are being made to recognize and understand organizations that are self-organizing, self-regulating and directing, and self-repairing, such as organisms, cultures, and social orders.[16] But we lack the concepts and the verbal symbols and expressions, and also the mathematics, for these "organized complexities," as Warren Weaver has named them.[17] Accordingly, we are handicapped when attempting to discuss and explore these organizations, finding it difficult to articulate and synthesize the findings of analytic study that have disclosed and often measured some of the components of these organizations when abstracted from their organized context. Frequently the results of this fractionation are measured and symbolized and reified into entities or mechanisms because they have been so symbolized. In this way many artifacts, developed through laboratory experimentation, become incorporated in the scientific symbol system which has provided a powerful instrumentality for manipulating events.

Whenever symbols are created and accepted and utilized by a group, they attain a status and become established so that it is exceedingly difficult to displace them or to persuade people that such symbols are no longer valid. This becomes understandable when we recall that a symbol is essentially a human creation that requires "full faith and credence" if it is to be meaningful and significant, capable of evoking from those who use it and those who are exposed to it, the meaning and the credibility necessary for its functioning as an operating symbol.

Symbols are coercive, providing the meanings and evaluations by which individual conduct and social order are so largely governed; but symbols are highly ambiguous and easily manipulated. Hence there have been many different efforts to test their validity. Historically, the major sanctions for symbols were provided by theology, with the assertion of a supernatural origin for its symbol system. Supported by these theological sanctions, the law has also asserted its symbols as compelling and reinforced the authority of rulers. But the major and more critical examination of symbols has come from philosophy, which has also contributed many symbolic formulations that have exercised widespread and prolonged direction over human thinking and activity. In recent modern times science has developed its symbol systems for interpreting the world of events, and has progressively developed its methods and criteria for testing the validity of its proposals. Each of these symbol systems, it should be emphasized, offers its specialized and often esoteric formulation for translating the signals from nature for human understanding and communication. Mathematics and symbolic logic have arisen as an effort to construct a symbol system independent of any specific referent and operating by a logic concerned only with the relations among the symbols of these systems. This represents a cumulative elaboration of the age-old endeavor to establish reason and logic in the conduct of human affairs by a rigorous control and regulation of the linguistic and related symbols for thinking and communicating about the world.

Through the three traditional symbol systems of art, science, and theology, we have attempted to rationalize the nonrational, and make it possible for each individual to develop his own psycho-logic and his own religion. But the professional guardians of these three symbol systems jealously protect their own domains, criticizing and rejecting the others because they do not meet the criteria established for each of these symbol systems.

We live as humans by and for symbols. When the symbol systems that we have relied upon to transform nature and human nature into a meaningful cultural world are in conflict and lose their once unquestioned and unquestionable acceptability, then indeed we are faced with a cultural crisis as variously described in terms of the existentialist crisis, which can be resolved only as we can reconcile and articulate the symbol systems of art, science, and theology. As we recognize and more fully understand these symbol systems, which man himself has created for establishing his various cultural worlds and providing for fulfillment of his varied potentialities, we will see that we have the needed instrumentalities for the cultural renewal we must undertake. To quote Whitehead again:

> The art of free society consists first in the maintenance of the symbolic code; and secondly, in fearlessness of revision, to secure that the code serves those purposes which satisfy an enlightened reason. Those societies which cannot combine reverence for their symbols with freedom of revision, must ultimately decay either from anarchy, or from the slow atrophy of a life stifled by useless shadows.[18]

1. New York, Atheneum (1962).
2. Alfred North Whitehead, *Symbolism, Its Meaning and Effect,* New York, Macmillan (1927).
3. Ernst Cassirer, *Essay on Man,* New Haven, Yale University Press (1944).
4. Suzanne K. Langer, *Philosophy in a New Key,* Cambridge, Mass., Harvard University Press (1942).
5. Cassirer, *op. cit.*
6. Arthur F. Bentley, "Kennetic Inquiry," in *Science,* vol. 112 (Dec. 29, 1950), pp. 775–783.
7. Lawrence K. Frank, *Tactile Communication, Genetic Psychology Monograph,* vol. 56 (1957).
8. *Cf. Sensory Communication* (Walter Rosenblith, editor), Cambridge, Mass., Massachusetts Institute of Technology Press (1961).
9. George A. Kubler, *The Shape of Time: Remarks on the History of Things,* New Haven, Yale University Press (1962).
10. John Dewey and Arthur F. Bentley, *Knowing and the Known,* Boston, Beacon Press (1948).
11. Suzanne K. Langer, *Feeling and Form: A Theory of Art,* New York, Scribner's (1956).
12. Benjamin Whorf, "Science and Linguistics," in *The Technology Review,* vol. XLII (April, 1940).
13. Dorothy D. Lee, *Culture and Freedom,* Englewood Cliffs, N.J., Prentice-Hall (1959).
14. Lancelot Law Whyte, *Essay on Atomism from Democritus to 1960,* Middletown, Conn., Wesleyan University Press (1961).
15. Joseph Needham, *Science and Civilization in China,* Cambridge, Cambridge University Press, 4 vols. (1954 ff).
16. *Cf. Principles of Self-Organization* (Heinz Von Foerster, editor), New York, Pergamon Press (1962).
17. Warren Weaver, "Science and Complexity," in *American Scientist,* vol. 3, no. 6 (1948).
18. Whitehead, *op. cit.*

SIGNS, IMAGES AND SYMBOLS

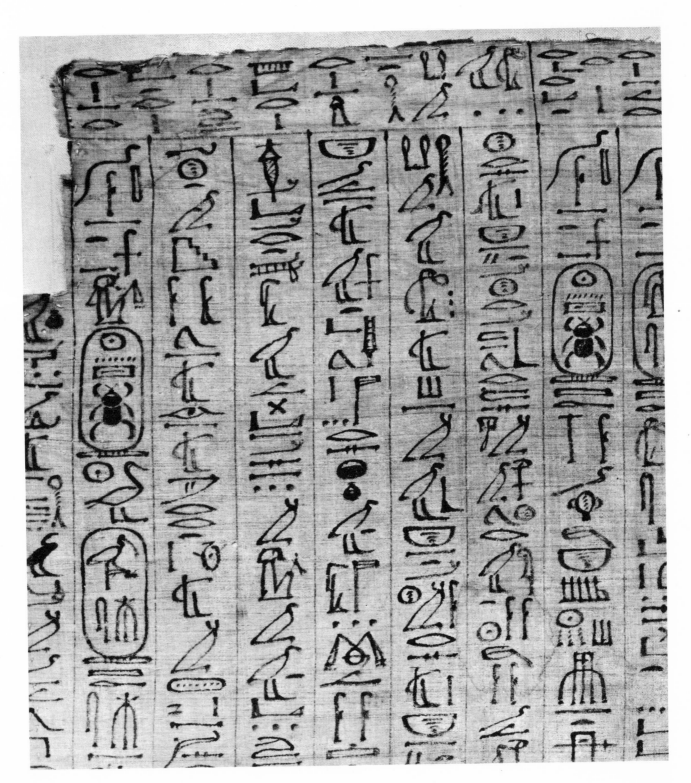

Inscription on an archaic stele from the *Lapis Niger* in the Roman Forum.

Head of a monk bearing an inscription on the interior.
By Koshon. Japanese, A.D. 1328. Wood.
Museum of Fine Arts, Boston.

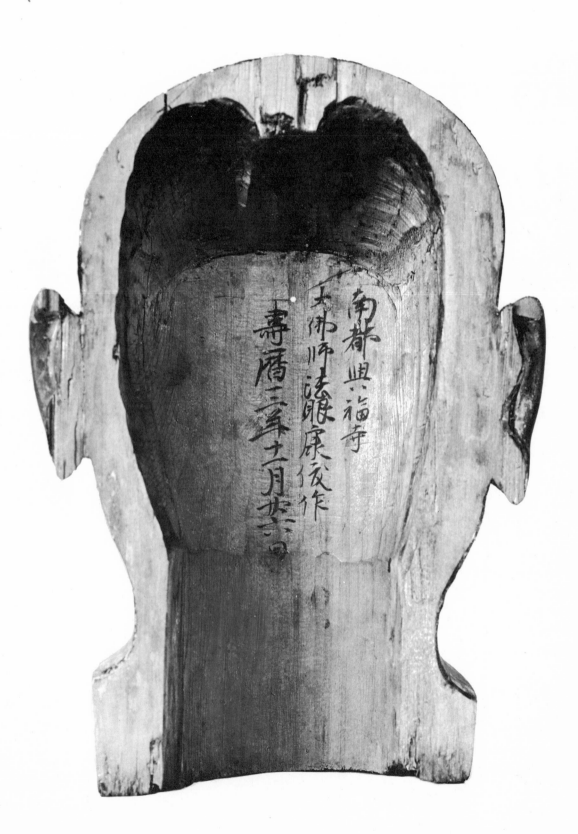

Upper left: Numerals. English engraving of the eighteenth century.

Lower left: John Dalton's Elements, 1806. Lecture diagram, Manchester Literary and Philosophical Society.

Below: Azimuth compass card by H. Gregory, about 1760.

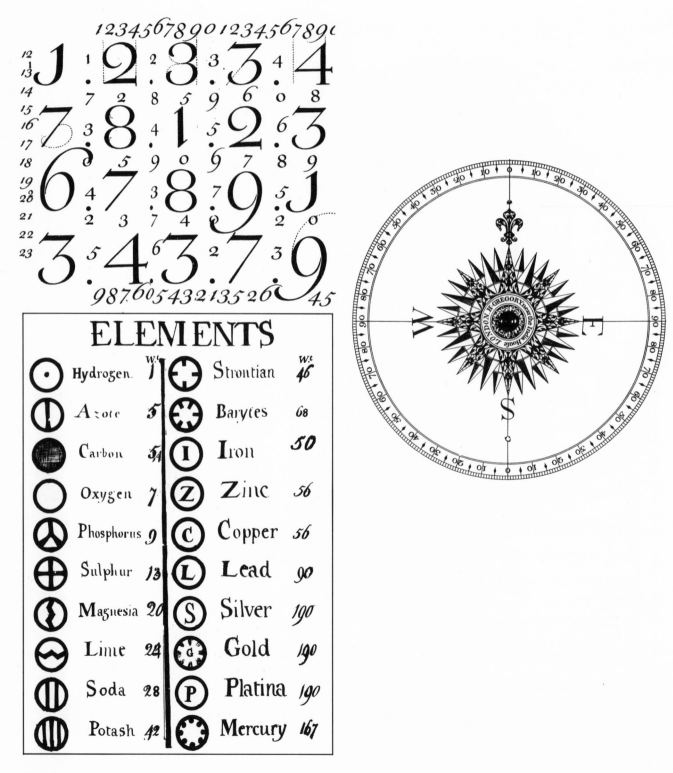

Upper left: John Cage. Score for *Cartridge Music.*

Lower left: John Cage. Page of score for *String Quartet in Four Parts.*

At right: Tomás Maldonado. Signs from a general purpose language for electronic data-processing machines.

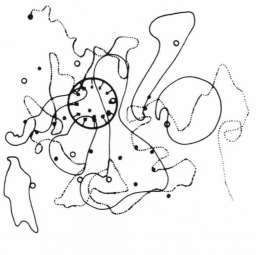

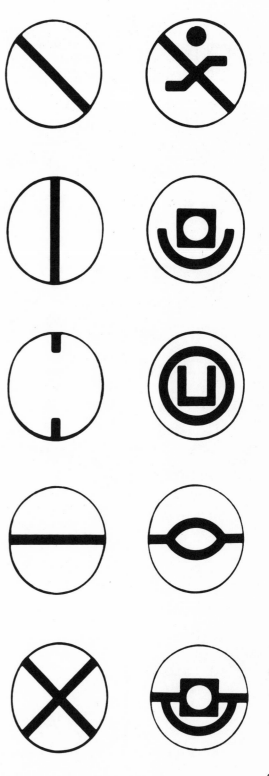

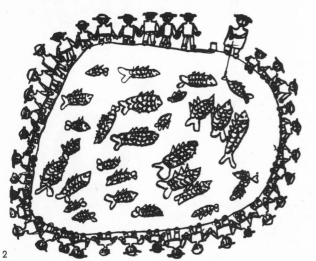

1. Child's drawing of a town.

2. Child's drawing of a pond and fishermen.

3. Model of polyethylene chain of 1000 links, paraffin molecule.

4. Time-lapse photo of the uranium atom.

5. Electron micrograph of myoglobin. Courtesy Dr. John C. Kendrew, Medical Research Center, Cambridge, England.

6. Herbert Bayer. Visualization of airport traffic controlled by radio beam, 1943.

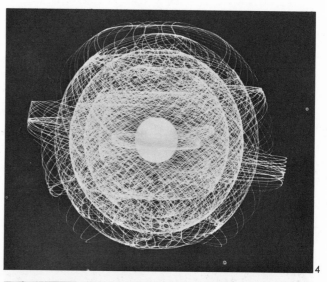

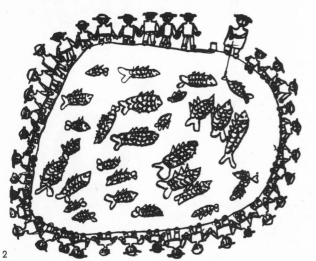

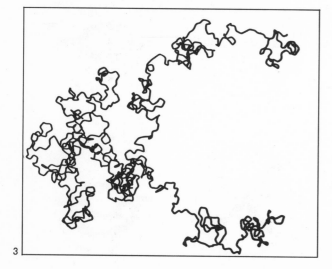

herbert bayer

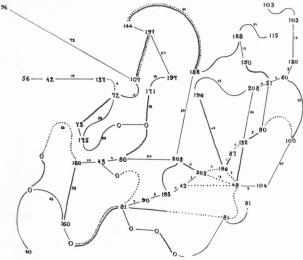

1. Scribblings on a playground. Student photo M.I.T.

2. Toschi Ichiyanagi. Score for music for electric metronome.

3. Integrated circuit. Courtesy Motorola Semiconductor Products, Inc.

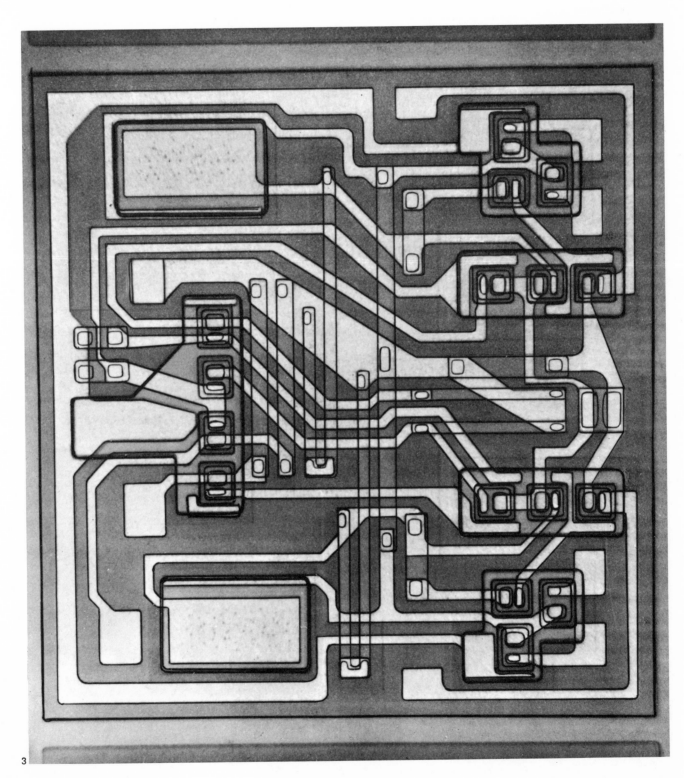

3

TRANSFORMATION OF SYMBOLS:

GRAPHIC ANALOGUES OF PHYSICAL EVENTS

1. Chladni figure.

2. Chladni figure. Courtesy Prof. H. Edgerton, M.I.T.

3. Oscilloscope pattern. Courtesy Ben F. Laposky.

4. Oscilloscope pattern. Courtesy General Electronic Laboratories. Photo G. Benenate and Ph. Hayden.

5. John H. Whitney. Graphic patterns. Analogue computer was used to generate designs in motion.

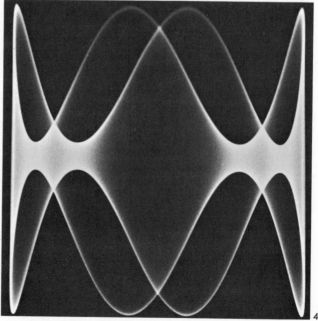

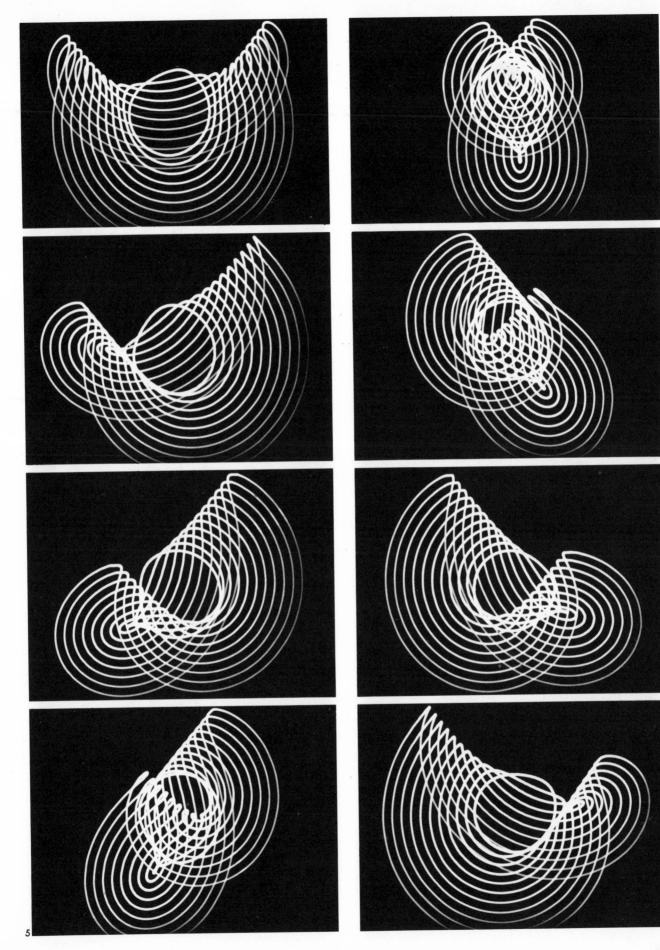

5

1. Electron micrograph. Courtesy J. A. Kessler, Lincoln Laboratory, M.I.T.

2. Electron micrograph, tobacco mosaic virus. Courtesy E. S. Boatman, University of Washington, Seattle.

3. Electron micrograph, bismuth telluride sample. Courtesy Machine Foundry Company, Springdale, Connecticut.

4. Electron micrograph, spiral growth of crystal of silicon carbide. Courtesy Prof. S. Tolansky.

5. Electron micrograph. Courtesy J. A. Kessler, Lincoln Laboratory, M.I.T.

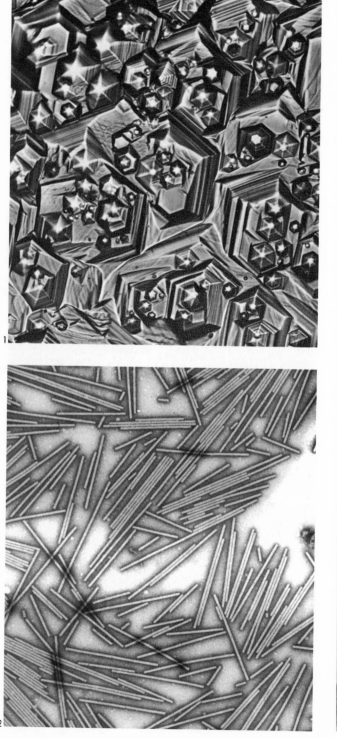

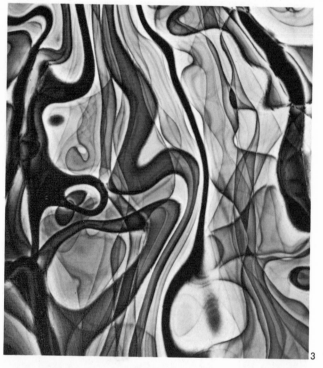

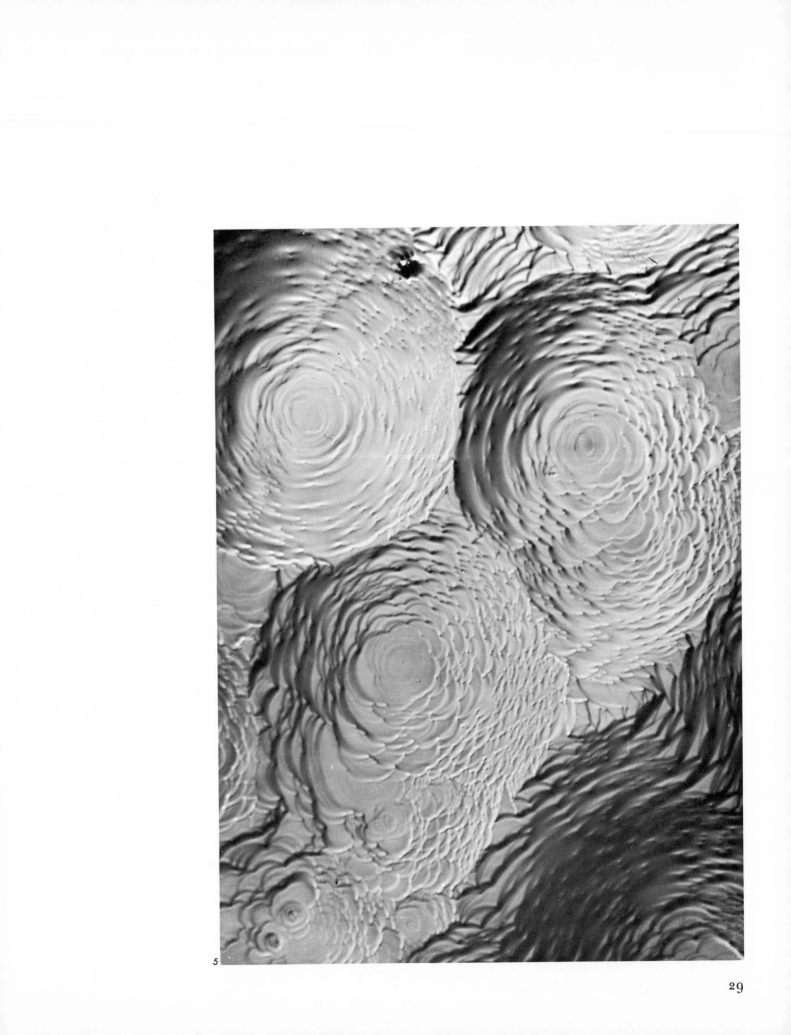

Fear Image: *The big bad wolves.* Imre Kepes, age 4.

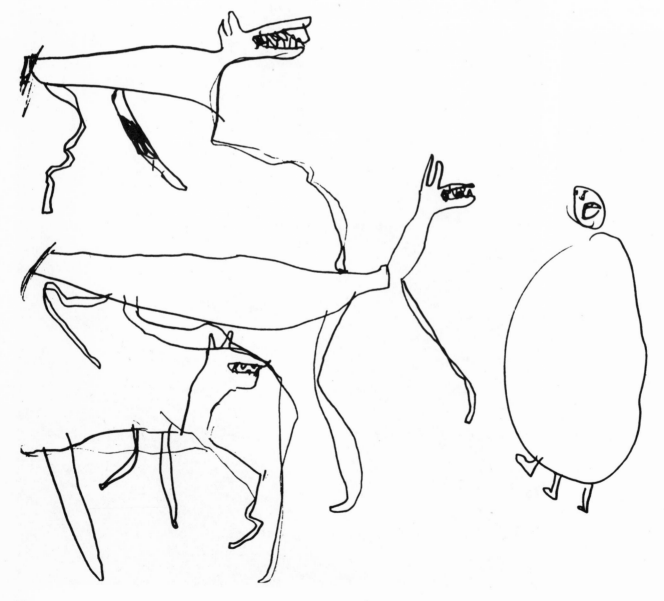

Franz Kline. *Painting Number 7*, 1952. The Solomon R. Guggenheim Museum, New York.

Gyorgy Kepes. *Light Image,* 1940. Museum of Modern Art, New York.

Jean Arp. Drawing, 1918. Museum of Modern Art, New York.

Cave Canem. Mosaic in House of the Tragic Poet, Pompeii.

Highway sign along U.S. route 5. Courtesy Standard Oil Company, N.J.

1

2

3

WORDS AND PICTURES: PUBLICITY IMAGES

1. Playbill for early American theater.

2. Paul Rand. Book jacket, Wittenborn Co. New York.

3. Melin & Österlin. A series of posters for the Modern Museum, Stockholm.

4. Paul Rand. Advertising Typographers Association poster, 1963.

5. Swiss Poster exhibition. Stedelijk Museum, Amsterdam, 1946.

Invasion of the environment by aggressive advertising:
New England roadside stand.
Lobstertorium, Portland, Maine.
Produce market, Baton Rouge, Louisiana.
Photos courtesy Standard Oil Company, N.J.

An attempt to introduce heraldic coding into the environment: Outdoor mural of tubular lights for the front of a radio store. Designed by Gyorgy Kepes, 1951. Photo Nishan Bichajian.

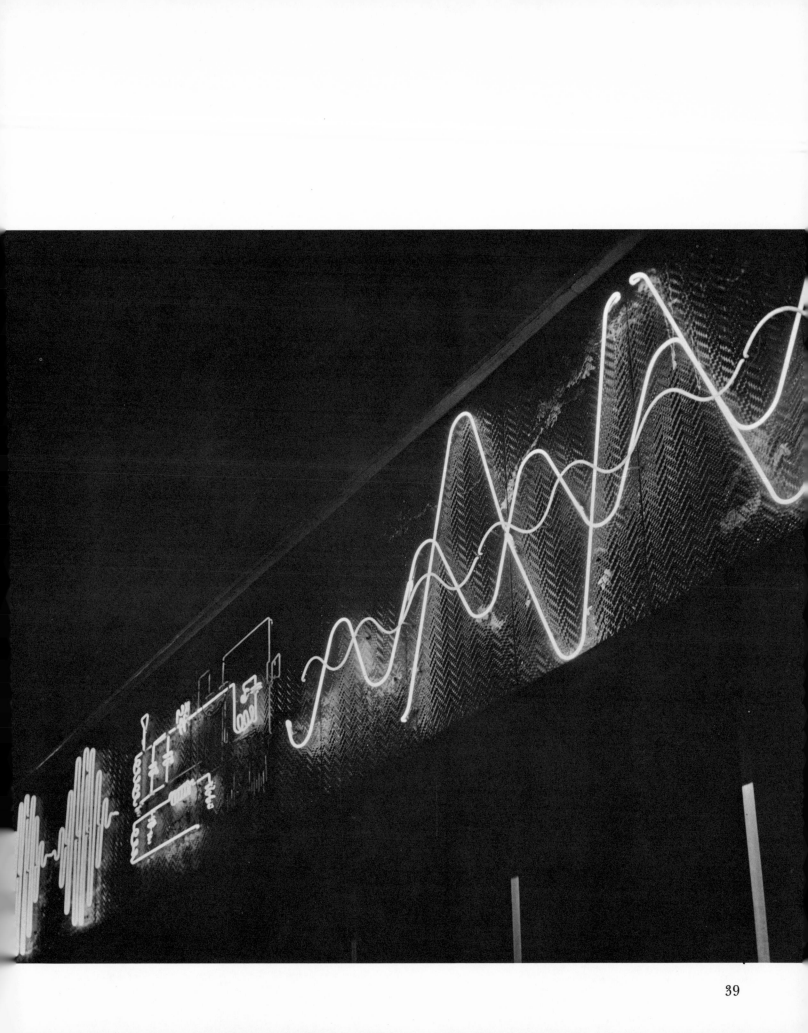

Stefan Lorant. Photomontage for *Picture Post*. Comment on the remark, "Peace for our time," made by Neville Chamberlain on his return from Munich in 1938.

French picture postcard of about 1901.

Alexander Rodchenko. Photomontage, 1927.

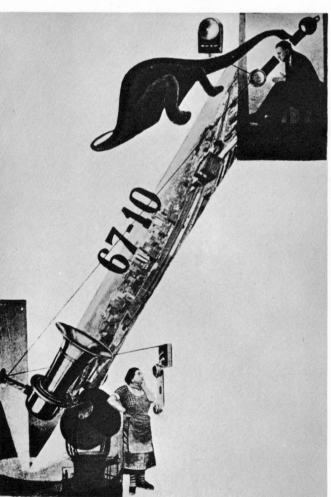

THE HAPPY ELEPHANTS.

The elephants are happy. They are flying about in the sky. The elephants are happy because they have got peace. For how long have the elephants got peace? Ah, that alas! no one can say.

HEINZ VON FOERSTER

FROM STIMULUS TO SYMBOL:
THE ECONOMY OF BIOLOGICAL COMPUTATION

Man's heritage is of two different kinds. One has been accumulated through perhaps two billion years of evolution and is encoded in the molecular structure of his genetic make-up. The other has been built up during approximately one million years of communication and is encoded in the symbolic structure of his knowledge.

While man evolved as a result of interplay between genetic mutability and environmental selectivity, his self-made symbols evolved as a result of interplay between his flexibility in expressing and his sensitivity in distinguishing. This observation links these two evolutionary processes in a not too obvious way, and gives rise to the formidable problem of demonstrating this link by tracing structure and function of the symbols he uses back to the cellular organization of his body.

It is clear that we are today still far from a solution to this problem. First, we do not yet possess a consistent comprehension of structure and function of our symbols, to wit, the Cyclopean efforts by various linguistic schools to establish a concise language for dealing with language; second, our knowledge of the cellular organization of the body is still meager, despite the incredible amount of knowledge accumulated over the past decades. As a matter of fact, it is indeed doubtful whether with presently available conceptual tools this problem can be solved at all. These tools, however, will permit us to get an insight into the magnitude of this problem.

An approach which considers symbolization in the framework suggested by the formulation of this problem does have the advantage that it can tie together evidences accumulated in a variety of fields. Moreover, within the framework suggested here it becomes impossible to talk about symbols in a static, ontological way and not consider the dynamic evolution of symbolic presentation. Likewise, it becomes impossible to separate a symbol from its symbolizer, his sensory motor and mental capabilities and constraints. And further, it becomes impossible to separate symbol and symbolizer from his environment which we have to populate with other symbolizers in order that symbolization makes any sense at all.

The following is an attempt to establish clues for the understanding of potentialities and limits of symbolization through the understanding of variety and constraints in the maker and user of symbols and in his environment.

The argument will be presented in three steps. First, the concept of "environment" and the relation "environment-environmentee" will be discussed. The second step will be to briefly sketch some basic principles and some hypotheses of the processes that permit internal representations of environmental features. Third, modes of projecting externally these internal representations will lead to the consideration of possibilities of interaction by symbolization.

ENVIRONMENT: AN ANALYSIS

Evolution, like memory, is an irreversible process. The man who once knew a datum, but has forgotten it now, is different from the man who never knew it. Irreversibility in evolution permits one to picture this process in the form of a tree with divergent branch points only. Fig. 1 is such a representation of evolutionary differentiation in vertebrates over the last 500 million years. Time runs from bottom to top and the number of different species at any time within each branch is indicated by the width of this branch. A subspecies among mammals called *homo sapiens,* including its entire temporal extension, occupies in this graph but a tiny speck of space in the upper right corner of the mammalian branch, number 8.

It is perhaps easy to see that this graph represents paleontological estimates of only those species that were sufficiently stable to leave detectable traces. All instable mutants escape detection, and thus cannot be accounted for. In other words, this graph is essentially a picture of the success story of living forms. This observation permits us to look at this representation in a slightly different way, namely, to consider each point in a branch as being an instant at which a crucial problem is presented to a particular species. If it solves this problem the point will be retained and moves upward an ever so slight amount. If not, the point will be removed, *i.e.,* the species is eliminated. It is clear that the crucial problem referred to here is how to survive, and it is also clear that this crucial problem is posed by the properties of the particular environment which is in interaction with elements of this species or its mutants.

Fig. 1. Evolution of vertebrates over the last 500 million years. Time runs from bottom to top. Width of branches corresponds to approximate abundance of different species within the branch (class). 1. Jawless fishes. 2. Cartilage fishes. 3. Placoderms. 4. Bony fishes. 5. Amphibians. 6. Birds. 7. Reptiles. 8. Mammals.

100

10 MILLION YEARS

From this viewpoint "environment" is seen in a two-fold way: as a set of properties of the physical world that act upon an organism; and also as an accumulation of successful solutions to the problem of selecting such conditions in the physical world which are at least survivable. In this discussion "environment" will always carry this relative notion as "environment of . . . ," where environment and the organism associated with it will be duals to each other in the sense that a particular organism O implies its particular environment E(O), and vice versa, that a particular environment E implies its appropriate organism O(E).

By carving out from the physical universe just that portion E(O) which is "meaningful" for this organism O, one has carved out a portion that is necessarily of compatible complexity with that of the organism. An organism that tolerates a variation of temperature of, say, thirty degrees Fahrenheit around a certain mean, cannot "dare" to move into places where temperatures vary beyond this tolerance.

This statement can be expressed differently. An organism that is matched to its environment possesses in some way or another an internal representation of the order and the regularities of this environment. How this internal representation within the cellular architecture of living systems is achieved will be taken up later in this paper.

At this point the concept of "order" needs further clarification. Intuitively one would associate order with the relation of parts in a whole. But what are parts? Again, intuitively, parts emerge as "separabilia," because the relation among their components is of higher order than that of the parts of the whole. Although this definition is circular, it points in the right direction, for it relates order to the strength of constraints that

Fig. 2. Globular star cluster NGC 5272 in the constellation *Canes Venatici*. Mount Wilson and Palomar Observatories.

control the interaction of elements which comprise the whole. These constraints manifest themselves in the structures they produce. The globular star cluster (Fig. 2) has simple spherical symmetry, because the weak gravitational forces that hold the approximately 100,000 elements of this system in statistical equilibrium have themselves radial symmetry. Of course, much more sophisticated structures are obtained if the constraints are more numerous and stronger. The volume *Structure* of this present series[1] abounds with beautiful examples from nature and art, where either strong molecular forces (*e.g.*, the paper by Cyril Stanley Smith) or the application of strong principles of construction (*e.g.*, the paper by R. Buckminster Fuller) generate structures of great intricacy and sophistication. Here only one shall be given, the almost inexhaustible variety of hexagonal symmetries in snow crystals (Fig. 3). The growth mechanism of these crystals is subjected to a major constraint, namely the triangular shape of the water molecule H_2O which has two hydrogen atoms attached to the big oxygen atom at angles which are close to either 30° or 60°. This slight deviation from the condition that would produce equilateral shapes introduces a certain amount of "freedom" for the molecules to attach themselves to each other, which in turn allows for the large variability within this constraint. Note that in spite of the great difference in the individual shapes of these crystals, no difficulty arises in recognizing these forms at a glance as snow crystals. This suggests that the cognitive apparatus that "figures out"—or computes—the answer to the question "What is this?" is the one thing that is common to all these shapes, and this is the constraint in their growth mechanism. The name we give to this constraint is simply "snow crystal."

Fig. 3. Snow crystals.

In the temporal domain order is again generated by the constraints of the "Laws of Nature" which, on the macroscopic scale of direct observation, control the chain of events. Chaos would permit transitions from any state to any other state, mountains transforming themselves into flying pink elephants, pink elephants turning into yellow goo, etc. Not only are organisms impossible in this world, for by definition, there is no law that holds the organism together, but also this world is indescribable, for description requires names, and names refer to the "invariabilia"—the constraints—in the environment.

One clue of how to compute these constraints from the apparent structure of the environment is suggested by the preceding examples. Structure in space was determined by a law in the growth mechanism that permitted attachment of new neighbor elements only at particular points; structure in time was determined by a law in the transition process that permitted only a particular event to be neighbor to an existing one. In other words, spatiotemporal order is generated by constraints that control spatiotemporal neighborhood relationships. Hence, if these can be "sized up," the constraints can be evaluated.

If chaos permits every event to appear with equal probability, order emerges from chaos when certain transitions of events become more probable than others. Certainty of an event following another creates a perfect, deterministic universe, and the problem of how to survive in such a deterministic universe is reduced to finding the constraints that govern the transitions from one event to the next. Clearly, the simplest of all such deterministic universes is the one where no transitions take place, i.e., where everything is at motionless and uniform tranquility. Hence, the oceans, where temperature variations, changes in the concentration of chemicals, destructive forces, etc., are kept at a minimum, were the cradle for life.

The dual interdependence of organism-environment permits a dual interpretation of the tree of evolution (Fig. 1). Instead of interpreting points on this graph as *species of organisms,* one may interpret them as *species of environments.* Thus viewed, this chart represents the evolution of environments which were successively carved out of the physical universe. These environments evolved from simple, almost deterministic ones, to ex-

tremely complex ones, where large numbers of constraints regulate the flow of events. An environmental subspecies among mammalian environments, called "E (*homo sapiens*)," occupies in this graph a small speck of space in the upper right corner of branch number 8. Hence, its dual, "*homo sapiens* (E)," sees "his universe" as a result of two billion years of environmental evolution, which step by step carved out from the physical universe an ever increasing number of constraints of all those in this universe that are computable within the limits of the evolving organism.

The diagram shown here below sketches the circular flow of information in the system environment-organism. In the environment constraints generate structure. Structural information is received by the organism which passes this information on to the brain which, in turn, computes the constraints. These are finally tested against the environment by the actions of the organism.

ENVIRONMENT

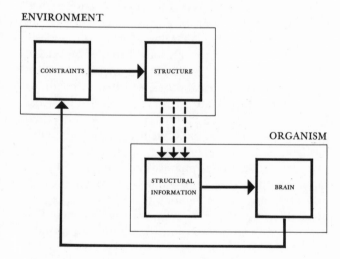

With the emergence of self-reflection and consciousness in higher organisms a peculiar complication arises. A self-reflecting subject may insist that introspection does not permit him to decide whether the world as he sees it is "real," or just a phantasmagory, a dream, an illusion of his fancy. A decision in this dilemma is important in this discussion, since, if the latter alternative should hold true, no problems as to how organisms represent internally the features of their environment would arise, for all environmental features would be just internal affairs in the first place.

In which sense reality indeed exists for a self-reflecting organism will become clear by the argument that defeats the solipsistic hypothesis.[2] This argument proceeds by *reductio ad absurdum* of the thesis: "This world is only in my imagination; the only reality is the imagining 'I.' "

Assume for the moment that the gentleman in the bowler hat in Fig. 4 insists that he is the sole reality, while everything else appears only in his imagination. However, he cannot deny that his imaginary universe is populated with apparitions that are not unlike himself. Hence he has to grant them the privilege, that they themselves may insist that they are the sole reality and everything else is only a concoction of their imaginations. On the other hand, they cannot deny that their fantasies are populated by apparitions that are not unlike themselves, one of which may be *he,* the gentleman with the bowler hat.

With this the circle of contradiction is closed, for if one assumes to be the sole reality, it turns out he is the imagination of someone else who, in turn, insists that *he* is the sole reality.

The resolution of this paradox establishes the reality of environment through evidence of a second observer. Reality is that which can be witnessed; hence, rests on knowledge that can be shared, that is, "together-knowledge," or *con-scientia.*

Fig. 4. *Reductio ad absurdum* of the solipsistic hypothesis. The hominid apparitions of the gentleman with the bowler hat have the gentleman with the bowler hat as apparition. Gordon Pask pinx.

INTERNAL REPRESENTATION
OF ENVIRONMENT: A PHYSIOLOGY

Distributed over the surface of multicellular organisms are highly differentiated cells that establish the interface between the proceedings of the external world and the representations of these proceedings within the organism. To some variables in the physical universe these cells, called sensory receptors, have become specifically sensitive: for example, cells sensitive to changes in pressure are insensitive to, say, the changes in the concentration of sodium chloride in the water surrounding the organism, etc., etc., and vice versa.

Sensitivity of a receptor cell to a specified perturbation is observed by its response in the form of a short electric discharge, which, after it has been initiated at the surface, travels into the interior of the organism along a thin fiber, the axon, which protrudes from the cell.

The approximate duration of this discharge is several thousandths of a second and its magnitude always about one-tenth of a volt, irrespective of the intensity of the

Fig. 5. Electrical pulse activity measured with a microprobe on the axon of a tactile sensor neuron under different pressures. High frequency corresponds to high pressure.

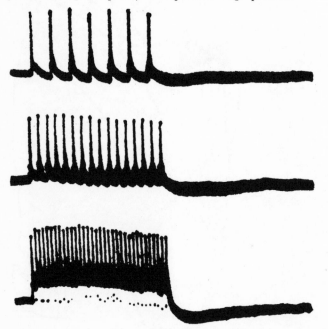

perturbation. A prolonged perturbation produces a sequence of discharges the frequency of which corresponds approximately to the logarithm of the intensity of the perturbation. A series of such pulse sequences measured with small electrodes in the axon of a tactile sensor is shown in Fig. 5. In engineering language the encoding of an intensity into frequency of a signal is called frequency modulation, or FM, and it may be noted that all sensory information—irrespective of sensory modality—is coded into this common language.

If a perturbation is permanently applied, the interval between pulses slowly increases until the sensor fires at a low frequency—called the resting rate—which is independent of the intensity of the permanent perturbation. This phenomenon, "habituation," is one example of computational economy in living organisms, for a property of the universe that does not change in space or time can safely be ignored. Air has no smell. It is the change of things to which an organism must be alerted.

A specific perturbation that elicits responses of a sensory receptor is called stimulus. Stimulus and receptor are duals in the same sense as are environment and organism. Consequently, a tree of the evolution of sensory receptors could be drawn which, at the same time, would show the successive acquisition of specified properties of the physical universe that are selectively filtered out from the rest of the universe.

In the higher animals the most intricately developed sensory system is that of their visual organs. Distributed over the human retina are 180 million sensory receptors of essentially two kinds, the rods and the cones. Rods respond to brightness in general and are more concentrated on the periphery, while cones respond to brightness modified by a variety of pigments and are more concentrated in the central part of the retina, the fovea. The fovea, by proper accommodation of the crystalline lens, has the lion's share in transducing the information contained in the inverted image focused on the retina.[3] The concentration of sensors in the fovea is very high indeed. An area on the retina of the magnitude of the small, black, circular spot that indicated termination of the previous sentence contains approximately 20,000 cones and rods. The projected image of this spot, when looked at under normal reading conditions, is "seen" by about 200 cells. Since each cell distinguishes about 60 levels of brightness, the number of images distinguishable by this small ensemble of 200 cells is exactly $(60)^{200}$, or approximately 10^{1556}. This is a meta-astronomical number which, if printed out on this page, spreads over 13 lines.

It is clear that this overwhelming mass of information is neither useful nor desirable, for an organism has to act; and to act requires making a decision on the available information, which in this case is so large that it would take eons of eons to initiate action, even if the evidence were scanned at lightning speed. Moreover, any accidental distortion of the image—may it be ever so slight—caused, say, by light scattering in the vitreous humor, by optical aberrations in the lens, such as achromatism, astigmatism, temporary failure of single receptors, etc., etc., would pass as evidence with equal weight and be admitted in the decision-making operation.

What, then, protects the brain from overflow of information?

A first clue was discovered by counting the fibers in the optic tract that is the bundle of nerves which connect the eye with the brain. Here one counts only one million fibers, a reduction by 1/180 compared with the number of sensors. Why this waste on the sensory level, or why this redundancy? Is all this tremendous sensory information just discarded? One has to look and to measure in order to answer these questions.

The anatomy of the postretinal neural structures is known over many decades; the knowledge of its functions emerges only slowly with advances in electronics and the refinement of microelectrodes that permit penetration of single fibers in vivo and thus permit the recording of their activity under controlled conditions of illumination.

Fig. 6 shows a semischematic sketch of the multilayered postretinal neural network that connects sensors with the fibers of the optic tract. Rods, and a few cones, with their associated cell bodies containing the nucleus, comprise layers 1 and 2, the light-sensitive nerve-endings in 1, the nuclei in 2. Their axons descend into layer 3 where contacts are established with fibers emerging from the nuclei of a second layer of cells, the "bipolars," in layer 4. Their axons, in turn, connect in layer 5 with branch-like ramifications, the "dendrites," emerging from cells of a third kind, the first ganglion cells in layer 6, which send their axons into deeper regions of the brain, making up the fibers of the optic tract, layer 7.

Fig. 6. Semischematic drawing of the postretinal neural network. 1. Rods and cones. 2. Nuclei of cones and rods. 3. Interaction between sensors and bipolars. 4. Bipolar cells. 5. Interaction bipolars and ganglion cells. 6. Ganglion cells. 7. Optic nerve.

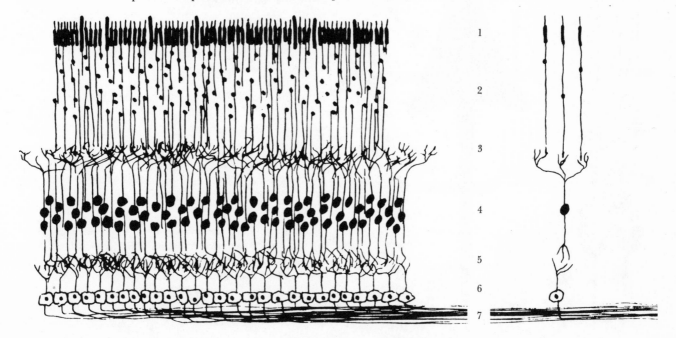

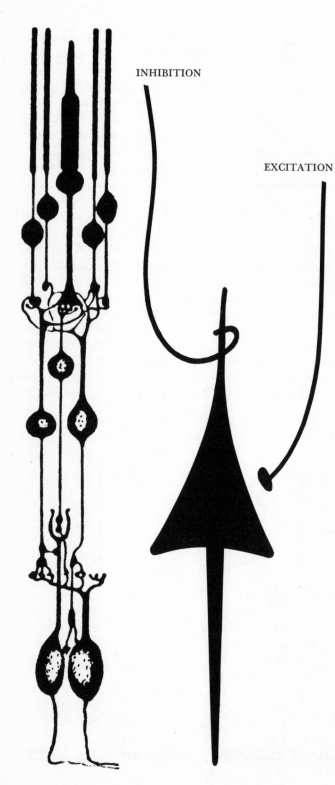

INHIBITION

EXCITATION

Two features of this network should be noted. First, that only a few sensors within a spatial neighborhood contribute to one ganglion cell, as can be seen more clearly in Fig. 7, which shows an elementary net of four rods, one cone, three bipolars and two ganglion cells, drawn directly from microscopic observation.[4] Second, that the signal pattern generated at the cones and rods may be modified only in two places, namely in layers 3 and 5 where cells in different layers connect, and thus may act on their successors according to rules of signal transmission from neuron to neuron and according to the local connection scheme.

The mechanisms that determine the response of a successor cell when stimulated by the activity of its predecessor at the place of their junction—the synapse—are still today not clear. Nevertheless, it is clear that two types of interaction can take place, excitation and inhibition. An excitatory synapse will transmit to the successor the oncoming discharge, while an inhibitory synapse will cancel the trigger action of another excitatory synapse. Fig. 8 suggests a symbolic representation of these two synaptic functions. The triangular figure represents the successor neuron with its axon extending downward. Axons from predecessor neurons forming excitatory synapses are indicated as knobs, those with inhibitory synapses as loops.

Fig. 7. Elementary net composed of four rods, one cone, three bipolars and two ganglion cells. Reproduced from S. L. Polyak, *The Vertebrate Visual System,* Chicago, The University of Chicago Press (1957).

Fig. 8. Symbolic representation of excitation (knob) and inhibition (loop) of a neuron.

This observation of the two kinds of signal transmission suffices to see neural interaction in a new light, for it suggests the possibility of seeing the function of a neuron in the form of a logical operation, the affirmative corresponding to excitation, negation corresponding to inhibition. Hence, a network of synapting neurons can be regarded as a system that computes certain logical functions depending upon the type and structure of the connections.

To see clearly the significance of this observation, an idealized two-layer neural network is drawn in Fig. 9. The first layer consists of "rods," each of which acts upon precisely three neurons in the second "computing" layer. Two fibers with excitatory synapses connect with the neuron just below, while two other fibers with inhibitory synapses connect with its left- and right-hand neighbor. This we shall call an elementary net. It repeats itself periodically over the entire strip, which is thought to extend far out to both sides of the figure.

What does this net compute? Assume that all sensors are uniformly illuminated. An arbitrary neuron in the computer layer receives from its corresponding sensor immediately above two excitatory stimuli which are, however, cancelled by the two inhibitory stimuli descending from the immediate neighbors of its corresponding sensor. Due to the perfect cancellation of the two "yeses" and the two "noes," the net result is no response at all. Since this is true for all other neurons in the computer layer, the whole net remains silent, independent of the intensity of light projected on the sensors. One property of this scheme is now apparent: the net is insensitive to a uniform light distribution.

What happens if a perturbation is introduced in the light path? Fig. 10 illustrates this situation. Again, under regions of uniform darkness or uniform illumination the computer cells do not respond. However, the neuron at the fringe between darkness and light receives no inhibitory signal from the sensor in the shade; double excitation overrides single inhibition and the cell fires. Due to the periodicity of the elementary net, this property, namely, the presence of an edge, will be computed independent of the position of this edge and independent of the level of over-all illumination. Hence, such a network may be called an "edge detector," which when the same principle is extended into two dimensions, may be called a "contour detector."

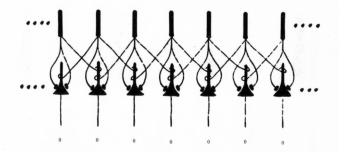

Fig. 9. Periodic network of idealized neurons incorporating lateral inhibition.

Fig. 10. Periodic network with later inhibition computing the property "edge."

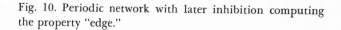

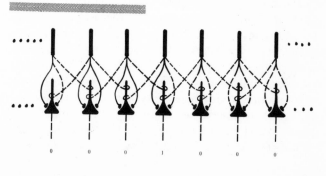

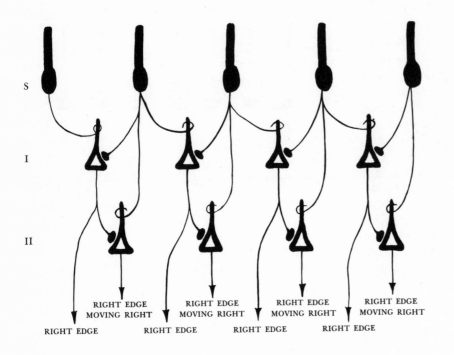

S

I

II

RIGHT EDGE
MOVING RIGHT

RIGHT EDGE
MOVING RIGHT

RIGHT EDGE
MOVING RIGHT

RIGHT EDGE
MOVING RIGHT

RIGHT EDGE

RIGHT EDGE

RIGHT EDGE

RIGHT EDGE

Fig. 11. Anisotropic periodic network computing the property "right edge" and the property "right edge moving right."

Other connections will compute other properties in the visual field. Fig. 11 shows a periodic net with two computer layers, 1 and 2, where layer 2 utilizes results computed by layer 1. Inspection of the connection scheme may easily show that layer 1 computes the presence of a right edge (light right, dark left); while layer 2, utilizing the synaptic delay in elements of layer 1, computes a right edge moving right. Of course, no responses are obtained for left edges (light left, dark right), left edges moving left or right, and right edges moving left.

These examples are intended to show that owing to the basic computational properties of the neuron, parallel, periodic arrays of elementary networks are capable of extracting a variety of useful "invariants" in an otherwise complex environment. The theory that connects structure and function of such networks with the invariants they compute is fully developed. Given any universal property to be computed, the appropriate network to carry out this computation can be synthesized.[5]

To establish similar correlations in actual physiolog-ical nerve nets is infinitely more difficult. Nevertheless, during the last couple of years in a series of brilliant experiments[6] the computation of invariants by postretinal networks in some vertebrates (frog, pigeon) has been demonstrated. The experimental procedure consists of observing responses of single fibers in the optic tract elicited by the presentation of various visual stimuli to the retina of an anesthetized animal. These observations show indeed that certain fibers respond only if the appropriate invariant is present in their receptor field. Some of these invariants are:

1. Local sharp edges and contrast.
2. The curvature of edge of a dark object.
3. The movement of edges.
4. Local dimmings produced by movement or rapid general darkening.
5. Vertical edges only.
6. Vertical edges moving.
7. Vertical edges moving right (left) only.
   etc.

Fig. 12. Topological mapping of the sensation of touch into the outer layers of the brain "homunculus."

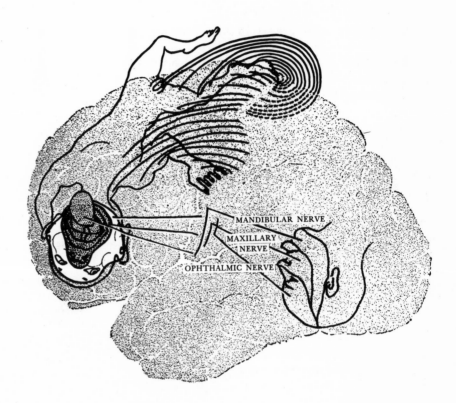

MANDIBULAR NERVE
MAXILLARY NERVE
OPHTHALMIC NERVE

These abstracts are still on a primitive level, but it is the way in which they are computed that invites further comments. Although only those operations of the perceptive apparatus have been described which are an immediate consequence of the stimulation of sensors, some basic principles are now visible which underlie the translation of environmental features into representations of these features within the cellular architecture of the organism. Perhaps the most fundamental principle involved in this translation is the correspondence between the *neighborhood relationships* that determine environmental structures, and the *neighborhood logics* that are incorporated into neural connectivity which determine the "whether" and "where" of certain environmental properties.

This suggests two levels of computation. First, computation on the grand scale of evolutionary differentiation which incorporates the environmental constraints into the structure of those networks which, on the second level, compute within the limits of their structure

spatiotemporal quantities of useful universal parameters. Clearly, the first level refers to the species, the second to the specimen. It is on the first level that the notion of "Platonic Ideas" arises, for they refer to the fabric without which experience cannot be gathered.

The importance of distributed operations that can be carried out on a distributed stimulus is further emphasized by a careful preservation of neighborhood relationships even after the original stimulus has been relayed over many cascades of computational layers into the deeper regions of the brain. Fig. 12 shows a topological mapping—that is, a mapping which preserves neighborhoods—of our body with respect to the sensation of touch into the appropriate cortical regions. This "homunculus" is obtained by registering with microelectrodes those regions in the brain which become active when certain regions of the body are stimulated.[7] Such a "signal representation" must not necessarily conform with original proportions, as seen by the emphasis of organs that convey most of the tactile information.

53

The importance is the preservation of neighborhoods which permit further computation of tactile abstracts.

The reliance on neighborhood relationships can cause peculiar breakdowns of the perceptive apparatus when presented, for instance, with a triple-pronged fork with only two branches (Fig. 13). Although in all details (neighborhoods) this figure seems right, as a whole it represents an impossible object.

Similar difficulties arise when the visual system is confronted with unusual projections which do not allow quick reconstruction of the unprojected image. Erhard Schön's anamorphosis (Fig. 14) seems to picture a somewhat peculiar landscape, but "actually" it portrays the three Emperors, Charles V, Ferdinand I, Francis I, and Pope Paul III. Faces of these personalities, including their names, can easily be recovered by looking at this engraving under a grazing angle from the left.[8]

Since all sensory modalities translate stimuli into the universal language of electric pulse activity, invariants computed by different senses may be compared on higher levels of neural activity. Since it is on this level where we have to search for the origin of symbolization, this point may be illustrated by an example.

A hypothetical anthropologist visits a fictitious tribe whose members use symbolic representations, two of which are shown in Fig. 15. One is referred to as "Ooboo," the other one as "Itratzky." It is significant that no further information is required to identify these symbols.

In the light of the preceding discussion it may indeed be argued that in this case the pattern of neural activity, which represents the visual stimulus configuration, is homologous to that generated by configurations of the auditory stimulus. This argument is going in the right direction, but it fails to cope with a strange situation, namely, that earlier experience and learning is not involved in this spontaneous identification process.

Since associations gained from experience are excluded, one must assume that this audio-visual correspondence rests upon the fabric without which experience cannot be gained. The structure of this fabric must permit some cross-talk between the senses, not only in terms of associations, but also in terms of integration. If this structure permits the ear to witness what the eye sees and the eye to witness what the ear hears then there is "together-knowledge," there is *con-scientia*.

SYMBOLIZATION: A SYNTHESIS

To survive is to anticipate correctly environmental events. The logical canon of anticipation is inductive inference, that is, the method of finding, under given evidence E, the hypothesis H which is highly confirmed by E and is suitable for a certain purpose. This is computation of invariants within the limits of insufficient information, and follows the principles of invariant computations as before, only on a higher level. Knowledge is the sum total of these hypotheses (invariants, laws, regulations) and is accumulated on three levels. First, on the molecular level in the genetic structure which tests the viability of its hypotheses, the mutations, through the vehicle of the developed organism; second, on the level of the individual organism through adaptation and learning; and third, on the social level through symbolic communication which cumulatively passes information on from generation to generation.

Since these are evolutionary processes, and hence irreversible, error would accumulate with knowledge, were it not for a preventative mechanism: death. With death, all registers are cleared and untaught offspring can freshly go on learning. This mechanism works on the first and second levels, but not on the third.

To cumulatively acquire knowledge by passing it on through generations, it must be communicated in symbols and not in signs. This separates man from beast. Communication among social insects is carried out through unalterable signs which are linked to the genetic make-up of the species. While signs refer to objects and percepts, and serve to modify actions and manipulations, symbols refer to concepts and ideas and serve to initiate and facilitate computation.

Since the ultimate relation between symbols and environmental entities is cascaded over the relations symbol/concept and concept/environment, it is in its logical structure very complicated indeed. This gives rise to breakdowns that manifest themselves on various levels of semantic morbidity.

Symbols share with concepts and ideas the property that they do not possess the properties of the entities they represent. The concept of roses "smells" as much, or as little, as the concept of jumping "jumps." The concept of a square is not quadratic. If this point is missed, a number would be just so many fingers and a square with area 2 would have nonexisting sides.

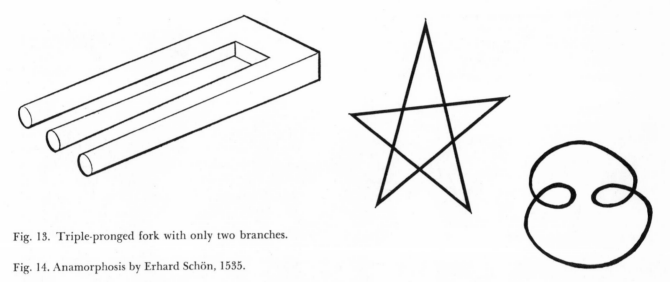

Fig. 13. Triple-pronged fork with only two branches.

Fig. 14. Anamorphosis by Erhard Schön, 1535.

Fig. 15. "Ooboo" and "Itratzky."

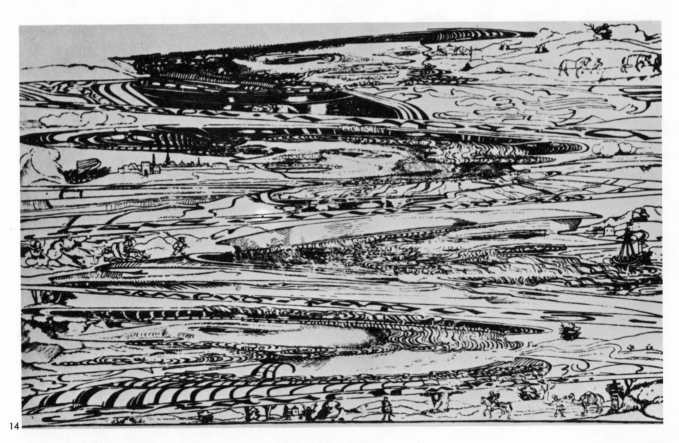

Fig. 16. *Nature Teaching Nature,* Allegory from *Scrutinum Chymicum* of Michael Maier, 1587.

Since symbols refer to concepts and ideas, they too may not have the properties they represent. The symbol of a square may not be quadratic, as can be clearly seen by the string of peculiarly shaped little marks on this paper that have just been used to refer to this geometrical figure. This was, of course, well understood when mystical experience was to be coded into symbols. Michael Maier's allegory, entitled *Nature Teaching Nature,* from the fifty allegories of his *Scrutinum Chymicum* of 1587[9]) is here presented for contemplation (Fig. 16). It may be noted that no commentary—except the title—accompanies these pictures.

What, then, determines the form of a symbol; is it an arbitrary convention, or does it convey its meaning by its shape? Again, ontologically this question cannot be resolved. One has to look into the ontogenesis of symbolic presentations.

We here repeat the diagram seen earlier which represents the information flow between a single organism and its environment:

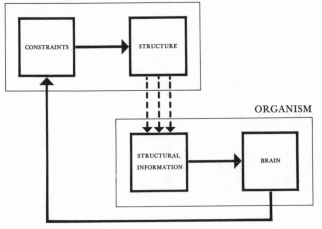

Since symbolization requires at least two interacting subjects who are immersed in an environment that is common to both, we must extend this diagram to admit a second subject. This is done here below:

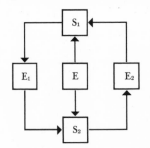

Subjects S_1 and S_2 are coupled to their common environment E. In contrast to the first diagram in which the organism is faced only with an environment with given constraints, now each of these subjects is confronted with the additional complication of seeing his environment populated with at least one other subject that generates events in the environment E. Hence S_2 sees, in addition to the events generated by E, those generated by S_1, and since these take place in E, they shall be labeled E_1; conversely, subject S_1 sees in addition to events generated by E those generated by S_2 which will be called E_2. Thus, in spite of the fact that both S_1 and S_2 are immersed in the same environment E, each of these subjects sees a different environment, namely, S_1 has to cope with (E, E_2), and S_2 with (E, E_1). In other words, this situation is asymmetrical regarding the two subjects, with E being the only symmetrical part.

Assume that E_1 and E_2 are initial attempts by S_1 and S_2 to communicate environmental features to each other. It is clear that these attempts will fail unless—and this is the decisive point—both subjects succeed in eventually converging to like representation for like universal features. This process may be expressed symbolically:

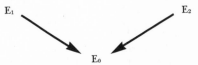

The arrows indicate the convergence process, and E_0 stands for the final universal "language" spoken by both subjects. At this point the initial asymmetry ceases to exist and both subjects see the same environment (E, E_0).

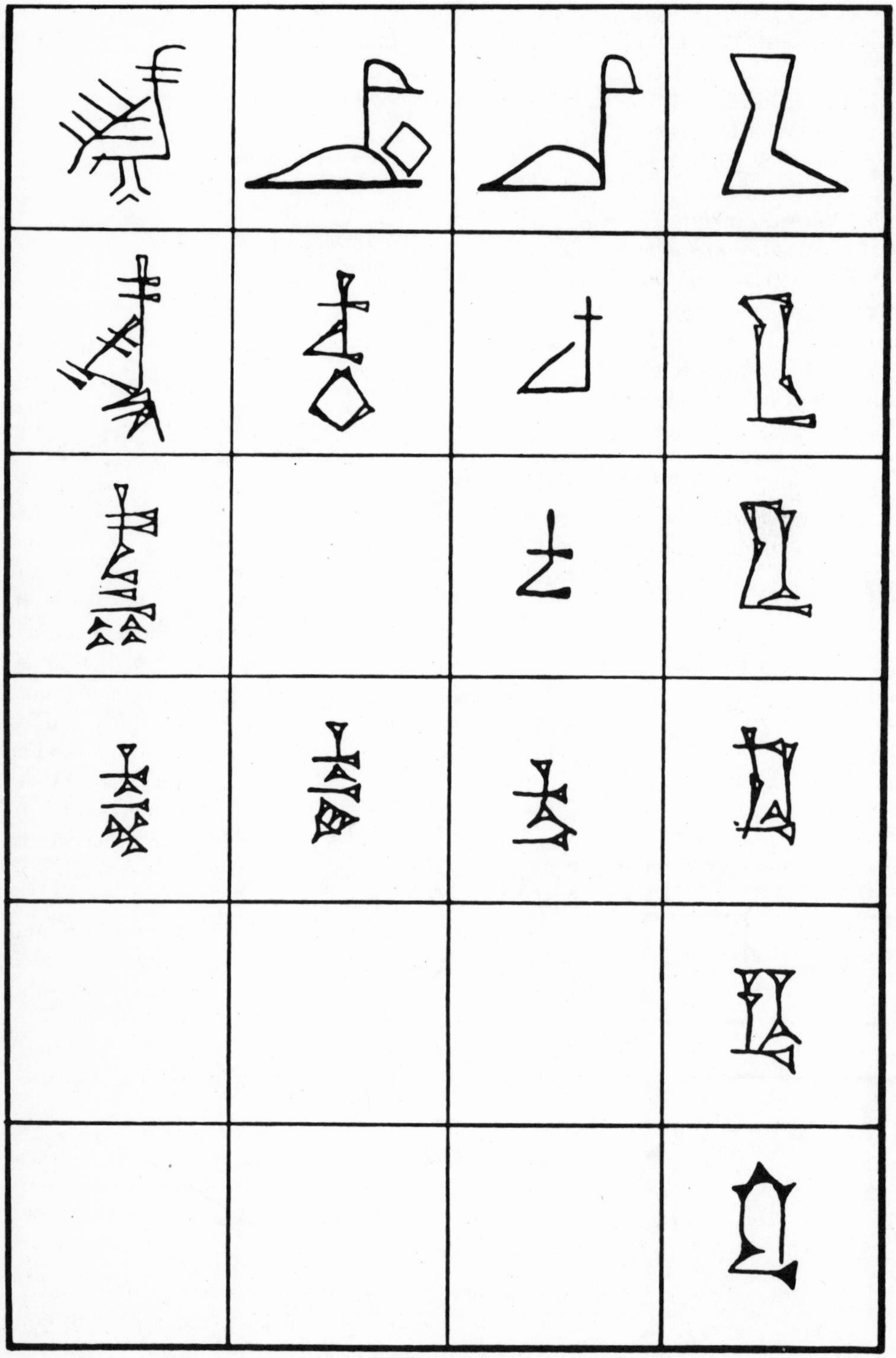

As in all evolutionary systems, the outcome of this process cannot be predicted in the usual sense, because the goal which establishes equilibrium is not directly visible in the final equilibrial state which is a communicable symbol, while the goal is communicability.

Symbols must not necessarily have the shape of the objects they ultimately refer to, yet within that freedom there are constraints working in the evolution of symbolic representation which confine their development within reasonable limits. One of these constraints is dictated by the tools with which these symbols are generated, the other one is their syntactical structure.

An example of the first kind of constraints operating on the development of written symbols is given in Fig. 17, which shows the development of highly stylized symbolic forms from initially representational pictograms.[10] This transition is believed to have taken place in the two millennia of Sumerian cultural activity between 4000 and 2000 B.C. As one goes down the rows it is clearly seen how the constraints imposed by the writing tools—a stylus with triangular cross-section pressed into soft clay—strongly modify the early pictograms given in the top row. It may be interesting to note that simultaneously with this departure from structural representation goes an increase in the possibility to add modifiers to the original meaning. While the pictogram at the top of the right-hand column indeed says "foot," after two thousand years of stylization (bottom row) it may stand for "walking," "running," "delivering a message," or other "foot-connected" actions if associated with appropriate modifiers. Nevertheless, in some instances it seems

to be possible to see behind the form of later symbols the shape of earlier pictorial representations.

The other kind of constraint is a structural one and does not show itself in an obvious way, for symbols carry rules of connectivity and not so much rules of entity. Symbols may be compared to atoms which react to particular atoms only to form the molecular compounds, but are inert to all others. Take, for instance, these "molecular" sentences:

> "Socrates is identical."
> "4 + 4 = purple."

The disturbing thing about these is that they are neither true nor false; they are nonsensical. The connection rules of the symbols have been violated in these examples. "Identical" sets up a relation between two entities. "Socrates is identical with Plato" is a sentence that makes sense although it happens to be a false proposition. The compound "4 + 4 =   " requires a number to follow. Putting "6" at the end is a good guess, but "purple" is an operator with an entirely different structure. This indicates that somehow structure is still preserved in symbolical discourse, but in a syntactical and not in a representational sense. The language of symbols has, so to speak, its own logical grammar.[11] Uniqueness in symbolic expressions is established in a way similar to that of a jigsaw puzzle in which pieces can be put together in one, and only one way. It is the sometime far-extending neighborhood relationship among the pieces—the symbols—that puts them into place.

It is clear that the constraints expressed in the neighborhood relationships of symbols reflect constraints in the environment. For instance, a sentence that refers to two particular persons must employ two proper names. To establish connection rules among symbols of speech is the linguistic problem. One of the most primitive connectivities among words is the probability of their succession. With the following two examples the emergence of order by tightening the constraints of succession will be demonstrated. These examples are random sequences of words generated by a chance device which, however, takes into account the various probabilities by which a particular English word follows a number of precursors. In the first example the number of precursor words is two:

Fig. 17. Formalization of pictograms through constraints imposed by writing tools. This development is estimated to have taken place in Mesopotamia during a period from the fourth to the second millennium B.C.

. . . . . THE HEAD AND IN FRONTAL ATTACK ON AN ENGLISH WRITER THAT THE CHARACTER OF THIS POINT IS THEREFORE ANOTHER METHOD FOR THE LETTERS THAT THE TIME OF WHO EVER TOLD THE PROBLEM FOR AN UNEXPECTED . . . .

In the second example the constraints are tightened by extending the neighborhood relationship up to four words:

. . . . . HOUSE TO ASK FOR IS TO EARN OUR LIVING BY WORKING TOWARDS A GOAL FOR HIS TEAM IN OLD NEW YORK WAS A WONDERFUL PLACE WASN'T IT EVEN PLEASANT TO TALK ABOUT AND LAUGH HARD WHEN HE TELLS LIES HE SHOULD NOT TELL ME THE REASON WHY YOU ARE IS EVIDENT . . . . .

Symbols are no proxy for their objects.[12] There are two morbid states of the mind, magical thinking and schizophrenia, in which this distinction is erased. In both cases symbol and object become indistinguishable. In purpose-oriented Jou Jou and in Voodoo the identity of symbol with object is used to manipulate the world by manipulating the symbol. In schizophrenia symbol and object are freely interchanged to produce peculiar hierarchies of identities. In order to comprehend in depth the modality of this affliction, a short passage of the extensive description of the case of a six-year-old boy by the name of Walter (= water) is given here:[13]

Late in November, 1936, presumably because he had heard a rumor about a child killed in an accident in an elevator there, he became terrified when taken to a department store. He trembled, cried, vomited and remained "hysterical" for two days during which time he made little jerking movements of his body and shoulders and said scarcely a word. The following day, Dr. Hamill was for the first time able to make out that he failed to distinguish between himself (Walter) and water. Walter shifted to water, thence to Deanna Durbin who played in "Rainbow on the River" and so to water again. Being water, he felt he could not be drowned, but might be imprisoned in the radiator. On hearing the knocking of water in the radiator, he said, "elevator just came up and gave the kid a knock" and again, "they are killing the kid,"

which terrified him because he was the kid. Then followed "the telephone burnt and got water after Suzy burnt."

(Dr.: "Where does water come from?") "I come from the show." (Dr.: "You thought water and Walter were the same thing.") "My father used to take me across the river." (Dr.: "And he called you Walter?") "And got drowned. I do not live on Springfield. Bad boys drink water. They do not drink milk. Good boys live on Springfield. I used to live on Springfield— Mississippi River."

It may be speculated that evolution did not weed out mental diseases that afflict proper use of symbols because the survival value of the ability to symbolize is so enormous that occasional morbid deviations of this ability in individuals and in whole cultures could still be tolerated. The enormous advantage of organisms that are able to manipulate symbols over those who can only react to signs is that all logical operations have not to be acted out, they can be computed. It is obvious that this saves considerable amounts of energy. But the really crucial point here is that errors in reasoning are not necessarily lethal.

The recognition of the fact that information is a precious commodity and can be processed by manipulating symbols gave rise to the quick emergence of the fast and large electronic computer systems. These systems manipulate symbols only and do not know objects. The laws of algebra and logic are incorporated in their structure. Hence, they cannot err by confusing modality as does a schizophrenic, nor can they err in syntax and generate nonsense. The only error they can make is confusing true with false and false with true.

The human retina with its associated, genetically structured networks may be compared to these computer systems from a purely quantitative point of view, namely, by the sheer amount of information that is processed. The retina, with its 180 million sensors which operate in parallel at millisecond intervals, performs equivalently to a modern digital computer system that occupies 800 square feet of floor space and uses 4 tons of highly sophisticated electronics. In comparison, the retina's extensions are 2 square inches by 4/1000 of an inch, and it weighs approximately 100 milligrams. This may be taken as an indication of the economy of biological computation.

Note: This article is in part based on work sponsored by the Air Force Office of Scientific Research under Grant 7–64 and by the National Institute of Health under Grant GM–10718.

1. *Structure in Art and in Science* (Gyorgy Kepes, editor), New York, George Braziller (1965).
2. H. Von Foerster, "On Self-Organizing Systems and Their Environments," in *Self-Organizing Systems* (M. C. Yovits and Scott Cameron, editors), New York, Pergamon Press (1960), pp. 31–50.
3. R. Held, "Object and Effigy," in *Structure in Art and in Science . . .*, p. 42–54.
4. S. L. Polyak, *The Vertebrate Visual System,* Chicago, The University of Chicago Press (1957).
5. W. Pitts and W. S. McCulloch, "How We Know Universals: The Perceptions of Auditory and Visual Form," in *Bulletin of Mathematical Biophysics,* vol. 9 (1947), pp. 127–147; H. Von Foerster, "Structural Models of Functional Interaction," in *Information Processing in the Nervous System* (R. W. Gerard and J. W. Duyff, editors), Amsterdam, Excerpta Medica Foundation (1963), pp. 370–383.
6. J. Y. Lettvin, H. R. Maturana, W. S. McCulloch, and W. Pitts, "What the Frog's Eye Tells the Frog's Brain," in *Proceedings of the Institute of Radio Engineers,* vol. 47 (1959), pp. 1940–1951; H. R. Maturana, "Functional Organization of the Pigeon Retina," in *Information Processing . . .*, pp. 170–178.
7. F. A. Mettler, *Neuroanatomy,* St. Louis, The C. V. Mosby Co. (1958), p. 432.
8. J. Baltrusaitis, *Anamorphoses,* Paris, Oliver Perrin (1955).
9. R. Caillois, *Au Coeur du Fantastique,* Paris, Gallimard (1965).
10. O. Neugebauer, *Vorgriechische Mathematik,* Berlin, Springer (1934), pp. 40–78.
11. L. Wittgenstein, *Tractatus Logico Philosophicus,* New York, Humanities Publications (1961).
12. S. Langer, *Philosophy in a New Key,* New York, The New American Library (1962), p. 61.
13. L. J. Meduna and W. S. McCulloch, "The Modern Concept of Schizophrenia," in *Symposium on Neuropsychiatric Diseases,* Philadelphia, W. B. Saunders Co. (1945), pp. 147–164.

Thinking is concerned with the objects and events of the world we know. Therefore, when thinking takes place, these objects and events must be present and acted upon. When they are bodily present we can perceive them, think about them, handle them. The handling is inseparably related to the thinking. Thoughtful exploring involves handling. We actually think with our hands when we are dealing with objects.

When the objects are not physically present, they are represented indirectly by what we remember and know about them. In what shape do memory and knowledge deliver the needed facts? In the shape of memory images, we answer most simply. Experiences deposit images, and these images are handled as though they were the originals themselves.

This simple view, however, raises questions. Are mental images in fact found to be present when thinking goes on? And, more disturbingly: Are we not facing the old problem that individual objects, presented either "in person" or through memory images, are supposed to be unsuitable material for thought? Aristotle, explaining why we need memory, maintained that "without a presentation intellectual activity is impossible." But immediately afterwards Aristotle encountered Berkeley's dilemma concerning generalization and anticipated the Englishman's answer. In geometrical demonstrations, he said, "though we do not for the purpose of the proof make any use of the fact that the quantity in the triangle is determinate, we nevertheless draw it determinate in quantity." Similarly, if the intellect deals with something that is not quantitative, "one envisages it as quantitative, though one thinks it in abstraction from quantity."

The dilemma is all here! In order to think about something, it must be present. But this presence is said to be an obstacle to generalization and therefore, it seems, it must be abandoned by the very thinking that requires it. But if visual presence is given up, in what other form of existence is the thought material handled? In what nonperceptual medium could it possibly exist? At what level of reality can a triangle without "determinate quantity" dwell?

Around the turn of this century, psychologists searched for an experimental answer. They asked their subjects questions that made them think and they inquired afterwards: What took place within you? From his results, Karl Bühler concluded in 1908 that "in principle any subject can be thought and meant completely and distinctly without any help of imagery (*Anschauungshilfen*)." At about the same time, Robert S. Woodworth was led to assert that "there is nonsensuous content" and that "according to my experience, the more effective the thinking process is at any moment, the more likely is imageless thought to be detected."

The doctrine of "imageless thought" did not hold that nothing observable goes on when a person thinks. The experiments did not indicate that the fruit of thought drops out of nowhere. On the contrary, the consensus was that thinking often takes place consciously; but this conscious happening was said not to be in the nature of imagery. Even skilled observers were at a loss to describe what went on in their minds while they were thinking. In order to define such imageless presence positively, Narziss Ach called it *"Bewusstheit"* (awareness). Karl Marbe called it *"Bewusstseinslagen"* (dispositions of consciousness). But mere names were of little help.

Not much is heard about this puzzlesome situation these days. Psychologists maintain that the nature of thinking is most reliably determined by what it accomplishes. And, in fact, the animal experiments on problem-solving have told us much about the kind of task a species of animal can perform and the conditions that help or hinder such a performance. But the experiments have also shown that if we wish to understand why an animal succeeds in one situation and fails in another we have to make inferences about the kind of process that goes on in the nervous system or mind of the animal. For example, the controversy on whether or not problem-solving may involve "insight" cannot be resolved by a mere description of the kind of task a pigeon or a chimpanzee is able to perform. We must inquire about the nature of the power needed for such achievements. Learning based simply on the practical experience of what "works" can be accomplished by a machine or its equivalent in the nervous system. The term "insight," on the other hand, refers to "sight" and raises the question of how much the perceptual awareness of the problem situation contributes. If an animal arrives at understanding, can it do so by simply handling the perceptual data in themselves or must it resort to nonperceptual thought? The same question has to be answered for human thinking. If we do not know what sort of process is at work, how are we to comprehend why certain conditions enhance understanding whereas others hamper it? And how are we to discover the best methods of training the mind for its profession?

Looking back at the controversy about the role of imagery in thinking, we can see now that its conclusions were unsatisfactory because two problems were confused. To ask whether or not thinking involves imagery was considered tantamout to asking whether such imagery is consciously experienced. Both contending parties seem to have agreed that if introspection did not reveal at least minimal traces of imagery in every thought process there was no way of asserting that such imagery was indispensable. The so-called sensationalists tried to cope with the negative results of many experiments by suggesting that "automatism or mechanization" could reduce the visual component of thought to "a feeble spark of conscious life," and that under such conditions experimental observers could not be expected to identify the "unanalyzable degenerate" (Edward B. Titchener) as what it actually was.

Even nowadays we would surely agree that to demonstrate the presence of a phenomenon in consciousness would greatly help in convincing us that it exists in the mind. But if we do not find it there, we can no longer conclude that it does not exist. Quite apart from the rather special mechanisms of repression described by the psychoanalysts, we have come to realize that a vast amount of mental processes—perhaps most of them—occur below the threshold of awareness. This includes much of the routine input of our senses. A great deal of what we notice and react to with our eyes and ears, with our sense of touch, and the muscle sense involves no consciousness or so little that often we cannot remember whether or not we saw our face when we brushed our hair in the morning, whether we felt the pressure of the chair when we sat down for breakfast, or whether we "saw" the elderly lady whom we avoided running into

when we walked to work. Sensory experience, then, is not necessarily conscious. Most certainly it is not always consciously remembered.

When it comes to thinking, there are many responses we give automatically, or almost so, because we hold them readily available or because the needed operations are so simple as to be almost instantaneous. They will tell us little about the nature of thought. Whether they involve imagery or not we have no way of knowing. We are more likely to learn from what can be observed when a person wrestles with a problem that mobilizes his mental resources. Such experiments were indeed performed, for instance, by Bühler and Woodworth. Even under these conditions, however, both men maintained that their observations supported the doctrine of imageless thought.

Here arises a suspicion concerning the nature of imagery. Perhaps the psychologists of those days and their subjects did not report the presence of images because what they experienced did not correspond to their notion of what an image is. In fact, the word "mental image" makes most of us feel uncomfortable. It suggests a complete, colorful, and faithful replica of some visible scene or object, floating tangibly in the mind. The German word *"Vorstellung,"* coined by a less empirically oriented tradition, avoids this connotation and therefore sounds more appropriate. But it has no clear meaning. It is untranslatable because it does not know what it is trying to describe. Sometimes it is rendered in English with "representation"—a term which indicates what function the phenomenon in question is supposed to fulfill, without, however, defining the nature of the phenomenon itself.

What, then, are mental images? According to the most elementary view, they are faithful replicas of the physical objects they replace. In Greek philosophy, the School of Leucippus and Democritus believed that a kind of image, which is shaped like the visible object and streams off from it, meets the eyes of the observer and penetrates them, whereby seeing comes about. These *eidola* or replicas, just as physical as the objects from which they had detached themselves, remained in the soul as memory images. They had all the completeness of the original objects. The closest approximation to

these faithful replications the modern psychologist has been able to discover are the so-called eidetic images—a kind of photographic memory that, according to the Marburg psychologist, Erich Jaensch, was to be found in 40 percent of all children and also in some adults. A person endowed with eidetic recall, for example, was able to commit a geographic map to memory in such a way that he could read off from the image the names of towns or rivers he did not know or had forgotten. Not much has been heard of eidetics since the 1920's, but the reports we have make it clear that the phenomena in question are more closely related to afterimages than to the sort of experience conjured up when somebody is asked to think of what his breakfast table looked like this morning. Just as an afterimage—*e.g.,* the ghostly white square appearing after we have stared at a black square—is not a percept in itself but the stimulus material for a percept, so is the eidetic image an objectively given stimulus, to be scrutinized, scanned, and selectively perceived. In studying direct perception we need to know with what kind of a pattern a person or animal responds to the stimulus material. Similarly it is an open question what sort of percept is produced in response to an afterimage or an eidetic image. We ask: How is such an image perceived? And the answer does not really concern the psychology of memory.

If the memory image does not simply duplicate some scene of the physical world, what is it like? As a first concession one may allow that memory can take things out of their context and show them in isolation. Berkeley admits being "able to abstract in one sense, as when I consider some particular parts or qualities separated from others, with which though they are united in some object, yet it is possible they may really exist without them." He can, for example, imagine "the trunk of a human body without the limbs." This sort of quantitative difference between the memory image and the complete array of stimulus material is the easiest to conceive theoretically. It leaves untouched the notion that perception is a mechanical copy of what the outer world contains and that memory simply preserves such a copy faithfully. The mind, it is said, can cut pieces from the cloth of memory, leaving the cloth itself unchanged. It can also make collages from memory material, by

In an experiment on eidetic imagery made around 1920 by August Riekel, a ten-year-old boy was asked to examine this picture for nine seconds. Later, looking at an empty white screen, he was able to glean details of the picture as though it were still present. He could count the number of the windows on the house in the back and the number of cans on the milk cart. When asked about the sign on top of the door he deciphered it with difficulty: "That's hard to read . . . it says 'Number,' then a 3, then an 8 or 9 . . ." He also could make out the name of the shop owner and the drawing of a cow beneath the word *Milchhandlung.*

imagining centaurs or griffins. Here we have the crudest concept of imagination or fantasy—a concept that concedes to the human mind nothing more creative than the capacity to combine mechanically reproduced "pieces of reality."

Piecemeal recall is indeed frequently reported in memory experiments. One of Kurt Koffka's subjects, asked to respond to the stimulus word "jurist," states: "All I saw was a brief-case held by an arm!" Even more frequently, an object, or group of objects, appears in memory on empty ground, completely deprived of its natural setting. I shall show soon that one cannot account for the refined abstractions commonly found in mental imagery by simply asserting that memory images often fail to reproduce some of the parts of the complete object. But even this unsophisticated motion presents us with a formidable problem, crucial to our present purpose and almost untouched by psychology.

There is an obvious difference between Berkeley's "human body without limbs" and the jurist's arm holding the brief-case. Berkeley refers to an incomplete object of nature—a mutilated trunk or a sculptured torso —completely perceived. In the second example, we have a complete object incompletely perceived. The jurist is no anatomical fragment; but all we see of him is a significant detail. This sort of incompleteness is typical of mental imagery. Paradoxically it presupposes the perceptual presence of things we do not perceive. The jurist is completely present, but much of him is not seen.

Artists are familiar with representing parts of objects or surroundings of objects by the empty ground of paper or canvas. A Baroque painter may sketch only the shadowed portions of a face; a Chinese scroll may show mountains dissolving into empty silk. In part, we are helped to understand the artist's purpose by what we know about the objects represented. But the artist must also indicate by visual means that he is offering an incomplete image. He may use open form instead of a delineating contour; he may make his shapes fade out gradually; he may indicate enough of the simple geometry of contour or symmetry of pattern to indicate what is not given by what is.

In some persons' imagery there may be similar visible distinctions between the mental image of a cut-off head

Chinese landscape painting with mountains.

Nicolas Poussin, bister wash drawing of shepherds presenting offerings. Musée Condé, Chantilly.

"It seems to me as though the back, which looks as though it were bent by lofty meditations, fashions for me the head, engaged in the joyful recollection of astonishing deeds. And as a head full of majesty and wisdom rises thus before my eyes, the other deficient limbs begin to take shape in my thoughts. There gathers an effluence from what is present, producing, as it were, a sudden supplement.

Description of the *Torso Belvedere* by Johann Joachim Winckelmann (1717–1768).

and that of a man of whom only the head is visible. But much imagery is too indefinite in spelling out detail to allow for such purely perceptual discrimination. No, the distinction is typically determined by what psychologists have alluded to as the "meaning" of an image. An observer may report: "I see it neither distinctly nor completely, but I know what it means!"

As usual, the problem of "meaning" in perception has found psychologists in two camps: those asserting that sensory images are supplemented by what the mind knows about the represented objects intellectually; and those who consider meaning the memory effect of past images upon present images. I side with the latter because I am convinced that intellectual knowledge as such cannot influence the character of a visual image. Only images can influence images.

On the other hand, much remains to be explained if we say that images give meaning to images. When a person visualizes a horse mentally as a vague, moving blotch but knows it is a horse, where is the better defined image of a horse to which he refers the present one? Surely it is not consciously given. Surely, the jurist whose arm and brief-case were clearly perceived was not visible as a shadowy complement—the way we see the dark portion of the moon. Nor was he available for comparison floating around somewhere in the observer's visual field. The referential image of the horse was not visually given; but it was active in the present situation. Its effect was conscious but the image itself was not.

At an elementary level, the phenomenon may be described as the partial visualization of nonconscious memory images. The "incomplete" faces or mountains in visual art are shaped in such a way as to call up memory traces of the complete objects, and the interaction between these nonconscious images and the perceived patterns produce the curious effect of fragmentary images seen as parts of a completeness that is perceptually present but not visible. It will be clear, I hope, that this phenomenon has nothing to do with "illusion," that is, with the erroneous sensation that something is present which in fact is not, or with so-called imagination, which is supposed to supply, from past experience, the missing pieces and thereby complete the visible picture.

We can now describe with some precision the difference between the mental image of a torso and that of a human figure of which only the trunk is visible. The torso coincides with the memory trace of an incomplete human body, let us say, a sculptured fragment. The image of the trunk carries a portion of a more comprehensive memory trace to the level of visibility and is therefore perceived as a part of a larger "known" entity. It is as though in the dark a flashlight revealed a part of an object, which, although visually isolated, is seen as belonging to a whole.

The capacity of the mind to raise parts of a memory trace above the threshold of visibility helps us to respond to the question from which we started: How can conceptual thinking rely on imagery if the individuality of images interferes with the generality of thought? Our first answer is that mental images admit of selectivity. The thinker can focus on what is relevant and dismiss from visibility what is not.

So far we have only taken care of the crudest definition of abstraction, namely, generalization through the picking out of elements. But a closer look at the experimental data leads us to suspect that mental imagery may actually be a much subtler instrument, capable of serving a less primitive kind of abstraction.

Let us remember that Berkeley had no difficulty in admitting the existence of fragmentary mental images. But he saw that fragmentation was not sufficient to produce the visual equivalent of a concept. In order to visualize the concept of a horse, more is needed than the ability to imagine a horse without head or without legs. The image has to leave out all references to attributes in which horses differ; and this, Berkeley contended, was inconceivable.

When, early in our century, the experiment was actually made, several reputable investigators found, independently of each other, that generality was precisely what observers attributed to the appearance of the images they saw. Alfred Binet, the father of intelligence testing, subjected his two young daughters, Armande and Marguerite, to prolonged and exacting inquiries. At one occasion, he had Armande observe what happened when he uttered the word "hat." He then asked her whether she had thought of a hat in general or of a particular hat. The child's answer is a classic of introspective reporting: *"C'est mal dit: en général—je cherche à me représenter un de tous ces objets que le mot rassemble, mais je ne m'en représente aucun."* [" 'In general' expresses it badly: I try to represent to myself one of all the objects that the word brings together, but I do not represent to myself any one of them."] Asked to respond to the word "snow," Marguerite first visualizes a photograph, then "I saw the snow falling . . . in general . . . not very clearly." Binet notes that Berkeley is being refuted when one of the girls reports "a lady, who is dressed, but one cannot tell whether her dress is white or black, light or dark."

Koffka, in a similar series of experiments, published in 1912, obtained many *"Allgemeinvorstellungen"* (generic images), which are often quite "indistinct": a waving tricolor flag, rather dark, no certainty as to whether the colors run vertically or horizontally; a train of which one cannot tell whether it is freight or passenger; a coin of no particular denomination; a "schematic" figure, which might be male or female.

In reading these experimental reports, one notices, in the formulations of the investigators as well as in those of their observers, a tendency to get around the paradox of images that are particular and at the same time generic. They describe these experiences as indistinct or unclear: You cannot tell whether the object is blue or red because the image is not sharp enough! Such a description tends to dismiss the phenomenon as a purely negative one, the implication being that if we could only discern the object a little better we would be able to tell whether it is red or blue. But there is no such thing as a negative phenomenon. Either the image is experienced or it is not, and if it is, the challenge to the Berkeleyan contention is fully with us.

Only Edward B. Titchener, among psychologists, had the gift and the courage to say exactly what he saw, no matter how offensive his observations were to common-sense theory. He reports in his 1909 *Lectures on the Experimental Psychology of the Thought-Processes:*

. . . my mind, in its ordinary operations, is a fairly complete picture gallery,—not of finished paintings, but of impressionist notes. Whenever I read or hear

Auguste Renoir, *San Marco*. The Minneapolis
Institute of Art, Minneapolis.
Whole painting and detail of left center-
ground showing strokes and patches of color
which indicate figures and pigeons.

that somebody has done something modestly, or gravely, or proudly, or humbly, or courteously, I see a visual hint of the modesty or gravity or pride or humility or courtesy. The stately heroine gives me a flash of a tall figure, the only clear part of which is a hand holding up a steely grey skirt; the humble suitor gives me a flash of a bent figure, the only clear part of which is the bowed back, though at times there are hands held deprecatingly before the absent face. . . All these descriptions must be either self-evident or as unreal as a fairy-tale.

This is the voice of a new era. As clearly as words permit, Titchener points out that the incompleteness of the mental image is not simply a matter of fragmentation or insufficient apprehension but a positive quality, which distinguishes the mental grasp of an object from the physical nature of that object itself. He thus avoids the stimulus-error or—as he rightly suggests it would better be called—the "thing-error" or "object-error," that is, the assumption that the mind's account of a thing is identical with all or some of the thing's objective properties.

The reference to painting and to Impressionism is significant. Titchener's descriptions of visual experience differ as fundamentally from those of other psychologists as did the paintings of the Impressionists from those of their predecessors. In spite of the considerable liberties which artists before the generation of Edouard Manet took in fact with the objects they portrayed, the accepted convention had it that the picture was a faithful likeness of the object. Only with the Impressionists does aesthetic theory accept the view that the pictorial image is a product of the mind rather than a deposit of the physical object, and as such fundamentally different. This is the doctrine of modern art. A similar fundamental break with the tradition occurs in the psychology of visual experience a few decades later.

The comparison with Impressionist painting can also help us to understand the exact nature of Titchener's "visual hints" and "flashes." Instead of spelling out the detailed shape of a human figure or a tree the Impressionist offered an approximation, a few strokes, which were not intended to create the illusion of the spelled-out figure or tree. Rather, in order to serve as the stimulus for the intended effect, the reduced pattern of strokes was to be perceived as such. However, we would again commit the stimulus-error if we identified the resulting experience with the strokes of paint that provoked it. The intended results were in fact hints and flashes, indicators of direction and color rather than defined outlines or patches. The assembly of colored strokes on the canvas was responded to by the beholder with what can only be described as a pattern of visual forces.

In order to suggest an explanation of these experiences we may refer to what I have described elsewhere as "induced perception." Show a person four dots in the configuration of a square and ask him to report what he sees or saw. Did he see a square? Did he not? The straight connections between the dots are an integral part of the percept; but they are not "seen," the way the dots are seen. What is going on here is not simply an interaction between the stored images of squares, preserved in memory from past experience, and the given configuration of dots. Instead, we are dealing with a much more basic physiological mechanism, not dependent on past experience although just as hypothetical as the effect of the past upon the present. The four dots

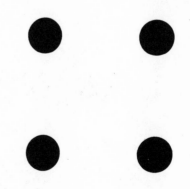

can be assumed to arouse in the brain the simplest configuration of forces compatible with them, that is, the pattern of squareness. Although these brain mechanisms are not reflected as such in visual experience, they are not the physiological equivalent of intellectual defini-

Hans Holbein, the Younger, *Portrait of Benedikt von Hertenstein,* detail. Metropolitan Museum, New York. Rogers Fund Purchase.

Oskar Kokoschka, *Portrait of Professor Forel,* detail. Kunsthalle, Mannheim.

70

tions either. They operate in the brain sector concerned with vision and they correspond therefore to visual concepts, not to intellectual ones.

The stimuli that arouse these configurations of forces may be as fragmentary as the four dots. They may also spell out the square explicitly by means of four lines drawn with a ruler. Or they may range somewhere in between on the scale of explicitness, as in Impressionist sketches. The less "complete" the stimulus, the more clearly will perceptual experience be revealed as a pattern of forces called up by the stimulus, imposed upon it, and organizing it in such a way as to provide it with a structural skeleton.

The elusive quality of such experiences is hard to capture with our language, which commonly describes objects by their tangible, material dimensions. But this quality is invaluable for abstract thought in that it offers the possibility of reducing a theme visually to a skeleton of essential dynamic elements. The humble suitor is abstracted to the flash of a bent figure. And this perceptual abstraction takes place without removal from the concrete experience, since the humble bent is not only understood to be that of the humble suitor but seen as such!

Note that these images, although vague in their outlines, surfaces, and colors, can embody with the greatest precision the patterns of forces called up by them. A popular prejudice has it that what is not sharply outlined, complete, and detailed is necessarily imprecise. In opposition to this view, we point out that, in painting, a sharply outlined portrait by Holbein or Dürer is no more precise in its perceptual form than the tissue of strokes by which a Frans Hals or Oskar Kokoschka defines the human countenance. In mathematics, a topological statement or drawing identifies a spatial relation such as "being contained in" or "overlapping" with the utmost precision although the statement leaves the actual shapes entirely undetermined. In logic, nobody contends that the generality of a concept makes for vagueness because it is devoid of particularized detail; on the contrary, the concentration on a few essentials is recognized as a means of sharpening the concept. But we are reluctant to admit that the same can be true for the visual image. And yet, the reduction of a human figure to the simple geometry of an expressive gesture or posture can sharpen the image in precisely the same way.

Here again we are helped by an observation of Titchener's, who invited his students to compare an actual nod of the head with the mental nod that signifies assent to an argument, or the actual frown and wrinkling of the forehead with the mental frown that signifies perplexity. "The sensed nod and frown are coarse and rough in outline; the imaged nod and frown are cleanly and delicately traced." To be sure, a sketchy image, painted on canvas or seen by the mind's eye, can be imprecise and confused, but so can the most meticulously detailed picture. This is a matter of shapelessness rather than of detailedness. It depends on whether the structural skeleton of the image is organized and orderly or not. The composite pictures of healthiness, illness, criminality, or family character which Francis Galton obtained by superimposing the portrait photographs of many individuals are fuzzy and unenlightening because they are shapeless, not because they are blurred.

The blurredness of the composite photographs does not prevent them, however, from being concrete. Nor are they "generic" in themselves because they are derived from many individual images. William James has made this point, reminding us that "a blurred thing is just as particular as a sharp thing; and the generic character of either sharp image or blurred image depends on its being felt with its representative function. This function is the mysterious plus, the understood meaning." The same point was made also by other psychologists, and it gave trouble to Titchener, who claimed that to speak, in psychology, of an abstract idea or a general idea is no more correct than it would be to speak of an abstract sensation or a general sensation. It was, he said, a "confusion of logic and psychology." He failed to see that concreteness and abstractness do not exclude each other, and that a concrete image may preserve its concreteness and yet be experienced as abstract, when viewed as the image of a kind of thing rather than merely as that of an individual.

So far we have limited ourselves to mental images of physical objects, such as human figures or landscapes. Some of these images, however, have been evoked by such abstract concepts as modesty or gravity or pride.

I give woodcuts of representative specimens of these Forms, and very brief descriptions of them extracted from the letters of my correspondents.   Sixty-three other diagrams on a smaller scale will be found in Plates I., II. and III., and two more which are coloured are given in Plate IV.

D. A. "From the very first I have seen numerals up to nearly 200, range themselves always in a particular manner, and

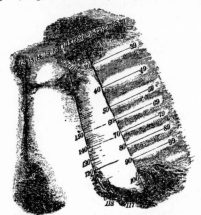

in thinking of a number it always takes its place in the figure. The more attention I give to the properties of numbers and their interpretations, the less I am troubled with this clumsy framework for them, but it is indelible in my mind's eye even when for a long time less consciously so.   The higher numbers are to me quite abstract and unconnected with a shape.   This rough and untidy [1] production is the best I can do towards repre-

[1] The engraver took much pains to interpret the meaning of the rather faint but carefully made drawing, by strengthening some of the shades.   The result was very very satisfactory, judging from the author's own view of it, which is as follows:—" Certainly if the engraver has been as successful with all the other representations as with that of my shape and its accompaniments, your article must be entirely correct."

senting what I see.   There was a little difficulty in the performance, because it is only by catching oneself at unawares, so to speak, that one is quite sure that what one sees is not affected by temporary imagination.   But it does not seem much like, chiefly because the mental picture never seems *on* the flat but *in* a thick, dark gray atmosphere deepening in certain parts, especially where 1 emerges, and about 20.   How I get from 100 to 120 I hardly know, though if I could require these figures a few times without thinking of them on purpose, I should soon notice.   About 200 I lose all framework.   I do not see the actual figures very distinctly, but what there is of them is distinguished from the dark by a thin whitish tracing.   It is the place they take and the shape they make collectively which is invariable.   Nothing more definitely takes its place than a person's age.   The person is usually there so long as his age is in mind."

T. M.   "The representation I carry in my mind of the numerical series is quite distinct to me, so much so that I cannot think of any number but I at once see it (as it were) in its peculiar place in the diagram.   My remembrance of dates is also nearly entirely dependent on a clear mental vision of their *loci* in the diagram.   This, as nearly as I can draw it, is the following :—

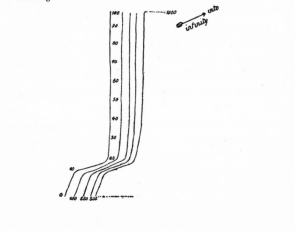

Images of numerical series from Sir Francis Galton's *Inquiries into Human Faculty,* first published in 1883.

Also, the visual content of some of these images has been reduced to mere flashes of shape or direction, so that what is actually seen can hardly be described as a likeness of the object. We ask: How abstract can a mental image be?

A reference to the so-called synesthesias may be helpful here because they commonly involve nonrepresentational images. In cases of *audition colorée* (color hearing), a person will see colors when he listens to sounds, especially music. In general, these visual sensations fail to make music more enjoyable or more understandable even when the correlation between certain tones and certain colors is fairly constant. On the other hand, the attempts to accompany music with moving colored shapes (Oskar Fischinger, Walter Ruttmann, Walt Disney) have been strikingly successful when the common expressive characteristics of motion, rhythm, color, shape, musical pitch, etc. strengthened each other across sensory boundaries. Whether or not such combinations of sensory modes are helpful or disturbing depends largely on whether structural correspondences can be experienced among them.

The same holds true when theoretical concepts, such as the number series or the sequence of the twelve months, are accompanied with color associations or spatial arrangements. These accompaniments, too, appear quite spontaneously in some persons, as Francis Galton established in his famous inquiries into imagery. They also can be quite stable. But although they are sometimes used as mnemotechnical aids, there is no indication that they are of help in the active handling of the concepts. This is so because the structural relations among the visual counterparts do not seem to illustrate those among the concepts. When one of the Fellows of the Royal Society whom Galton interviewed saw the number series from zero to a hundred habitually arranged in "the shape of a horseshoe, lying on a slightly inclined plane, with the open end towards me" and the 50 located on the apex, no benefit to the professor's arithmetic is likely to have come from this image.

Theoretical concepts are not handled in empty space; they may associate with a visual setting. The images resulting from these associations may appear more accidental than they actually are. Titchener, after sitting on the platform behind "a somewhat emphatic lecturer, who made great use of the monosyllable 'but' " had his "feeling of but" associated ever since with "a flashing picture of a bald crown, with a fringe of hair below, and a massive black shoulder, the whole passing swiftly down the visual field, from northwest to southeast." Although Titchener himself cites this example as an instance of association by circumstance, it would seem evident that the image took so firmly to the concept because there was an intrinsic resemblance of the barrier character of "but" and that of the turned-away speaker and his massive black shoulder. And although the image is not likely to have helped Titchener's reasoning, it will have added a substantial flavor to his attitude toward "but"-clauses, *i.e.*, toward the kind of reservation these clauses impose on affirmative statements—and this attitude was surely not irrelevant to his thinking.

Some visualizations of theoretical concepts can be described as routine metaphors. Herbert Silberer has reported on the "hypnagogic states" which he frequently experienced when he made an effort to think but was hampered by drowsiness. Once, after a futile effort to confront Kant's and Schopenhauer's philosophy of time, his frustration expressed itself spontaneously in the image of a "morose secretary," unwilling to give information. At another occasion, when he was about to review an idea in order not to forget it, he saw, while falling asleep, a lackey in livery, standing before him as though waiting for his orders. Or, after pondering how he might improve a halting passage in his writing, he saw himself planing a piece of wood. Here the images reflect an almost automatic parallelism among activities of the mind and events in the physical world. Rather similar examples are cited in Darwin's studies on the expression of emotion. While a person is struggling with an irritating problem of thought he may scratch his head, as though trying to assuage a physical irritation. The organism functions as a whole, and the body produces a physical equivalent of what the mind is doing. In Silberer's hypnagogic states, this physical counterpart is conjured up by spontaneous imagery.

This sort of simple-minded illustration may be more of a distraction than a help to the thinker. When Galton discovered, to his astonishment, that "the great majority of the men of science to whom I first applied protested that mental imagery was unknown to them," he finally concluded that "an overready perception of sharp mental images is antagonistic to the acquirement of habits of highly-generalized and abstract thought, especially when the steps of reasoning are carried on by words as symbols, and that if the faculty of seeing the pictures was ever possessed by men who think hard, it is very apt to be lost by disuse."

But there is only a fine line between the pedestrian explicitness of the illustrative image and a well-chosen example's power to test the nature and consequences of an idea in a kind of thought experiment. I said earlier that thinking begins with the handling of objects and that when the objects are not present they are replaced by some sort of imagery. These images need not be lifelike replicas of the physical world. Consider the following instance from Silberer's half-dreams. In the twilight state of drowsiness he reflects on "transsubjectively valid judgments." Can judgments be valid for everybody? Are there some that are? Under what conditions? Obviously there is no other way of searching for the answers than to explore pertinent test situations. In the drowsy thinker's mind there arises suddenly the image of a big circle or transparent sphere in the air with people surrounding it whose heads reach into the circle. This is a fairly schematic visualization of the idea under investigation, but it also makes some of its aspects metaphorically tangible: the dwelling of all heads in a common realm, the exclusion of the bodies from this community, etc. It is a useful working model. We also notice that the image presents natural objects—human figures, a sphere—but in a thoroughly unnatural constellation, not realizable on our gravity-ridden earth. The visual constellation is dictated by the dominating idea in the mind of the dreamy thinker. The centric symmetry of the converging figures is the simplest, clearest, most economical representation of "shared judgments," brought about without any concern for what is feasible in practical space. Also the transparency of the sphere, this paradoxical solid into which heads can reach, indicates that the image is physically tangible only to the extent that suits the thought and is compatible with it. While thoroughly fantastic as a physical event, the image is strictly functional with regard to the idea it embodies.

Galton, although critical of "overready perception of sharp mental images," realized that there was no reason to starve the visualizing faculty. He suggested that if this faculty is free in its action and not tied to reproduce hard and persistent forms "it might then produce generalized pictures out of its past experiences quite automatically."

One step further, and we are ready to point out that imagery is not limited to the representation of objects and events. The reduction of the object to a few essential flashes of direction or shape leads to the imaging of "abstract" forms, that is, spatial configurations or happenings without any direct reference to the inventory of the physical world. In the arts, the same continuum has led to the nonrepresentational painting and sculpture of our century. I pointed to Impressionism when I referred to Titchener's descriptions of imagery; and indeed one can date with some precision the phase of modern painting corresponding to such examples as: "Horse is, to me, a double curve and a rampant posture with a touch of mane about it; cow is a longish rectangle with a certain facial expression, a sort of exaggerated pout." But Titchener can sound even more modern. He describes the "patterns" aroused in him by a particular writer or book: "I get a suggestion of dull red . . . of angles rather than curves; I get, pretty clearly, the picture of movement along lines, and of neatness or confusion where the moving lines come together. But that is all,—all, at least, that ordinary introspection reveals." While Titchener was recording his introspections, artists such as Wassily Kandinsky were exploring the mysterious zone between the representational and the abstract. Titchener visualizes the concept of "meaning": "I see meaning as the blue-grey tip of a kind of scoop, which has a bit of yellow above it (probably a part of the handle), and which is just digging into a dark mass of what appears to be plastic material"—an image that would have qualified for exhibition at Kandinsky's *Blaue Reiter*.

Nonrepresentational images are rarely reported in the psychological literature—for reasons I have indicated. At the time when the studies of mental imagery were

Wassily Kandinsky, *Improvisation, Number 27*, 1912.
Metropolitan Museum, New York. Alfred Stieglitz Collection.

CHAP. XL.

I AM now beginning to get fairly into my work; and by the help of a vegetable diet, with a few of the cold feeds, I make no doubt but I shall be able to go on with my uncle Toby's story, and my own, in a tolerable straight line. Now,

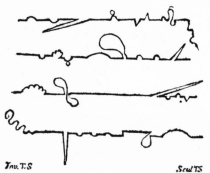

Inv. T.S   *Sculp TS*

Thefe were the four lines I moved in thro' my first, second, third, and fourth volumes *. —In the fifth volume I have been very good, —the precife line I have defcribed in it being this :—

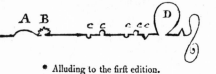

* Alluding to the firft edition.

By

By which it appears, that except at the curve, marked A, where I took a trip to Navarre;— and the indented curve B, which is the fhort airing when I was there with the Lady Baufliere and her page,—I have not taken the leaft frifk of a digreffion, till John de la Caffe's Devils led me the round you fee marked D;—for as for *c c c c c*, they are nothing but parenthefes, and the common *ins* and *outs* incident to the lives of the greateft minifters of ftate; and when compared with what men have done,—or with my own tranfgreffions at the letters A B D,—they vanifh into nothing.

In this laft volume I have done better ftill, —for from the end of Le Fever's epifode, to the beginning of my uncle Toby's campaigns,—I have fcarce ftepped a yard out of my way.

If I mend at this rate, it is not impoffible,— by the good leave of his Grace of Benevento's Devils,—but I may arrive hereafter at the excellency of going on even thus :—

————————————

which is a line drawn as ftraight as I could draw it by a writing-mafter's ruler (borrowed for that purpofe) turning neither to the right hand nor to the left.

This *right line*,—the path-way for Chriftians to walk in! fay Divines,————

————The emblem of moral rectitude! fays Cicero,————

————The *beft line!* fay cabbage-planters,———— is the fhorteft line, fays Archimedes, which can be drawn from one given point to another.

I wifh

An example of visual thinking from the opening pages of Book VI, Chapter 40, of *Tristram Shandy* by Laurence Sterne, first published in 1761.

made, the nonobjective depiction of definite contents was not yet conceivable, and it takes a bold mind to acknowledge the presence of what it cannot conceive. Théodule Ribot, who collected nine hundred replies, gives only an occasional example; one of his observers saw the infinite represented by a black hole. And yet, I venture to guess that "abstract" imagery belongs to the ordinary equipment of the mind. We are likely to find it not only as the idle accompaniment of speculation but as the indispensable means of demonstration and experimentation, resorted to when we think about theoretical matters. These nonobjective metaphors, often faint to the point of being barely observable, are likely to have been the "nonsensuous content," those "nonsensorial feelings of relation" that produced so much trouble in the discussions on imageless thought because of their paradoxical status. They were existing nonexistent things. No wonder that an observer described his thinking as "imageless" if by images he meant the floating likenesses of rather substantial human figures or breakfast tables. Brought up on the realism of traditional painting, such an observer was perhaps unable to conceive of "abstract" images. Even so, such images may be quite common and indeed indispensable to any mind that thinks generic thoughts but needs the tangible generality of pure shapes to think them. "I am inclined to believe," admitted Ribot, "that the logic of images is the prime mover of constructive imagination."

BIBLIOGRAPHIC REFERENCES

The foregoing essay is the first draft of a chapter from a book by Rudolf Arnheim, to be devoted to visual thinking. Consult Arnheim's *Art and Visual Perception* (Berkeley and Los Angeles, University of California Press, 1964) for induced perception and perceptual concepts. The reference to Aristotle is *On Memory and Reminiscence*, 450a. For Berkeley, see *A Treatise Concerning the Principles of Human Knowledge,* especially the Introduction. The history of the theories on the perception of form is briefly surveyed by Richard Held in *Structure in Art and in Science,* G. Kepes, editor (New York, Braziller, 1965); the passage about Democritus is given by G. S. Kirk and J. E. Raven, *The Presocratic Philosophers* (Cambridge, Cambridge University Press, 1963, p. 422). Samples of the literature on imageless thought are reprinted in J. M. Mandler and G. Mandler, *Thinking: From Association to Gestalt* (New York, Wiley, 1964). Herbert Silberer's report on hypnagogic imagery is reprinted in *Organization and Pathology of Thought,* D. Rapaport, editor (New York, Columbia, 1951). For the other original sources see:

Alfred Binet, *L'Etude expérimentale de l'intelligence,* Paris, Costes (1922).

Francis Galton, *Inquiries into Human Faculty and its Development,* London, Dent (1907).

Erich R. Jaensch, *Über den Aufbau der Wahrnehmungswelt und ihre Struktur im Jugendalter,* Leipzig (1923).

Kurt Koffka, *Zur Analyse der Vorstellungen und ihrer Gesetze,* Leipzig, Quelle & Meyer (1912).

Théodule Ribot: *L'Evolution des idées générales,* Paris, Alcan (1915).

Edward B. Titchener: *Lectures on the Experimental Psychology of the Thought-Processes,* New York, Macmillan (1926).

S. GIEDION

SYMBOLIC EXPRESSION IN PREHISTORY AND IN THE FIRST HIGH CIVILIZATIONS

Ours is a period of transition: a transition from the mechanistic age to the electronic age; a transition from the tangible, logical laws to intangible, irrational phenomena of the invisible world, from the normal bodies to the particles of the atoms, which cannot be seen by our eyes, but only the effect evaluated.

In other words, we are in a period of transition from the logical to the irrational. There are signs today that we are again approaching an age of symbolism, and that a prolonged phase of naturalism is giving way to new conceptions of reality, one of multiple dimensions and renewed significances. The present revival of interest in the symbol and its meaning leads us back to its origins in prehistory. It is there that the whole process of symbolization can best be studied. Indeed, symbolization is the key to all Paleolithic art, from the grandiose engravings and paintings in the caverns of southern France and Spain to small artifacts made from reindeer antlers. In every case actuality has been translated into symbolism, however realistic it may appear. This transmutation persisted throughout Paleolithic art until the Neolithic period, when abstraction reigned supreme.

It is only in recent years that scholarship has recognized the importance of a systematic study of the symbolic content of prehistoric art. The further we proceed in such investigations, the more we are astonished at the amazing richness of imagination displayed. Here, it seems, may be the sources of much of the imagery which has been attributed to Greek art. However, the previous work of all serious prehistorians and anthropologists has concentrated on the classification of material objects such as hand axes and other such tools. Consequently there still exist great gaps in our understanding of what symbols meant to prehistoric man.

Today the common denominator in creed and ritual that once linked man to man has lost its force. Whereas in primitive eras magic, myth, and religion provided man with a spiritual armor against a hostile environment, today he stands stripped and naked. In the effort to compensate he has had to create symbols and inner images out of himself. Half-ironically, the Surrealist painter Max Ernst wrote, "In 1930, after having composed with violence and method the *Femme 100 têtes,* I was visited nearly every day by my private phantom attached to my person—the superior of birds named Loplop."[1]

Today the average man appears to have lost the key to his own being, even though he still believes that he knows what he likes and that he can express what he feels. The ruling taste of the times demonstrates the result of this loss, for it affects the entire sphere of emotional activity. The average man, whether governed or governing, has grown indifferent to the flood of surrogates, to *ersatz* in art and architecture, to falsity in expression; and this process has been called "the devaluation of symbols."[2] For a century and a half it has been apparent, and it is still going on. The decline in our community life, our helplessness in finding forms for celebration or leisure, our lack of imaginative power to develop forms to counteract the maladies of our culture —all indicate the extent of man's present disorientation.

It is not difficult to understand how this has come about. The man of today has to bear an enormous and increasing load of intellectual knowledge, while at the same time his emotional world has been steadily atrophying. His emotional apparatus has shrunk to a mere appendage, quite unable to absorb and humanize the knowledge accumulated by his brain. He stands alone. It may be that from new developments in the communal sphere some new suprapersonal spirit will emerge. But at the moment, man must rely on himself. This situation may give us a clue to the nature of those symbols which are today emerging in the work of contemporary painters and poets.

THE REAWAKENING OF SYMBOLS

Jean-Paul Sartre (however his existentialism is regarded) is a poet with visions of what kinds of symbols are possible today. In *L'Imaginaire* he asserts that, in contrast to the situation in former periods, symbolic function is no longer derived and explained from the outside world: "We would not accept a conception according to which the symbolic function has to be added to the image from outside. The image is in essence symbolic by its very structure."[3] Without any kind of intermediary, the symbol through its very form finds a direct access to the emotions.

Forms that have no apparent significance and yet seize directly upon the senses are the dominant constituent elements of contemporary art (Fig. 1). These symbols differ not only from the magical potent symbols of prehistory but also from the conceptualized symbols of the Greeks. Today's symbols are anonymous; they seem to exist for themselves alone, without any direct significance. Yet they are imbued with an inexplicable attraction: the magic of their forms. In a sense, they represent a regenerative or healing process, a flight from technological frenzy. Beside these anonymous symbols or forms without direct significance, age-old symbols from the remote past have been revived and integrated into new contexts, as is discerned in the work of Joan Miró and Paul Klee, among others. It would be a rewarding though difficult task to carry out some form of research which could give us an insight into the process of this development and its manifold ramifications.

It cannot be said today that the forces of symbolization no longer exist. A great picture that seizes all our senses simultaneously (as does Picasso's *Guernica*) can become a great composite symbol. As we become aware of the multilayered fabric of the soul, we try to ascertain not only the limits within which logical argument operates as a reliable tool, but also the areas in which that tool cannot be used, areas of different psychic dimensions. The laws of logic have colored philosophic thought ever since the Renaissance, especially since the seventeenth century. This influence is closely paralleled in the optical sphere by the influence of perspective on our view of the world. It is just these narrow criteria of logical cause and effect and of optical perspective that the present period resents and rebels against.

One no longer has to ask why. Our eyes are not blinded to the marvelous artistic achievements of recent centuries; but we have become ever more conscious of the situation to which rationalism led us throughout the nineteenth century: that of living only for the moment, lacking all certainty regarding decisions that take on psychic dimensions. The one-way street of logic has landed us in the slum of materialism.

Fig. 1. Joan Miró, *New Year's Card for José Luis Sert,* 1949.

THE SYMBOL IN PRIMEVAL ART

Before art, man created the symbol. The name arose late—the symbol, early. It appears at the very dawn of man's urge for expression. Its first rudimentary form emerged in the Mousterian era as the traces of Neanderthal man's first attempts at a spiritual organization transcending simple materials and a utilitarian existence. Bones engraved with parallel and diagonal lines (Fig. 2) or with red circles have been found, but these are so fragmentary that no safe conclusions can be drawn from them. It is quite otherwise, however, with the small hemispherical hollows carved out of stone, called *cupules*. Prehistorians report that the earliest surviving man-made signs were found on a triangular grave slab discovered in the rock shelter of La Ferrassie in the Dordogne (Fig. 3). These were small hollows in the slab, which was placed face down over a child's body. These hollows, which had no practical function, are a widespread phenomenon of Paleolithic art whose symbolic significance is undefined.

The magic symbols that appear most frequently and over the longest periods of prehistory are simple. They consist of fragments, the part standing for the whole: a hand, for example, represents the entire human being, and the genitalia represent fertility. But it is more difficult to give meaning to the circle. It appears in a great number of forms, large and small—as cup-shaped depressions in stone (*cupules*), colored dots and disks (*ponctuations*), *holes* (*perforations*), often varying in shape.

In primitive times symbols sometimes stood alone, though usually several were associated and interrelated, *e.g.,* dots were related to hands, animals, or tectiforms, and *cupules* were arranged in rows or placed singly in association with an animal or upon the animal. Greater precision could thus be given to certain of the manifold meanings inherent in any one symbol, and also a single overriding meaning could be accentuated, such as the desire for increased fertility. Such designs, in which different symbols with many meanings were combined in order to stress one specific meaning—as genitalia and *cupules*—may be called "composite symbols."

In addition to simple straightforward symbols, a host of complex and entirely abstract forms were developed in primitive times. Man's power in this direction seems to have been inexhaustible, but the meanings are all the more obscure. The names given these more complex symbolic forms are mere labels—tectiforms, claviforms, naviforms (Fig. 4). In contrast to the simpler symbols, individual imagination here seems to have been given free play, and in many cases only a single example of certain types is as yet known. These symbols are usually in the most inaccessible parts of the caverns, as at Altamira, El Castillo, and La Pasiega. The fact of their inaccessibility may be interpreted as referring to the special potency of the magic emanating from them. Even today many of these configurations exert a strangely powerful impression on the beholder, as in Altamira, where blood-red zigzag symbols as large as the drawings of the bulls traverse the whole ceiling.

Symbolization arises from the need to give perceptible form to the imperceptible. Symbolization emerged as soon as man felt the need of expressing the disquieting and intangible relation between life and death, first expressed in very primitive ways. When Johann Jakob Bachofen said that it was in the tomb that the symbol was formed, he was thinking of the Etruscan necropolis that was the starting point for his pioneer researches on symbolism.[4] His supporting material was provided by tomb reliefs, long ignored by the archaeologists, and by his profound knowledge of classical authors. Since then, both material evidence and our understanding of symbolism have increased enormously, and our newly acquired knowledge of primitive art has largely sustained Bachofen's theories.

Fig. 2. Pink pebble engraved with parallel and diagonal lines.
Proto-Magdalenian, from Laugerie Haute (Dordogne).

Fig. 3. Triangular grave slab with the first man-made *cupules*.
Mousterian, from La Ferrassie (Dordogne).

Fig. 4. Tectiform symbols from Altamira.

Let us repeat: the symbols of primitive art are rooted in the primary demands of human existence, in the idea of the continuity of life and death. The main purpose of primitive existence was to obtain food. Food implied the animal. Where direct attack on the animal was not successful, rituals, magic signs, and magic symbols were invented, by which man hoped to be invested with power to bewitch the animal. But the killing of beasts was not enough to ensure a continuous food supply. That depended also on the fecundity of the stock; to ensure this, primitive man was even more powerless. Only magic held out hope.

We can therefore understand that most early symbols, though they appear in highly varied, even opposing, combinations, were concerned with the perpetuation of the animal species, and in one way or another were designed to promote fertility through magic. We see this more clearly in the primitive Aurignacian than in the later and more highly developed Magdalenian era. In the former, one symbol of fertility is the vulva; it appears constantly, generally alone, but sometimes in combination with the animal whose increase is desired. Such representations of female organs have certainly nothing to do with human sexual instincts, nor do the much rarer representations of male organs, or the small female figurines with enormous breasts and abdomens, or the ithyphallic male figures (Figs. 5, 6).

Signs of a belief in the continuance of life after death appeared in the early Mousterian age. Things come to no abrupt end, and death does not completely extinguish life. Some possibility of re-entering the earthly cycle emerges, both for men and for animals—though how this is to be achieved is very unclear. In that age man lived close to his dead, who were buried within his dwelling place. Tens of thousands of years later the same custom was practiced in the Nile Delta (Merimde), just before the dawn of history. The dead influenced the fate of their descendants, they shared in the family meals. Today in parts of Polynesia it is customary to bury the dead within the dwelling or outside beneath the eaves. This area is otherwise sacrosanct. "People do not turn their backs on it, and when they lie down to sleep they orient their heads in that direction."[5]

The animal, too, possessed magic power after death. Both in the interests of the food supply and also to placate the spirit of the dead animal, it was reasonable to take steps to facilitate its return to life. "In short, everything was done as though the animal had magic powers at its command which must be propitiated or dominated by other magic forces."[6]

Fig. 5. Stone slab with vulvas and *cupules.*
Aurignacian, from La Ferrassie (Dordogne).

Fig. 6. Detail of the Venus of Laussel.
Early Magdalenian, from Laussel (Dordogne).

SYMBOL AND MYTH

Premythological man was completely embedded in the world which surrounded him. He formed one with it, he did not stand above it, he did not feel himself to be the center, but a humble element in it. His fate was ruled by powers he could not comprehend. To him the animal was a superior being, a creature greater than he, and at the same time a personification of invisible powers. All primitive symbols are rooted in this zoomorphic age. However simple or complex these symbols, they all represent invisible forces in a universe not yet reduced to a battleground between man and man.

Myths, on the other hand, are based on the relationships and destinies of men, or of men and gods. In myths, time (the succession of events) plays a determining part. In primeval times, today, yesterday, tomorrow were all one. Myths grew out of the huge transformation from the zoomorphic to the anthropomorphic age in which we still live, and thus they arose relatively late. It would be hazardous to assign any precise dates; yet from their content, the conflicts they embody, and the context in which they are described, we may assume that they roughly coincided with the first formal communities, such as the small temple settlements that flourished in the north and south of Mesopotamia in the fourth millennium B.C.

In the Sumerian epic of Gilgamesh, the cities had already become the acknowledged centers of religion and authority, and Gilgamesh the epic hero ruled the city of Erech. According to the evidence, Gilgamesh did not live before 2700 or 2600 B.C. Therefore, the epic recording his heroic deeds can date from no earlier than about 2600 B.C. In this period a new world of gods, whose hierarchical structure precisely reflected the contemporary social order, came into being.

If we consider the situation immediately before this, as reflected in Persian and Mesopotamian pottery of the fifth millennium B.C., we find no trace of myth and the world of the gods, such as appears on the cylinder seals of the late fourth millennium. The abstract designs on the earlier pottery, with their artistic intensity and great charm, are rich in prehistoric concepts, and they have far more in common with the symbolic world of the Magdalenian era (eight to ten millennia earlier) than with the anthropomorphic myths of a thousand years later (Fig. 7).

Yet it must not be forgotten that vestiges of prehistory still cling to the anthropomorphic myths. Like the signs and symbols in the primitive world, they indicate the eternal polarity of life and death, and are embedded in the cosmos. Now all has been given anthropomorphic form, and the stars themselves have become deistic personifications. This mingling of men and gods with the cosmos is the prime characteristic of myths.

Fig. 7. Buff-ware jar with female figure on the handle and sexual triangle hatched below. From Kish, Mesopotamia, fourth millennium.

84

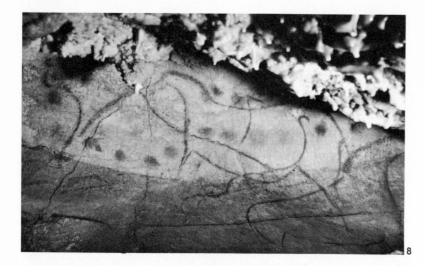

Fig. 8. Wounded lioness, three horses, and red dots. Aurignacian-Perigordian, from Le Combel, Pech-Merle (Lot).

Fig. 9. Tracing of a bison. Magdalenian, from Niaux (Ariège).

The golden age of the symbol was in prehistoric times. "Since then it has been overwhelmed by the hostile pressure of rational thought, which, reinforced by experience and reason itself, has steadily gained ground . . . The *raison d'être* of the symbol lies in the human urge to express that which is inherently inexpressible."[7]

The essential nature of the symbol has always consisted in this urge to express the inherently inexpressible, but in primitive times the crystallization of a concept in the form of a symbol portrayed reality before that reality came to pass. The symbol itself was reality, for it was believed to possess the power of working magic, and thus of directly affecting the course of events: the wish, the prayer, or the spell to be fulfilled.

Herein lies the contrast between the function of the symbol in prehistory and in later periods. In Greece the symbol was not only a means of recognition, it also developed a spiritual content and became an abstract concept. It was not an independent agent.

Bachofen calls the kinds of symbols found on Roman mortuary reliefs "reposing in themselves"—that is, complete in themselves. The symbols employed in the Christian catacombs up to the middle of the fifth century embodied the hope of future bliss: wine signified the feasts of Paradise; a dove sipping water, the soul refreshing itself in the waters of life; flowered meadows represented Heaven. These all point to the life beyond the tomb and are transcendental, whereas primitive symbols were neither complete in themselves nor transcendental.

It is difficult to determine the limits of symbolism in prehistory. It was believed to be a potent agent, and by force of sympathetic magic was called upon to help achieve a certain purpose, with positive results. Yet the border line between the symbol and other representations is indeterminate, as in the spellbinding forms of animals on cavern walls, with their inextricable mingling of magical intent and straightforward realism (Figs. 8, 9).

SYMBOLS IN THE FIRST HIGH CIVILIZATIONS

As I have tried to show elsewhere,[8] the strong cord which connected prehistory with the first high civilizations was never wholly severed, because the Egyptians never lost the cord which connected them with prehistory. Indeed the continued linkage was at the basis of their nature. For the Egyptians, the animate had direct relations with the unanimated: the live with the dead. The most important primeval tradition stressed the community with the animal world. The reference was changed, but this community was maintained.

Their attitude toward the animal was their strongest link with the prehistoric conception of the oneness of all life. To a certain extent this relation existed also in Mesopotamia. The best evidence are the pottery fragments of the fourth millennium, found in both the North and the South. All are submitted to abstract design. On a sherd found in the North, at Tepe Kazineh, not far from the Black Sea, the body of an ibex is reduced to a single line, and the horns, the sources of power and life-force, are stressed above all other parts of the body (Fig. 10). The same can be observed on a pottery fragment from the South with the incised design of an ibex (Fig. 11). Abstraction can go so far that, as in the bowl shown here from Tall-i-Bakun (Fig. 12), the bodies of the ibexes are reduced to the utmost while an enormous stress is given to the monumental horns.

The changes in hierarchy which occurred in the first high civilizations had their impact on the position of the animal: in creating the anthropomorphic gods there came about the transition from the prehistoric sacred animal to deity. The animal considered as sacred changed to the animal considered as god. In the newly emerging pantheon of gods they became the living incarnation of a deity. Ptah, the supreme deity of Memphis, was incarnated in the bull Apis; in the South the God Khnum was incarnated in a ram.

The abstract symbols also lived on in the high civilizations. They could have the meaning of signs for life (Ankh) or signs of lasting existence (Djed). But more important was their use for a new invention: writing.

Fig. 10. Pottery fragment painted with the figure of an ibex. From Tepe Kazineh, northern Mesopotamia, fourth millennium.

Fig. 11. Pottery fragment with incised figure of an ibex. From Kish, Mesopotamia, fourth millennium.

Fig. 12. Buff-ware bowl painted with ibex. From Tall-i-Bakun, Mesopotamia, fourth millennium.

88

10

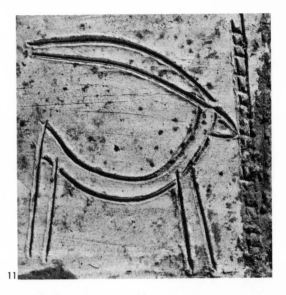

11

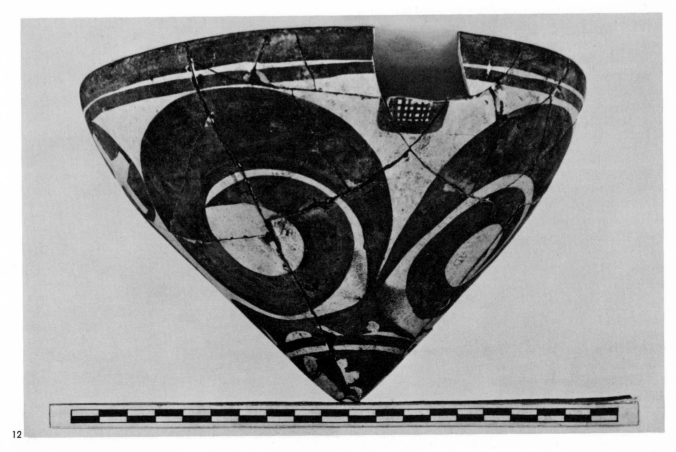

12

ABSTRACTION AND WRITING

In writing, signs, symbols, and abstraction flow together. Thousands of years of abstract representation lie behind the development of writing. Without this the discovery would have been unthinkable. Abstraction shaped its direct development and its final consistency (Fig. 13). In primitive times, abstract representation remained in the magical and symbolical realms. With writing, abstraction took on the aspect of everyday currency. Just like the animal which, when deprived of its freedom, becomes domesticated, so the magical meaning of abstraction was put to everyday use through writing.

Expression depends upon a connection between sound and image. A sound complex is created through a picture. That is, the picture no longer retains its original, physical meaning. The name borne by the physically represented picture is transformed into sound, which emanates from the picture.

In Chinese writing, which goes back some four thousand years, primitive customs live on to this day, for Chinese writing never progressed to the syllabic stage. It depicts the complex word in the form of a complex image. The origin of Chinese writing remains unclear. Attempts to derive it from the considerably earlier Sumerian writing do not seem to be acceptable. It is interesting that leading Sinologists have sought the origins of the earliest development of Chinese writing in the work of professional deviners.[9] This forms a natural connecting link with the formation of a differentiated society, which was controlled by priests. In any event, the earliest findings in Mesopotamia were traced to the temple community. On the earliest tablets from Uruk-Warka, of about 3000 B.C., the transformation of abstract form from the magical to the everyday is particularly apparent (Fig. 14). On one of these tablets are drawn two abstractly conceived heads of cattle, as we know them from the Magdalenian cultures, and next to these heads, several dots. A. Falkenstein assumes that the number of dots refers to the number of heads of cattle delivered.[10]

Fig. 13. Symbols from eastern Spain; from Le Mas d'Azil, Ariège [next to last symbol shown], and the Egyptian ankh hieroglyph [last symbol shown].

Fig. 14. Tablet of Enannatum I, Governor of Lagash, with an inscription recording the delivery of cedar trees to roof a temple, and the appointment of a watchman. Mesopotamian, *circa* 2900 B.C.

In the early advanced cultures of Egypt and Sumer, we note, in general, a more extensive process of abstraction, ranging from the recognizable images of 3000 B.C. to totally abstract and hastily scrawled signs.

That the development from pictorial writing to pure sign-writing proceeded more quickly and more radically on Mesopotamian soil than in Egypt can perhaps be explained in two different ways. First, in the Sumerian and all the later Mesopotamian cultures, tablets were used for writing on which cuneiform could be most easily scratched: short, vertical, or crooked, wedge-shaped impressions, which did not resemble the original pictorial image in the slightest. Secondly, the Sumerians and those who came after them, the Assyrians and Babylonians, all possessed a considerable logical-scientific bent, but on the whole were not inclined to an optical-physical approach as were the Egyptians. Thus in Mesopotamia, in contrast with Egypt, the primitive picture-writing sank into oblivion. Even in the most solemn stele, such as that bearing the code of laws of Hammurabi (eighteenth century B.C.), cuneiform was used.

The originally "holy" signs—the Egyptian hieroglyphics—have, in their completed form, the solemn character of reliefs. Their careful execution occasionally approaches the discipline of a work of art. And yet it is assumed today that they came into existence, not within a few hundred years, but rather, within a couple of generations.[11] The Egyptians also witnessed various stages of the transformation of writing to unrecognizable signs. On monuments, hieroglyphics were indeed retained in their original imagery; but in daily use, greatly simplified written signs were used.

We are again approaching an age of symbolism. No one will deny the laws of logic; they are as valid today as yesterday. Yet we are compelled to ask: Does everything come under the sway of logical reasoning? Are there not many aspects of human experience to which the cause-and-effect reasonings of logic are not applicable? In considering history—even the life history of the simplest creature—we cannot help but observe how most actions evade a clear explanation in terms of cause and effect. We can always discover certain causes after the event, but we are unable to predict a future effect of a cause, or its development, of which we ourselves are a part and with which our personal destiny is unremittingly involved.

Once again we begin to recognize the wisdom of bygone periods, when so much less was known but when the world was conceived as free and untrammeled, not caged within the bounds of logical cause and effect.

1. Max Ernst, *Beyond Painting,* New York, Wittenborn, Schultz (1948), p. 9.
2. S. Giedion, *Mechanization Takes Command,* New York, Oxford University Press (1948).
3. Jean-Paul Sartre, *L'Imaginaire: Psychologie phénomenologique de l'imagination,* Paris, Gallimard (1940), p. 128. This remark is based on the work of a Wurzburg psychologist who had experimented with forms and shapes that had no significance in themselves.
4. Johann Jakob Bachofen, "Versuch über die Gräber Symbolik der Alten" (1859), reprinted in Bachofen's *Gesammelte Werke,* vol. IV, Basel (1954).
5. Raymond Firth, *We the Tikopia,* New York, American Book Company (1936), second edition, London, Allen & Unwin (1957), p. 77.
6. Lucien Lévy-Bruhl, *La Mythologie primitive,* Paris, F. Alcan (1935), p. 52.
7. Théodule Ribot, "La Pensée Symbolique," in *Revue Philosophique,* vol. 49 (1915), pp. 386–387.
8. S. Giedion, *The Eternal Present,* vol. 2.: *The Beginnings of Architecture,* New York, Bollingen Foundation (1964).
9. David Diringer, *The Alphabet,* New York (1953), p. 102.
10. A. Falkenstein, *Archaische Texte aus Uruk,* Leipzig, (1936). This study presents an extremely comprehensive survey of the first written signs and their meanings, to the extent that they can be deciphered.
11. S. Schott, "Hieroglyphen," in *Abhandlungen der Mainzer Akademie der Wissenschaften* (1950).

JAMES J. GIBSON

A THEORY OF PICTORIAL PERCEPTION

A distinction is possible between what is commonly called experience at firsthand and experience at secondhand. In the former, one becomes aware of something. In the latter, one is *made aware* of something. The process by which an individual becomes aware of something is called perception, and psychological investigators have been concerned with it for generations. The process by which an individual is made aware of something, however, is a stage higher in complexity, and this has scarcely been touched upon by modern experimental psychology. It involves the action of another individual besides the perceiver. Although a precise terminology is lacking for this two-stage process, it is readily described in ordinary language: we speak of *being informed, being told, being taught, being shown,* or *being given to understand.* The principal vehicle for this kind of indirect perception is, of course, language. There is another vehicle for obtaining experience at secondhand, however, and this is by way of pictures or models. Although much has been written about language, there is no coherent theory of pictures. The attempt to analyze how a picture conveys information is a necessary but highly ambitious undertaking. The following essay cannot claim to do anything but set up working hypotheses for an important field of investigation.

I. *Words, Pictures, and Models as Substitutes for Realities.* An obvious fact about perception is that it is different for different things, that is, our percepts are specific to the various features of the physical environment surrounding us. We discriminate among these features and we can identify objects, places, and events when we encounter them on another occasion. This discriminating and identifying of things is an important part of what goes on when we say that we *learn.* Learning requires not only that we make the appropriate reactions but also that we be sensitive to the appropriate stimuli. An important aspect of education, or of any kind of special training, is an increasing ability to discriminate and identify things.

The training situation, however, is not always the same situation as that for which the individual is being trained. The learner must ordinarily be given an acquaintance with objects, places, and events which he has never physically encountered. The expedient is to train the individual in artificially constructed situations and expect that his learning will *transfer* to the novel situation, and this is essentially what any teacher does. The artificial construction of these situations is the crux of the matter. They must present adequate substitutes for the objects, places, and events later to be met with, if the latter are to be successfully discriminated and identified. The teacher can use oral and written words to induce this kind of secondhand experience, but he has always felt the need for other substitutes in addition. Pictures, films, drawings, models, and displays, along with diagrams, graphs, charts, and maps are also, he is convinced, useful. Precisely why they are useful needs to be understood.

What kinds of substitute stimuli are best for informing or teaching, or which kinds are better for what purposes? What are the advantages of pictures and motion pictures? What are the advantages of words? What are the limitations of both? Should pictures be realistic or schematic? Do pictures reproduce the perception of real three-dimensional space? These are all practical questions, but they involve difficult theoretical problems.

II. *Definition of the Term "Surrogate."* In order to understand how pictures convey information it will be necessary to have some general theory of how information is conveyed. Before attempting to specify the difference between pictures and words we should examine them to see how they are alike. The term *surrogate* is proposed to cover both, and a theory of surrogates will be formulated as a first step toward a theory of pictures.

The traditional or common-sense explanation of how one man conveys information to another is simply that men have ideas, and that ideas are transmitted. The idea is said to be "expressed" in language, the words "carry" the idea, and the idea is then "grasped" or "taken in." An idea may be expressed by a picture as well as by words. It is hardly necessary to point out that this is no explanation at all. The "transmission of ideas" by words and pictures implies, when taken literally, that these vehicles carry their ghostly passengers unaltered from one mind to another. We shall therefore dispense with the term "idea" and state our definitions objectively.

A surrogate will be defined as a *stimulus produced by another individual which is relatively specific to some object, place, or event not at present affecting the sense organs of the perceiving individual.* The implications of this definition should be explored both for what it includes and what it does not include. It says, in the first place, that a surrogate is an artificial stimulus constituted or produced by the behavior of another organism. Consequently, a surrogate is *not* the same thing as a substitute stimulus or a preparatory stimulus or a conditioned stimulus, as these are ordinarily defined in psychology, for these include merely physical conjunctions of events. Clouds are not a surrogate for rain, nor is the smell of food a surrogate for food. These are *signs,* but not surrogates.

In the second place, the definition says nothing about what the stimulated individual will *do* in the presence of a surrogate. All it implies is that he may have a kind of mediated or indirect perception of what the surrogate is specific to. It is true, of course, that perception is a form of organic activity, but this kind of response probably has the primary function of identifying or discriminating features of the environment; it is implicit rather than overt and it does not in any reliable way tell us what the individual will do.

Thirdly, the definition implies the action of one individual on another, a social influence, or an elementary form of communication, but the emphasis is on one aspect of communication only. The definition is concerned with the *mediating of a perception* rather than the *arousing of an action* in one's fellow man. Long ago, De Laguna pointed out that speech had two general functions, that of "proclamation" and that of "command."[1] An act of speech might at one extreme merely proclaim the existence of a certain state of affairs, or at another extreme merely command a certain action. Usually it did both, but the two functions were said to be distinguishable. More recently, Skinner has distinguished between the "tact" and the "mand" in verbal behavior.[2] Many social scientists have contrasted the transmitting of knowledge with the effort to control action, or "information," as against "propaganda." Surrogate-making as here considered, then, will apply only to the first kind of communication, not to the second. A general theory of communication including the function of persuasion would require many definitions and assumptions about human motivation and conduct, and is a greater undertaking than the writer here intends.

Fourthly, the definition says that a surrogate must be relatively specific to an absent object, place, or event. "Specific" here means a one-to-one relationship between different surrogates and different things; it does not mean that the things specified are necessarily concrete objects or particular places or never-to-be-repeated events. On the contrary, they may be abstract or universal things. Evidently the meaning of specificity is a crucial part of the definition. (Perhaps it is also the part of the theory to follow which most needs criticism and elaboration.) The specificity of surrogates to their referents is analogous to what was called an obvious fact about direct perception—that it, is different for different physical things. We assume that direct perceptions correspond to realities, or rather that they come more and more to do so as the perceiver learns. Accordingly, we are primarily interested in how perceptions *mediated by surrogates* also come to correspond to realities. Clearly, this kind of apprehension can only be specific to a referent if the intervening surrogate was itself specific to a referent in the first place. The interesting fact about the specificity of a surrogate is that it depends on the psychological activity of its producer, that is, on the precision of *his* apprehension. Surrogate-making, whether it be naming, drawing, or modeling in clay, consists largely in what the writer has elsewhere called *identifying* reactions.[3]

The above definition of surrogates may usefully be compared and contrasted with an explicit definition of *signs* by Charles Morris.[4] The present formula owes much to his rigorous discussion, but there are fundamental differences between them. Morris distinguishes between *iconic* signs and *non-iconic* signs. The former include images and pictures; the latter include words. Morris understands that no sharp line can be drawn between them. But he has very little to say about the former and his theory is applied not to them, but to language. In contrast, the present theory is directed toward pictorial communication and language is slighted. A surrogate as defined here is less inclusive than a sign as defined by Morris, in that the former is always something produced by an organism whereas the latter may be any feature of the stimulating situation. Moreover, surrogates exclude in large part the difficult category of "expressive" or "emotive" signs, that is, reactions which are specific to the state of the organism rather than to the features of his environment. The present emphasis, in short, is cognitive.

III. *The Production of Surrogates.* Human organisms are chronic makers of surrogates. Some of their reactions yield only temporary stimuli (sounds, gestures, and so-called expressive movements) while others yield permanent stimulus objects (picture-making, modeling, writing). It would be useful to classify and list, first, the fundamental motor acts which either constitute or produce surrogates and, second, the complex motor acts or technologies which man has learned for producing them. These sources of stimulation are necessarily such as always to be either easily seen or easily heard by normal perceivers.

The fundamental motor acts are: a) the making of vocal sounds, such as cries or speech; b) the making of movements of the face, hands, arms, or body, which includes gestures, postures, and mimicry;

c) the making of tracings on a surface of some kind, which includes drawing, painting, and the special case of writing; d) the shaping of a substance by molding it, cutting it, or fitting pieces together, which includes sculptures, toys, and models of all kinds, and finally; e) the making of mechanical sounds by manipulating an instrument or blowing into it, which includes sound-signaling and above all, music. If this list is exhaustive, it suggests that there are only a limited number of basic reactions appropriate for surrogate-making.

During recent history, to be sure, complex operations have been invented for making all these fundamental surrogates, which enable them to be conveniently reproduced, stored, and transmitted. Secondary surrogates are the result. The earliest technique of this sort, writing, is an instance of making a permanent surrogate to substitute for a simpler but temporary surrogate, *i.e.*, tracings which are a substitute for speech. Writing probably evolved in the history of civilization from drawing, which is a primary surrogate.[5] The main technologies for secondary or tertiary surrogates seem to be a) printing, which substitutes for writing; b) sound-recording and reproducing, which substitutes for speech and music; c) photography, which substitutes for drawing, painting, engraving, and other methods of altering a surface by hand, and which, together with photoengraving, has flooded our environment with pictures; d) cinematography, which enables a picture to represent time as well as space; e) vacuum-tube images, both pictorial (television) and symbolic (radar), the end of which is not yet in sight, and finally; f) various techniques for replicating things in three dimensions and thereby making models, displays, exhibits, panoramas, and simulators intended to produce all kinds of "synthetic" realities.

It should be noted that there is a characteristic of primary surrogates which the secondary or tertiary surrogates tend to lack, namely the personal style of the producer. Speech, gesture, handwriting, drawing, and artistic style are notably "expressive" of the person who performs them.[6] His reaction is specific, in other words, to himself or to his mood in addition to being specific to an object. The more complex products tend to lack this personal character. A painter is usually identifiable from his pictures but a photographer seldom is.

IV. *The Consequences of Surrogate-Making for the Perceiver and the Producer.* The most obvious consequence of surrogate-making is that another person can apprehend objects, places, and events perceived only by the first person. This makes possible a sort of vicarious experience for other individuals. The writer of a book, for instance, can produce mediated perceptions in many other people, and they may be people who live in distant places or even will not be living until future times. He can make them see what he has seen and hear what he has heard. A similar power is commanded by the painter, the movie-maker, the teacher, and the parent. One person can, as we say figuratively, transmit knowledge to others. What is equally important, however, is the fact that the first person can *exchange* surrogates with other persons. This makes possible a common body of perceptions among the group; it influences their direct perceptions and it may lead to a sort of consensus of experience, a common world in which mediated percepts and direct percepts are no longer separate.

The making of a surrogate, we must remember, necessarily involves self-stimulation whether or not it ever stimulates anyone else. Stimulation is fed back into an organism synchronously with its action. A speaker hears his own voice; an actor feels his own gestures; an artist sees his own pencil movements. As a result, the perceptual process and the surrogate-making process tend each to lead into the other, and the two become inextricably mixed. As Morris[7] and others before him have pointed out, this circular response in children, in conjunction with the facts of social stimulation, eventually converts a vocal sound into a symbol. The symbol process then comes to occur in the absence of another person and even in the absence of the stimulating object to which the original perception was specific. At this stage of development the individual "thinks." Since the same circular operation occurs for other surrogates as well as for vocal ones, it is not unreasonable to suppose that a person can learn to think in terms of drawings or graphs or models (and of the manipulations which produce them) as well as in terms of words. It may even be possible to infer, later on in this essay, that in certain respects such thinking is more easily performed than is verbal thinking.

V. *Conventional and Nonconventional Surrogates.* An attempt can now be made to formulate the difference between words and pictures. All surrogates are specific to their referents, but the correspondence between a word and its object is not the same as that between a picture and its object. Morris faced the same problem when he considered that a great many signs are, as he put it, "iconic."[8] His formula is very simple: a sign is iconic to the extent that it has itself the properties of what it denotes, or to the extent that it is similar to what it denotes. An image or a portrait of a man has many (but not all) of the properties of the man himself.

This statement is illuminating but it does not go very far, as Morris might be the first to admit. What *kinds* of properties can a surrogate share with the thing it stands for? In what respects is it similar? Can a surrogate be wholly unlike its object? And what if the object be abstract, so that there is little to be denoted?

Consider two extreme cases of what can be meant by the correspondence of one thing to another, first the correspondence of a license plate to an automobile and second the correspondence of a shadow to the tree that casts it. The plate is specific to the car because of an arbitrary pairing of the two and because of a rule of social conduct that says plates may not be exchanged or duplicated. The shadow is specific to the tree because it is a geometrical projection of the tree on the surface of the ground by rays of light from the sun.

By analogy with the license plate and the shadow, one may suggest that surrogates at one extreme are specific to objects, places, and events by *convention*, while surrogates at the other extreme are specific to the same things by *projection*. Language and algebraic symbols tend to fall toward the former pole and pictures or motion pictures toward the latter. Diagrams and graphs fall somewhere in the middle. Considering a language as a set of sounds produced by vocal reactions (or an equivalent set of tracings produced by manual reactions), the obvious fact to consider is that some groups of men have one set while other groups have different sets. A given object has different names in different languages. On the other hand, the enormous number of photographic snapshots existing all over the world constitute a single set. A given object could be matched with its photograph by any human being without having to learn laboriously a special vocabulary of photographs. The object and its name have an extrinsic relation, whereas the object and its picture have an intrinsic relation.

Nonconventional, projective, or replicative surrogates seem to be characterized by a very interesting possibility, which will require closer examination later. It is the theoretical possibility of the surrogate becoming more and more like the original until it is indistinguishable from it. For visual perception, and under certain viewing conditions, a model can be elaborated until the artificial scene is equivalent to the natural one. Under very special viewing conditions a motion picture can probably also be so elaborated that the perceiver is led to suppose that what he sees is an actual situation and an actual sequence of events. This possibility is not characteristic of a conventional surrogate.

Both conventional and nonconventional surrogates may, of course, be relatively unspecific to their referents, and to this extent the resulting perceptions will also be unspecific. Language may be vague or ambiguous[9] and so also may pictures. *In the case of pictures the relation will be called one of greater or lesser fidelity; in the case of words the relation will be called one of greater or lesser univocality.* Maximum fidelity of a picture or model will be defined later, in terms of geometry and optics. Maximum univocality is very difficult to define; the task will be left to the students of semantics and of information theory.

From the foregoing assumptions a number of propositions about words and pictures seem to follow, of which four will be stated.

1. In general, children have to learn the correspondence of a surrogate to its object in order to make use of it. *The more nearly a surrogate is projective or replicative, the less does associative learning need to occur. The more nearly a surrogate is conventional, the more does associative learning need to occur.* Pictures and models give closer approximations to direct perception than do words and symbols.

2. Distinguishing between concrete objects, places, and events on the one hand, and abstract properties, qualities, or variables of them on the other, *the more nearly a surrogate is replicative or projective the less is it capable of referring to abstractions and the more must its referent be concrete.* Conventional surrogates, however, do not have this limitation. *The more arbitrary a surrogate, the more is it free to specify anything, abstract or concrete.* Verbal responses, for example, may be either names which identify objects or adjectives and adverbs which specify their properties. Picture-making can also identify objects and specify properties, but it cannot name an object and describe it *separately.* Verbal surrogates enable us to separate abstractions from concrete things and respond to them in a special way. With symbolic responses we can make propositions and hence perform logical and mathematical thinking. A realistic picture, on the contrary, cannot state a logical proposition.

3. If purely conventional surrogates exist at one extreme and purely replicative surrogates at the other, there are "mixed" surrogates which are intermediate. These are specific to their referents partly by virtue of univocality and partly by virtue of fidelity. This applies particularly to pictures made by hand, which will be called "chirographic." The shift in human prehistory from picture-making (such as cave paintings) to picture-writing (such as Chinese characters) is apparently a develop-

ment away from fidelity toward univocality. The development of Western painting up until the advent of photography is partly a matter of striving for fidelity, but artists at all times have also sought to specify general or abstract features of the world. Cartoonists, for instance, do so. *Mixed surrogates, especially chirographic pictures, specify both concrete objects, places, and events and general or typical objects, places, and events.* In other words, graphic conventions or graphic symbols may be incorporated in a picture as distortions of line, shape, proportion, or color. This reduces fidelity, but it may increase univocality. The latter effect, however, depends on the *establishment* of the convention.

4. A conclusion seems to follow from the foregoing paragraph, which may be controversial. *A chirographic picture cannot at the same time possess high fidelity for something concrete and high univocality for something abstract.* The introduction of graphic symbolization into a picture necessarily sacrifices its capacity to represent. The effort to gain abstractness entails a loss in concreteness. The sacrificing of fidelity, that is to say, distortion, should have the result of making the observer's perception vague and his behavior unspecific, *as a general rule.* Only when the distortion is such that artist and observer both accept it as a univocal symbol is the sacrifice worthwhile. The artist's intention may have been to make evident some typical or significant feature of the original, but if his distortion is not established as specifying it, the observer is only puzzled. If his distortion *does* specify it, the picture can evoke not only a mediated perception of something concrete, but also an apprehension of its general, abstract, or universal features.

VI. *The Fidelity of a Model.* Certain types of surrogates, it was asserted, are characterized by fidelity (replicative or projective). Models and pictures are examples. Other types of surrogates are characterized by univocality, without fidelity. Words and symbols are examples. "Fidelity" must now be defined. It should be treated as a matter of degree, and the definition should be mathematical. The geometry of fidelity needs to come up for discussion. We will begin with models.

A faithful model can be defined as a physical object whose various surfaces have the same dimensions as the corresponding surfaces of the original object, and hence are geometrically congruent with them, but which is made of a different substance than the original. When the ratios of dimensions are the same, and the surfaces are geometrically similar instead of congruent, it is a *scale* model, and this is the commonest kind. Color can be reproduced as well as shape and structure. A model as thus defined will produce a retinal image identical with that of the original and, as an object, will be visually indistinguishable from the original. The *surroundings* of the original are not reproduced, however, and the ground on which the figure appears will then be different.

A model can be fabricated for a *place* as well as for an object, with the same definition as above. An example is a stage setting, or the simulated cockpit of an airplane. A *working model* can be constructed in which movements and the course of events are replicated, although this begins to be difficult. Theoretically, this simulation of a total situation could be elaborated indefinitely, but if the purpose is a visual surrogate, it will soon become more economical to utilize a *picture* or a *motion picture* instead of a model if the observer's viewing position can be confined to one spot.

A model has several dimensions of fidelity: shape and proportion, motion, size, color, texture, and the like. Since a learner does not need to become familiar with *all* the properties of an absent situation in order to learn how to deal with it, there is theoretically no need to simulate all its properties in a model. The properties which are relevant or significant for his future behavior are the important ones.

The most obvious kind of nonfidelity of a model is any distortion of shape. Consider, for instance, a set of scale models of different military aircraft used for the purpose of learning to identify and name the originals. As a general rule, distortion of the models would lead to confusion and poor aircraft recognition. There is evidence to suggest, however, that a distortion which exaggerates some *unique* or *characteristic* feature of an airplane relative to all the others may lead to *improved* identification of it.[10] The phenomenon may be related to the caricaturing of faces by drawing, and it is consistent with the fourth proposition cited in section V of this article. This predication can be tested experimentally.

VII. *The Fidelity and Scope of a Picture.* The fidelity of a picture, like that of a model, has to be defined geometrically, and only as an extreme case. *A faithful picture is a delimited physical surface processed in such a way that it reflects (or transmits) a sheaf of light rays to a given point which is the same as would be the sheaf of rays from the original to that point.* This definition is intended to apply to paintings, drawings, color prints, photographic prints, transparencies, projected slides, movies, television pictures, and the like, when taken as cases of pure representation. The definition is equivalent to saying that a picture may be considered as a geometrical projection, and that the relation of a picture to its original is given by a polar projection of a three-dimensional solid on a plane. If the center of projection is taken as infinitely distant from the solid, the polar projection becomes a parallel projection, and the picture correspondingly becomes a map, or a plan view, such as is employed in engineering drawing. This unique point for every picture is what makes the viewing position for a picture important, as will be later evident.

In the above definition a sheaf of rays is "the same as" another when the adjacent order of the points of color in the cross section of one is the same as the adjacent order in the cross section of the other. As the light energy varies along any cross-sectional axis of one, so must it vary along the corresponding axis of the other. *To the extent that this condition is fulfilled, the picture will be said to have fidelity.*

All the above applies to a "still" picture, and the fidelity defined is momentary only. *If in addition to the same adjacent order of color points, there exists the same successive order of color instants, the picture will be said to have temporal fidelity.* If the temporal pattern in the picture is that of the original, complex qualities like the motion, sequence, change, growth, and pace of the original can be reproduced. The motion picture and the television image are techniques for approximating this state

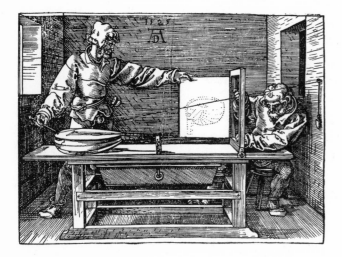

Woodcut illustrations of techniques for the pictorial rendering of a three-dimensional subject, from Albrecht Dürer's *Instructions for the mensuration of line, plane, and three-dimensional bodies, by the use of the circle and the rule,* first published, Nuremberg, 1525.

The plate above illustrates a device probably invented by Dürer, in which the human eye is replaced by the eye of a large needle. The needle, driven into the wall, is threaded with a string to which is attached at one end a pin, and at the other a weight. Between the eye of the needle and the subject (in this case a lute) is placed a frame with two movable strings which cross each other at right angles. The pin at the end of the string is then repeatedly placed at points along the contours of the subject. At each move of the pin the point where the string passes through the two movable threads of the frame determines the location of that point on the picture surface. The point is fixed by adjusting the two movable threads and is immediately recorded on the picture surface, which is the paper hinged to the frame.

In the plate shown below, the eye of the artist is fixed by a sight (in this case an obelisk). Between him and the subject is a frame divided into squares by black threads. The artist records the image thus perceived upon a paper divided into squares which correspond exactly to those formed by the threads of the frame. By this device the fidelity of the drawn image is greatly facilitated.

of affairs. It should be noted that the points and instants referred to above do not have to be the theoretical points and instants of mathematics, but may be finite units of area and finite intervals of time. The unit areas of the halftone photograph exemplify the former, and the 1/24 second intervals of the standard motion picture exemplify the latter.

[*Author's note added in 1965:* The above two paragraphs now seem unsatisfactory since this article was first published eleven years ago. The writer would now define fidelity not in terms of color spots and color movements, but wholly in terms of the "information" which two optic arrays have in common. This information is given by variables of structure, not by points and instants. Relational fidelity is not the same as point-to-point fidelity. The new definition depends on a conception of "ecological" optics which is quite distinct from classical energy optics, and was not yet developed at the time this paper was originally written. Ecological optics substitutes borders and transitions in the optic array for rays of light conceived as beams of energy shrunken to lines.]

Along with fidelity, another important property of a picture is its scope. A picture was defined as a *delimited* surface, which is to say, a picture has edges, commonly rectangular. If the surface is flat, the sheaf of rays projected by it to the "given point" is necessarily less than 180° in solid angle, and usually much less. Some pictures, such as murals, intercept a wide angle; other pictures, such as portraits, intercept a narrow angle. *The scope of a picture is the angular sector of the original environment intercepted by it.* One picture, in other words, may be a surrogate for a wide piece of the absent scene and another may be a surrogate for only a narrow piece of the absent scene, or perhaps only for a single object in it. When an environment needs to be represented, or when the background of or relations between objects, people, or events is important, a picture of wide scope is called for. When only a single object, person, or event needs to be represented, a picture of narrow scope may be sufficient. The scope of a photographic picture, for instance, is the angular amount of light intercepted by the lens of the camera. Scope should not be confused with degree of enlargement of a photograph. It is determined wholly by the lens used. A picture taken with a telephoto lens has a narrow scope and one taken with a wide-angle lens has a wide scope no matter what the size of the print in either case may be. The scope of a picture may be reduced by masking or cropping it, but it cannot be increased by photographically enlarging it. Neither can it be increased by holding the picture close to the eye or coming toward it for a close look. The retinal image of the observer is thereby magnified but the scope of the picture remains unaltered.

The fact that a picture is a surface with a boundary means that a picture can never, practically speaking, fill the entire field of view of its observer, which at any one moment occupies nearly a solid angular hemisphere. It is always surrounded by something else *not* the picture (the room, for instance); it is a figure on a ground in psychological terminology. An effort to overcome this limitation can be made by increasing the scope of the picture and employing a *curved* instead of a flat surface. Panoramic still pictures have long existed, and semipanoramic motion pictures are now being exploited. The psychological effect of this increased scope is very striking. Even a completely circular panorama, however, cannot surround the observer below his feet as well as to his right and left, since there has to be a physical floor to stand on. Only a full-scale model of a situation can do that.

VIII. *Space in Pictures*. A serious misunderstanding has existed for a long time about the physical fact that a picture is a two-dimensional surface. The misunderstanding takes the form of asserting that one cannot see three dimensions or depth in a picture. What one "sees" is a patchwork of flat surface colors which serve as clues, and then one "infers" depth in the scene. This account of the matter is mixed up with a second more basic misunderstanding which assumes that the retinal image itself is a picture (this assumption being false) and then goes on to assert that we can only see flat sensations of color in the world around us and must infer its depth. There is at least a germ of truth in the first misunderstanding, for anyone who looks at a picture can see a flat surface, if he attends to it as such. (The second misunderstanding is less excusable, for very few people who look at the world can see a flat surface in front of their eyes.) If, however, the man who looks at a picture does *not* give special attention to the surface as such, he perceives a three-dimensional scene. How is it possible to assert that he can see a flat surface and can also see a three-dimensional scene?

The misunderstanding about pictures arises because it is only half of the fact to say that a picture is a two-dimensional surface. It is a surface *and it is also a peculiar sheaf of rays*. The sheaf of rays is an essential part of the total fact of a picture. The fact of physical optics (the sheaf) and the fact of physical chemistry (the processed surface) must be combined. The surface as such is flat, but the surface as the source of a sheaf of rays may be equivalent to that of the original scene, and the latter is not flat. The sheaf of rays yields a *virtual* scene. The hypothesis to be proposed is that a picture can ordinarily be perceived in two different ways, as a surface and as a three-dimensional scene, and that this is so because the sheaf of rays ordinarily contains within it elements which are specific to a flat surface and also elements which are specific to a three-dimensional scene.

There can be no doubt whatever that a picture is capable of yielding a perception of depth and distance. It is, no doubt, the kind of depth and distance obtained when we close one eye, but this is not so different from the kind obtained with two eyes as the traditional theory asserts. The supplementary stimulation for depth perception obtained from the second eye is not, on the one hand, negligible, but neither is it, on the other hand, basic or essential for depth perception.[11]

When, under very special circumstances, a picture *cannot* be seen as a flat surface—when an observer who compares a photograph with the original scene cannot say which is which—it is because the elements in the sheaf of rays which are specific to a surface have been carefully eliminated. This involves a) arranging for the picture to be viewed through an aperture, and for the original scene to be viewed through a similar aperture; b) making the physical texture of the surface very fine; and c) processing the surface so that the ray bundle has high fidelity. A good deal of informal evidence for the success of this experiment exists, but it needs to be systematically performed.

It should be noted that our definition of a faithful picture implies not only a surface and a sheaf of light rays, but a unique viewing point. A picture is unlike a model in that theoretically it should be viewed with a single eye placed at its center of projection and kept motionless. Actually, and in practice, people do not satisfy these conditions very well when they look at a picture. They use two eyes, move about, and look from positions farther or nearer, above or below, and to the right or left of the center of projection (although they do, at least, always keep the picture nearly upright). These circumstances make the sheaf of rays *at the eye* (actually a pair of them at two eyes) rather different from the ideal sheaf of the theoretical picture, and plenty of stimulation is thus ordinarily provided for seeing the picture as a delimited flat surface.

Several propositions can now be formulated about space perception relative to picture perception.

1. Since two distinct systems of stimuli operate when a picture is viewed in the ordinary way, two kinds of perception ought simultaneously to occur: first, that of a three-dimensional scene (the situation represented) and second, that of a delimited flat surface which is part of a different scene (the room, say, in which the picture is shown). The first is perception of a *virtual* object; the second of a *real* object. There is simultaneously a *mediated* perception and a *direct* perception. There is evidence for this proposition, and more should be obtained.

2. The mediated perception evoked by a picture is a space perception, that is to say, it is three-dimensional. There is already evidence that the size of distant objects can be accurately judged in a photographic scene,[12] or in other words, that size constancy holds for this kind of perception. There is need for more evidence of this kind. We need to know whether accuracy of spatial judgments is increased when the fidelity of the photograph approaches a maximum, and also what happens to the perception when the fidelity is much reduced.

3. If two distinct spaces are capable of being seen when viewing a picture, two correspondingly different sets of spatial judgments should be obtainable from the observer. One set would consist of judgments of the distance from the point of view of the picture to a specified object in the picture. Phenomenally, the first distance would be in the space of the room and the second would be in the space of the picture. These two spaces should prove to be incommensurable. A similar experiment might require judgments of the size of the picture in contrast with judgments of the size of an object represented in the picture.

IX. *The Unique Viewing Point for a Picture.* Insofar as any picture is a geometrical projection, it must have a unique center of projection. Although this point lies in the air on a theoretical perpendicular to the plane of the picture, it is just as important for the picture as the deposits of pigment (or silver halide or dye) on its surface. In the case of a chirographic picture, constructed with some regard to the laws of perspective, it is the "station point" for the "picture plane."[13] In the case of a photographic picture it is at the perpendicular distance given by multiplying the focal length of the lens of the camera by the degree of enlargement of the picture.[14] This is the point at which an eye must be stationed if the eye is to be stimulated by the same sheaf of light rays which was included in the angular scope of the picture. In other words, the visual solid angle of the picture at the eye should equal the scope of the picture, or, in still other words, the eye should be so stationed relative to the picture that it takes in the same array that the camera did when the picture was taken (or that the painter's eye did when he made the picture).

The point has already been made that this ideal viewing position is departed from rather widely in looking at paintings, snapshots, projected slides, movies, and especially television pictures. The question which naturally arises is *what happens to the phenomenal space of the picture when a departure is made from the unique viewing point?*

Compare the sheaf of rays to the center of projection and the sheaf of rays to the eye, when these are not the same. The latter is *magnified* when the eye is nearer the picture. It is *diminished* when the eye is farther from the picture. (It is also *compressed horizontally* when the eye is to the right or left of the center of projection, and is *compressed vertically* when the eye is above or below the center of projection, but these deformations will not be considered at present.) We may now put this question: How is the three-dimensional object corresponding to a given sheaf of rays related to the three-dimensional object corresponding to a *magnified* (or diminished) but otherwise similar sheaf of rays? Would the latter object be simply *enlarged* (or reduced), or would it also be *deformed?* Geometrical analysis demonstrates that the object would have to be deformed as well as altered in size. The deformation consists in a relative shortening of its depth dimension in the case of magnification, and a relative elongation of its depth dimension in the case of diminishment. The implication is that depth in the space of a picture viewed from "too near" is shortened, whereas depth in the space of a picture viewed from "too far" is elongated. Whether this geometrical analysis will predict what happens to the *phenomenal* space of a picture is an empirical question which ought to be put to the test.

There is good evidence, obtained with groups of aviation cadets during the last war, that various types of abstract perceptual discrimination *not involving any discriminations of depth,* when tested by the projecting of motion pictures in a classroom, are not affected by the distance of the eyes from the screen, that is, by the angular magnitude of the picture.[15] This fact seems to suggest that the importance of the unique viewing point for a picture depends on the kind of perception the picture is intended to produce. Perhaps the chief consideration is whether the perception needs to be correct with respect to depth or distance.

The issues involved in picture viewing are highly complex, including as they do problems of spatial perception and perceptual constancy. The main puzzle for a general theory of perception can be put in this way: there is evidence to show that a retinal image which is magnified, diminished, or laterally compressed is in some respects equivalent to the unaltered image as a stimulus for perception. There is also evidence to show that a retinal image which undergoes such an elastic deformation is in other respects *not equivalent* as a stimulus for perception. What are the viewing conditions under which the first statement holds and what are the conditions under which the second statement holds?

The perception of pictures viewed *obliquely, i.e.,* at an angle to the surface, presents a similar set of problems regarding phenomenal distortion and phenomenal constancy. A method of investigating them has been described by the writer.[16]

X. *The Approximation of Pictorial Perception to Direct Perception.* References have already been made to the experiment of arranging that a picture and the original scene represented be viewed successively, under aperture conditions, and the possibility that the observer will be unable to distinguish one from the other. The picture most likely to yield success in this experiment is probably a large photographic color transparency; if the original scene involved movement, it would have to be a motion picture. Indistinguishability from the original has long been attained with *models* of certain things, for example, wax flowers, and there seems to be no reason why it could not be realized in pictures.

The experiment is theoretically important since it constitutes a test of the validity of the definition of a picture with fidelity given here in section VII. It exemplifies the limiting case in which an object and the surrogate for it can have precisely the same effect on an organism, and in which the pictorial quality of a picture perception vanishes. But its greatest importance, perhaps, is in demonstrating negatively the visual factors which, under ordinary viewing conditions rather than aperture conditions, make a picture seem what it is, namely, a surface, a substitute, or a mediating object.[17] These factors constitute a second system of optical stimulation, we postulated, which makes possible two kinds of spatial impressions and two kinds of judgments for the observer.

It is possible to add "realism" to a still picture in various different ways besides the aperture method described. The semipanoramic picture, and the circular panoramic picture constitute one way. The motion picture is another way. It is possible to combine these effects in semipanoramic motion pictures, as Waller has done in the "Cinerama." The stereoscopic picture and the stereoscopic motion picture is still another way. Color, sound, "stereophonic sound," the "subjective camera" method of shooting motion pictures, and perhaps others, are all techniques for increasing realism. It is the writer's opinion, however, that there are basic discrepancies among these lines of effort, at least between the stereoscopic and the panoramic, which will make it impossible to use them simultaneously in one grand effort to achieve "complete realism."

The *graphic* method of constructing a surrogate for a situation is fundamentally different from the method of building a *model* for it, or a full-scale replica. The replica for a situation has a ground on which one can stand. Any graphic method (including photography, cinematography and stereophotography) presupposes the use of either a *room* or a *viewing device*, and this limits the ultimate illusion of reality. A viewing device eliminates the sight of one's nose, hands, body, and one's feet on the floor, which is an important component of direct visual perception. A panoramic picture includes this component but necessarily introduces some kind of a junction between the room one stands in and the picture itself. The dilemma might be expressed by saying that it is intrinsically impossible to get the ego of the observer completely into the space of the picture. There will probably always be some tendency to experience *two* spaces, one incompatible and incommensurable with the other.

XI. *The Fidelity of Chirographic Picture.* Little has been said so far about handmade pictures as distinguished from lens-made pictures. Handmade or chirographic pictures include paintings, drawings, cartoons, caricatures, animated drawings, and a host of others. Their fidelity, as defined, is generally lower than that of photographic pictures, although this is not true of necessity. As early as the seventeenth century, some paintings of still life achieved a level of fidelity barely reached by modern color photography. The reason for chirographic lack of fidelity, perhaps, is this. A picture, like a model, has many dimensions of fidelity to the object, rather than a single dimension. The object has many visual properties, but the most important ones (for most human purposes) are the form, shape, and proportion of its edges and surfaces. These can be rendered by *outlines,* which are very easy to trace on a surface by hand. If we assume that a perceiver does not need to be given *all* the properties of an absent object in order to know how to deal with it, but only those which are *relevant* or *significant,* it is a waste of effort to simulate them all. The photograph reproduces them all indifferently. The chirograph reproduces them selectively. It can be (and has been) argued by artists that such selective emphasis may clarify the observer's perception of the object in a way that no photograph can do. The truth of this assertion is a problem in perception and cognition for which there is no present solution, but at least the assertion is not unreasonable. The danger of low fidelity is vagueness or nonspecificity. When the artist either omits some dimensions of fidelity or departs from fidelity by distorting form, he takes the risk, but he may achieve a picture which clarifies and specifies instead.

XII. *The Advantages and Disadvantages of Realism in Pictures.* Why, one might ask, do picture-makers strive for increased realism or, more exactly, why does a certain class of them do so? Why do children like realistic toys? Why the appeal of photography? of the movies? of television? of color movies? of stereoscopic color movies? Only an intuitive kind of answer can be given until a workable theory of surrogates is more fully developed, but it might be of this sort: that human beings have a need for firsthand experience; that an increasing proportion of experience comes at secondhand in the modern world; and that they therefore need the closest thing they can get to firsthand experience.

A realistic picture, notably a movie, makes the observer "forget himself," or "lose himself in the scene," or "takes him out of himself." So also, of course, does the reading of history, or a novel, or a book on how to do carpentry, but the realistic picture does so with less effort on the part of the observer. And there are good reasons for the greater simplicity and directness of this kind of perception, as we have seen. Pictures and models are better than words and symbols for learning about concrete things, tools, mechanisms, or organisms, about particular places, scenes, and environments, and about existing events, processes, and sequences. If this is what needs to be learned, the surrogates for them should be "realistic."

On the other hand, proponents of the spoken and written word have argued that this kind of learning makes no demands on the "imagination" of the learner. No one knows what the imagination is, precisely, but it does seem likely that men need to apprehend abstract things and general rules, as well as to perceive concrete objects. Words and symbols (including graphic symbols and geometrical drawings) are essential for learning about properties, variables, groups, classes, and universals. Men can make propositions with symbols, and discover new ones by manipulating old ones. They can mutually exchange propositions, and formulate general laws. If this is what needs to be learned, the surrogates for them should be arbitrary and conventional. Both kinds of surrogates have their value.

1. G. A. De Laguna, *Speech: Its Function and Development,* New Haven (1927).
2. B. F. Skinner, *Verbal Behavior,* New York (1957).
3. J. J. Gibson, *The Perception of the Visual World,* Boston (1950).
4. Ch. Morris, *Signs, Language and Behavior,* New York (1946).
5. L. Hogben, *From Cave Painting to Comic Strip,* New York (1949).
6. G. Allport and P. Vernon, *Studies in Expressive Movement,* New York (1933).
7. Ch. Morris, *Signs, . . .*
8. Ch. Morris, *Signs, . . . ,* pp. 23 and 191.
9. M. Black, *Language and Philosophy,* Ithaca (1949).
10. J. J. Gibson, editor, *Motion Picture Testing and Research* (Report No. 7, AAF Aviation Psychology Research Reports). Washington, D.C., U.S. Government Printing Office (1947), Chapter 7.
11. J. J. Gibson, *The Perception of the Visual World,* Chapter 6; *Motion Picture Testing, . . . ,* Chapter 9.
12. *Motion Picture Testing, . . . ,* Chapter 9.
13. W. R. Ware, *Modern Perspective,* New York (1900).
14. K. Henny and B. Dudley, *Handbook of Photography,* New York (1939).
15. *Motion Picture Testing, . . . ,* Chapter 4.
16. *Motion Picture Testing, . . . ,* p. 170 ff.
17. J. J. Gibson, "What Is a Form?" in *Psychological Review,* 58 (1951), pp. 403–412.

RUDOLF MODLEY

GRAPHIC SYMBOLS FOR WORLD-WIDE COMMUNICATION

INFORMATION

STATION RESTAURANT

BAGGAGE LOCKERS

DRINKING WATER

TELEPHONE

We are on the threshold of truly historic events in graphic communication. Steps are under way to create graphic symbols which can be understood by large groups of people—maybe even by people speaking all languages and living and working in all stages of technical and cultural development. Moreover, more effective graphic symbols may soon remake the many different written or printed languages which are still being used all over the world.

Evidence of the demand for change is piling up. The International Union of Railways and the International Civil Aviation Organization are developing new "international" graphic symbols. The United Nations has prepared a new "Protocol" for a world-wide road sign system. Writers and educators, disturbed by the phonetic shortcomings of the English language, have come up with several proposals to develop a new, truly phonetic alphabet. Even more ambitiously, C. K. Bliss of Australia has developed an auxiliary graphic language system. And Margaret Mead, the American anthropologist, has proposed the development of glyphs—universal graphic symbols.

Why this new intense and widespread concern with the basic graphic elements of communication, the symbols of the alphabet which represent sounds and the "higher" symbols which represent whole words or even broader concepts? The answer is that we are experiencing the long-delayed rediscovery that our common graphic symbols are not God-given and unchangeable, but mere man-made devices and thus subject to analytical review and meaningful shaping, reshaping, and development. Thus, progress is in the cards. But it will not come easily.

A selection of symbols proposed by the International Union of Railways to aid in the orientation of passengers.

GRAPHIC SYMBOLS BASIC TO OUR CIVILIZATION

In our culture, the most important graphic symbols inherited from the past are the twenty-odd letters of the alphabet, each of which stands for a specific sound. In some other cultures, the written language is not based on such sound symbols, but on symbols which represent syllables or even words. Syllabic languages require as many as a hundred different graphic symbols, word-based languages even more. Whatever the number of graphic symbols, "the invention of writing had a greater influence in uplifting the human race than any other achievement in the career of man." It enables man to make a permanent record of his achievements upon which later generations can build further.

More recent than the alphabet are the punctuation marks such as the period (.), the comma (,), the question mark (?), etc., and the handful of other graphic symbols such as the number sign (#), the ampersand (&), the dollar and pound signs ($ and £), and others.

Relative newcomers, too, are the ten numbers from 0 to 9 and the "operators" such as the plus sign (+), the minus (–), the "equals" (=), the multiplier (×), and others.

The symbols which have been added to the sound symbols of the alphabet are "word" symbols—they stand for a whole word. They are precise in meaning and avoid ambiguity, which so often makes words written with sound symbols understood differently by different persons.

The numerals 0 to 9, together with the "syntax" in which position (to the left or right of the real or im-

A selection of symbols from the auxiliary picture language developed by C. K. Bliss. From his book, *Semantography*, Sydney (1946–1949). Some of his symbols are closely related to generally accepted concepts.

WATER

FIRE

MAN

ENTRANCE

EXIT

The Cypriot syllabary, with symbols for each syllable:

a	e	i	o	u
ka	ke	ki	ko	ku
ta	te	ti	to	tu
pa	pe	pi	po	pu
la	le	li	lo	lu
ra	re	ri	ro	ru
ma	me	mi	mo	mu
na	ne	ni	no	nu
ja			jo	
wa	we	wi	wo	
sa	se	si	so	su
za			zo	
	xe			

The Cypriot syllabary: each symbol represents not a single letter but a whole syllable, either a vowel or a consonant plus a vowel. From John Chadwick, *The Decipherment of Linear B*, Cambridge University Press (1958).

agined decimal point) indicates "rank," had a decisive influence on our entire civilization. The invention of the "zero" (0) permitted positional numeration so that we can write 13, 103, 130, and 1003 without the need for more than three different numerals and can add, subtract, multiply, and divide at ease. One can go so far as to say that without the invention of the Indo-Arabic numerals and the letter symbols of modern algebra our modern technical civilization would be impossible.

In spite of their contribution to our civilization, only a few graphic symbols have been accepted into the inventory of commonly used symbols. And the last significant additions were made quite a few hundred years ago. The inventory is woefully inadequate today. We are paying the price for this in industrial, home, and traffic accidents, in misused and damaged appliances and machines, in failure of communication between peoples, in delays, confusion, and errors.

GROWTH OF NEW SYMBOL SYSTEMS FOR LIMITED USE

While only a few new symbols have been commonly accepted, there has been a rapid growth in recent time in the development of graphic symbols for limited use. Such symbols are being used extensively by scientists, technicians, and professional men.

Words alone are often found ineffective for written communication by these specialists. The geographer, the mathematician, the chemist, the architect, the electrical engineer, and the plumber have found it necessary to look for more precise and more efficient communication through graphic symbols. These symbols—or symbols systems—used on maps, in multiplications and divisions, in chemical formulas, in architectural drawings, and in the blueprints used by electrical engineers and other technicians and craftsmen are clearly defined, brief, and easy to manipulate. Many of them have been standardized through the efforts of professional societies.

VALVES

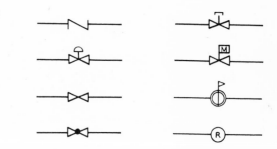

American Standard: Graphical Symbols for Heating, Ventilating, and Air Conditioning. American Society of Mechanical Engineers.

MECHANICAL MOTION

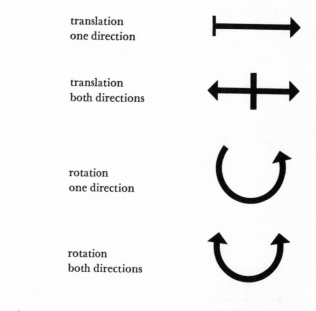

translation
one direction

translation
both directions

rotation
one direction

rotation
both directions

American Standard: Graphical Symbols for Electrical Diagrams. American Standards Association.

ROUGH ROAD

CURVE

CROSSING

LEVEL CROSSING

To take away these graphic symbols and to force these specialists to fall back on the written or spoken word alone would bring confusion, if not chaos. Yet, many of these symbols were developed before there was available even a rudimentary knowledge of the requirements and limitations of symbol development which are now gradually becoming apparent.

The American Standards Association, other national standards associations, and the International Standards Organization in Geneva have played an important role in the standardization of technical symbols and will undoubtedly play an even greater role in the future.

The enormous increase in foreign trade and travel and the deeper involvement of industrialized countries in the development of less developed ones have done much to focus attention on the need for graphic devices which can be understood even where language barriers make other spoken or written communication impossible.

Early European highway symbols, adopted in 1909. Reproduced from Martin Krampen, "Signs and Symbols in Graphic Communication," in *Design Quarterly*, 62 (1965).

Some of these devices go back for quite some time. Martin Krampen points out that the earliest road signs for drivers were installed by automobile clubs in Europe at the turn of the century and that four road symbols were conventionalized as early as 1909 at an international congress held in Paris. Symbols warning drivers of animal-drawn vehicles to apply brake shoes on steep hills go back even further. More recently, railroads, airlines, and tourist services have also made efforts to develop graphic symbols which can be understood by all travelers. As of now, however, no such symbol system has gained world-wide acceptance.

PROPOSAL FOR A UNIVERSAL GRAPHIC SYMBOL SYSTEM

A proposal to create a system of universally recognized graphic symbols was made in 1964 by Margaret Mead. Under this proposal, there would be developed a minimum number of symbols (called "glyphs" by Dr. Mead) which have meaning that is separable and independent from the names which are given to the symbol in different languages.

In an article in *Daedalus* (Winter, 1965) entitled "The Future as the Basis for Establishing a Shared Culture," Dr. Mead calls for a system that will make it possible for all peoples to start their intercommunication on a relatively equal basis. "No single geographical location, no traditional view of the universe, no special set of figures of speech . . . can provide an adequate basis," she says. "It must be such that everyone, everywhere, can start afresh, as a young child does, with a mind ready to meet ideas uncompromised by practical learning."

To meet the problem of "shared contribution," Dr. Mead thinks the fashioning of a new set of communication devices is required. Here is how Dr. Mead develops the idea:

In recent years there has been extensive discussion of the need for a systematic development of what are now called *glyphs,* that is, graphic representations, each of which stands for an idea: male, female, water, poison, danger, stop, go, etc. . . . What is needed internationally is a set of glyphs which does not refer to any single phonological system or to any specific cultural system of images but will, instead, form a system of visual signs with universally recognized referents. But up to the present no sustained effort has been made to explore the minimum number that would be needed, or to make a selection that would carry clear and unequivocal meaning for the peoples of the world, speaking all languages, living in all climates, and exposed to very different symbol systems.

The call for a universal symbol system offers a challenge to those concerned with graphic symbols. If we want to avoid a Tower of Babel of conflicting symbol languages, an international effort to lay the groundwork for a system of universally useable symbols is clearly indicated.

Yet there are many factors which will make this a difficult undertaking. The fact that in the thousands of years of man's cultural development only a limited number of graphic symbols has found wide acceptance (and even these only in limited areas) proves that evolution by "survival of the fittest" is a slow process. Those who want more precise, speedy, and widely understood communication through graphic symbols will have to know more about the nature of graphic symbols—and their intended users.

ALL GRAPHIC SYMBOLS MUST BE LEARNED

Because of the important role which graphic symbols are playing in modern communication, we might assume that they have been the subject of intensive study. This, however, is not the case. There are only a few pioneering works in the field. We shall try, therefore, to develop a framework which might be of help to those concerned with symbol development.

Symbols are among the millions of "messages" which are directed to man in any given moment by other men, by other living organisms, or even by inanimate matter. In a paper contained in this present volume, these messages have been classified by Lawrence K. Frank as signals, signs, and symbols.

Signals are messages for which we have inherited sensory capacities. We see trees, flowers, houses, people, and cars. We smell and we touch them. To some signals we respond instinctively. We close our eyes in strong light; we react to sounds, to heat and cold. Other signals we ignore as mere "noise."

Signs are messages which occur so regularly in conjunction with important signals that, after a number of occurrences, they evoke the same response as the signal. The best known example of such a response occurred in Pavlov's dogs which salivated at the sound of a bell that regularly preceded the serving of food. We, too, react to signs—the cloud in the sky which signifies rain, the sound of distant thunder, the smell of smoke, the voice raised in anger.

Man and other mammals respond to signals and signs. But only man communicates through symbols. Symbols are exclusive human creations for a world of meaning.

Symbols are created by man to communicate with others and with himself. Elsewhere in this volume Lawrence K. Frank has stated that a symbol "becomes meaningful and evokes human responses when, and only when, a perceiver of that symbol projects meaning into it and responds to it in terms of the meaning which he has learned as appropriate for that symbol." Thus a symbol must be "group-recognized and commonly used," either by tradition or, if it is newly created, by general acceptance.

Knowledge and acceptance of a symbol's meaning is therefore a prerequisite of its effectiveness. We may express this in other terms: a "message" will fail if the "sender" uses symbols which the potential "recipients" have not learned or have refused to accept. This is equally true for spoken or written language symbols, as we discover in a country whose language we do not know. To be successful in reaching a wider audience, therefore, our message must be expressed in symbols known and accepted by the potential recipients.

Here the designer of graphic symbols faces his first problem: unless he is able to use a graphic device that is already known and accepted, he must have the means to have his proposed symbol taught—otherwise it will not be a symbol but a mere graphic device subject to different interpretation by different people, or ignored entirely.

Because we are taught reading, writing, and arithmetic at a very early age, we tend to forget that letters and numerals, punctuation marks and mathematical operators had to be taught to us. Likewise, other graphic devices must also be learned before they can become symbols—recognized and accepted in terms of a clearly specified meaning.

Further on, we shall point out that many new and modern graphic symbols may well turn out to be much easier to learn than letters and numerals; yet they too will have to be taught and learned and accepted.

Some conclusions may be drawn from these facts:

1. Any project to develop graphic symbols needs broad public support or support from public or quasi-public agencies.

2. Only comparatively few graphic symbols are so urgently needed as to warrant the effort and expense of teaching them to the general public.

3. The effort and expense involved indicate that any project should be started only after the most careful preparation and study of its implications. Otherwise, it is likely to fail.

CLASSIFICATION OF GRAPHIC SYMBOLS

We have already pointed out the fact that the letters of our alphabet are mere sound symbols, but that other graphic symbols stand for complete words or even concepts. Krampen calls graphic signs which convey mere speech sounds "phonograms." He calls all other graphic symbols (which are independent of speech sounds) "logograms." A simple classification system of graphic symbols, adapted from Krampen with some changes by the author, is given here.

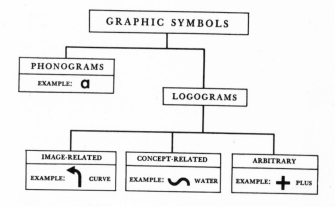

Phonograms do not concern us too much in this study. Yet this branch of symbols too needs further attention. Here we merely need to point out that there still exist different alphabets and that even among people using the same alphabet the sound-meaning of certain symbols differs. And still worse, some languages, especially English, make the same sound symbol stand for several different sounds; and in some English words, the pronunciation has little relation to the sound symbols which form them.

æ face	b bed	c cat	d dog	ⅇ key
f feet	g leg	h hat	ie fly	j jug	k key
l letter	m man	n nest	œ over	p pen
r red	s spoon	t tree	ue use	v voice	w window
y yes	z zebra	ʒ daisy	wh when	ch chair
th three	th the	ſh shop	3 television	ŋ drink
a father	au ball	a cap	e egg	i milk	o box
u up	ω book	⊚ spoon	ou out	oi oil

For this study it is sufficient to refer to the Shavian Alphabet, the Augmented Roman Alphabet (the Initial Teaching Alphabet), the World English Spelling Alphabet, and the New Single Sound Alphabet to indicate that spelling reform has many adherents. The difficulty of teaching English with our current alphabet and the advent of machine reading make it logical that there should be a growing demand for a more rational alphabet in which each letter means one specific sound and each sound one specific letter.

All phonograms are arbitrary symbols; the points which we shall discuss below under arbitrary logograms will therefore generally apply to phonograms, too.

Image-related graphic symbols (often called pictographs) refer to the real objects by resemblance. Let us assume the real object is a walking man (or a locomotive or a telephone). The symbol will then most likely be a stylized silhouette or a drawing of a walking man, a locomotive, or a telephone. Assuming that the potential recipient of a message (the driver of a car) has had past experience with pedestrians, locomotives, or telephones, we can assume that he will have little difficulty "learning" what these symbols mean.

One's quick conclusion might therefore be that image-related symbols are the ideal answer for those

The Augmented Roman Alphabet. This is one of several alphabets intended for beginners in reading, proposed by Sir James Pitman. Each letter of this alphabet denotes only its own one particular sound.

seeking easily taught, easily learned, and generally accepted effective symbols.

With limited audiences in limited geographic areas and within a limited historical period this conclusion is correct. But we may be wrong if we assume that symbols which appear self-explanatory to some of us must be equally self-explanatory to others.

Let us take the three symbols of the man, the locomotive, and the telephone. Will the fact that the walking man wears distinctly Western-style clothing confuse people from regions with other clothing habits? Will the fact that the locomotive shown is completely out-of-date lead American drivers to expect a museum of historical railroad engines rather than the level railroad crossing which this symbol is supposed to represent? And how long will the telephone symbol be recognized if the instruments generally used should change their form drastically?

These questions are far from trivial. Many once image-related symbols have become meaningless because the objects whose image they represented have vanished. The old-fashioned automobile horn is still being used in Europe as a symbol to indicate that horn-blowing is forbidden. To most drivers this symbol has no relation to a known image; it has become an unnecessarily complex, arbitrary symbol.

PEDESTRIAN

LOCOMOTIVE

TELEPHONE

Symbols taken from "standard" European highway signs. Note that each item is either dated or characteristic of local customs.

Pictorial symbols designed by Gerd Arntz, one of the designers who worked with Otto Neurath on the Isotype Institute.

The conclusion, then, is that there are only few image-related symbols which are unique in meaning, clearly recognizable, and permanent in time. Such symbols may be those representing "man" (provided the symbol is both realistic and simple, such as a stick drawing or a silhouette), animals, and some others. Symbols of this type deserve the fullest use.

Many other image-related symbols will have only limited use—geographically and historically. As such, they should be used with caution so as to avoid possible faulty interpretation by "outsiders." If used with caution, they can be useful. Most of the graphic symbols which have, or will come, into use for travelers will probably fall into this category. The fact, for instance, that telephone instruments may well change in time (or look different in different locations) is no reason why telephone facilities should not be clearly marked with currently valid symbols. Some day, however, a universally recognized arbitrary symbol for long-distance communication may replace these limited symbols.

Concept-related graphic symbols refer to perceptual concepts rather than to real objects. Thus, one or two parallel, horizontal wavy lines may represent water; an arrow pointing right may indicate that one should turn right; the Roman numerals I, II, and III are evidently concept-related.

The concept-related symbol may not be as easily recognizable as the image-related one. However, because its graphic form portrays the perceptual content of the object or concept which it represents, it is easy to learn. Once learned, it is easily retained.

The other advantage of concept-related symbols is that they are generally not subject to change; they can be used permanently because the basic concepts which underlie them are not likely to change. The symbols for water, direction, etc., once developed, taught, and accepted are likely to remain unchanged, yet up-to-date.

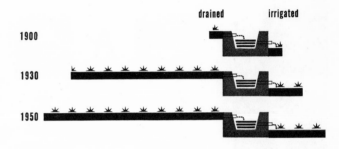

Image-related symbols used in a pictograph from *U.S.A. and Its Economic Future,* by Arnold B. Barach, graphics by Rudolf Modley, New York, Macmillan (1964).

ONE, TWO, THREE

WATER

RIGHT

Concept-related symbols like the Roman numerals for one, two, and three, the wave for water, and the directional arrow, are symbols which are comparatively easy to learn and remember. They are rarely subject to change.

TOOTH

TREE

HOUSE

EYE

HAND

Arbitrary graphic symbols do not resemble real objects; nor are they related to the objects or concepts which they represent. Their shape is arbitrarily assigned to them. Because of this lack of reference, arbitrary symbols are more difficult to teach, more difficult to learn, and harder to retain. They have to be learned by rote.

Regardless of their possible origin as image- or concept-related symbols, the graphic symbols in current general use—letters, numerals, punctuation marks, and mathematical operators—are all arbitrary symbols. Only in the more recent symbol systems used by professional groups or proposed for public use do we find heavier reliance on image-related or concept-related symbols.

The new symbol systems used by scientists and technicians have greatly facilitated transnational communications, economized on time and space in printed reports, and increased the accuracy of the transmission and reception of messages.

Arbitrary symbols, once fully accepted, tend to be permanent. Recently, however, technical developments, such as machine reading, have begun to have a modifying influence on the shape of numerals.

$$1\ 2\ 3\ 4\ 5\ 6\ 7\ 8\ 9\ 0$$
$$abcdefghijklmnop$$
$$+ - .,-:,!?\ '\ ""\ ()\ \&$$
$$\male\ \female\ R\hspace \$\ ¢ = \quad \flat :6 \#$$

A selection of the ancient symbols redesigned by Augustin Tschinkel in 1937, using Egyptian, Chinese, Hebrew, and other symbols.

Some of the best-known arbitrary symbols. All of these have to be learned, yet once accepted such symbols tend to be permanent.

GRAPHIC SYMBOLS TO STIMULATE VISUAL THINKING

A road sign indicating a right curve is more effective than a marker merely spelling out "Right Curve." The graphic sign stimulates visual thinking. The driver "sees" the coming curve ahead and adjusts to it. A word sign appeals to his intellectual thinking. He has to interpret the meaning of the words before he can adjust his actions. Rudolf Arnheim, in his contribution on "Visual Thinking" in the *Education of Vision* volume in the present series, describes other examples of visual thinking, such as chess-playing, map-reading, and even furniture-moving.

The symbol designer should always approach his task with the aim of stimulating visual thinking where this is possible. This will not always be easy. He will often be given tasks in verbal, intellectual terms. He will have to have the courage to think through these tasks visually. He will often find that he must take a completely new approach to a problem in order to find a visually satisfactory solution. The term "fragile," for instance, is a meaningful term when expressed in verbal form. It means that the contents of a container are easily damaged and one must therefore exercise special care in handling. Visually, it would be poor judgment to try to transpose the term "fragile" directly into pictorial content (as some misguided designers have tried to do by showing a broken glass or a broken egg). In some instances, an effective visual solution may be to illustrate one or more proper handling techniques. Where an effective solution is not possible, it will be better to stick to verbal warnings.

The difference between verbal and visual thinking may lead to several different visual solutions for a single verbal instruction. An example: the term "push," to be properly presented for perceptual action may show pushing a door (with the palm of the hand), a button (with the index finger), or a heavy object (with the shoulder). This depends on a given situation.

FRAGILE

THIS SIDE UP

At times designers fail to "think visually." This is the case with the attempts to translate the terms "fragile" and "this side up" into visually meaningful presentations.

121

INTERDICTION

WARNING

INFORMATION

Background shapes recommended for safety signs and symbols by the International Organization for Standardization.

BACKGROUND SHAPES AND COLOR

Signs and symbols are frequently placed on backgrounds of different shapes. In some cases, the background shapes themselves have been arbitarily assigned specific meanings. This is particularly true of traffic signs.

Thus, according to the U.S. Manual on Uniform Traffic Control Devices, "Stop" signs are octagonal in shape, "Yield" signs are equilateral triangles with one point downward, other regulatory signs are rectangular in shape with the longer dimension vertical. Warning signs in the United States are generally diamond-shaped, but railroad crossing signs (advance warning) are disk-shaped. The so-called international highway symbols also use arbitrarily assigned background shapes.

This multiplication of shapes and lack of relation of shapes to the message is unfortunate. A drastic simplification of background shapes to three might well be advisable, with some effort to relate the shapes to the concept groups which they represent.

Of particular importance would be the development of a shape to indicate the urgent need for attention or action. An equilateral triangle with one point downward may well represent the concept of instability and danger and attract maximum attention. It could be used for "Stop". signs, "Railroad Crossings," and exceptional danger warnings. The diamond-shaped backgrounds could still serve for warning signs. Rectangular shapes could continue for regulatory signs unless they are in the "major danger" category.

Color, too, has symbolic meaning. The most prominent, consistent use of color is in traffic-control devices. The use of red for negative orders, green for permissive, and amber or yellow for warning may well be "universal." It will be advisable, however, not to use color as the only identifying medium (as is now the case on power-operated circular traffic-control signals) because of the substantial incidence of color blindness.

Colors have frequently been used to indicate temperature: red for hot, blue for cold are often found and may be universally acceptable. However, careful experimental testing seems indicated.

FURTHER THOUGHTS ON GRAPHIC SYMBOLS

Two-dimensional symbols in a three-dimensional world. The fact that graphic symbols generally must be in two-dimensional form can lead to problems. This is particularly true of highway signs, but occurs with other symbols, too.

Highway signs are two-dimensional signs mounted approximately at right angles to the direction of, and facing, the traffic they are intended to serve. It is obvious that a two-dimensional, vertical sign cannot realistically display a horizontal direction. There is no horizontal surface on such a sign. We have therefore come to accept a vertical directional arrow (pointing up) as meaning "straight through" or "straight ahead." In most cases this arrow points straight up although in some cases the down-pointing arrow is still used. We thus have a widely used sign in which the vertical arrow means not "up" but "straight ahead." However, the same sign is used, for instance, on elevators and escalators to indicate "up," or when pointing down, to indicate "down."

The use of the vertical arrow as meaning straight ahead and the diagonal or horizontal arrow as indicating a direction makes it impossible to use this type of representation to express an up or down in the roadway itself, *i.e.,* uphill or downhill. This has forced the designers of highway signs to shift from the straight-on view represented by the directional sign to a cross-section view. Head-on views and profile views are thus arbitrarily intermixed in traffic signs.

While most traffic-control devices seem to have been accepted in the areas in which they are in use, the designer will have to test carefully to determine if the intended public really is able to go along with the artificial interpretations which the design medium imposes on him. Tests made by the United Nations indicate considerable areas of misunderstanding. Symbols therefore must be taught and learned.

For whom is the symbol intended? While the designer, or a symbol-issuing authority, may want to limit the use of its symbols to a specific group, the symbol will be seen, and interpreted, by others.

The confusion arising from the lack of clear definitions as to who is supposed to be subject to the commands and instructions conveyed by symbols is clearly apparent in urban traffic symbols. Most of us are both drivers and pedestrians. Yet traffic symbols do not always have identical messages for drivers and pedestrians. In some cases there are different symbols intended for drivers and others for pedestrians. But most often there are not. And drivers and pedestrians often have to "read" the same signal differently. In some localities a driver may be allowed to turn left or right on a green signal. A pedestrian generally may only cross in the direction of the green light. In some cases, he may not even do that, but must wait for the special "pedestrian" signals.

This is true of traffic lights and it is even more complex with other traffic signals. Thus, the European traffic symbol for "no entry" is definitely directed to vehicular traffic only. It generally means that pedestrians are free to pass. But would it not be logical for driver-pedestrians to expect that there should be a universally useable symbol for "no entry" and that one prohibiting the entry of vehicular traffic should be clearly identified as to its limited application?

Should a prohibited action be shown visually? Designers should carefully ponder if negative commands such as "No left turn," "Don't smoke," "Not fit for drinking" are best shown by two combined symbols, one showing the prohibited item and the other the negation. The answer is not always easy.

Where the prohibited item is represented by an arbitrary or even a concept-related symbol, the combination may well be acceptable. Thus the "No Parking" symbol which combines the arbitrarily selected blue background for parking with the red circle and diagonal crossbar appears effective. Similarly, a concept-related symbol for fire or smoke may make an effective "No smoking" or "No fires" symbol if negated.

In many cases, however, the designer will want to recall that a positive command, visually expressed, will be clearer and more effective than showing the prohibited concept or action graphically. Thus, instead of a "No Left Turn" symbol, he may want to develop a "Straight Ahead Only" symbol which expresses a clear command to follow the direction which the driver is supposed to follow without showing him what he is *not* to do.

REQUIREMENTS FOR PROGRESS

The demand for effective graphic symbols to supplement the limited number of generally used symbols is increasing. An expansion of the number of such generally used symbols could make a substantial contribution to better communication. It would lead to greater safety on our highways, easier and better information for travelers, quicker instruction in the use of machines and equipment.

The need for such symbols is urgent. An industrialized, technological civilization demands an almost unceasing alertness and a readiness to respond to the increasing variety of demands and constraints, and the growing possibilities and opportunities confronting individuals. Accordingly, the need will increase for rapid and unambiguous communications for living in this kind of a world, where sheer sensory awareness and acuity of vision must be supplemented by the learned capacity to recognize and respond appropriately to the meanings of situations and events as conveyed by graphic symbols.

The problems of creating effective and efficient graphic symbols are serious. Designers alone are not able to solve these problems. William Capitman's remarks on the role of the designer in another connection● can also apply here:

> I think it is arrogant for a designer to believe that it is his function not only to produce the design itself but to interpret in advance what the meaning is that should be built into this particular design. He is not capable of doing this in most instances. Basically, design is the job of a translator (researcher) and communicator (designer).

A satisfactory solution will require the combined efforts of public and private organizations. Industrialists, businessmen, scientists, and designers will have to pool their skills to make sure that the symbols of tomorrow properly fit the public need.

It might be appropriate and highly desirable for the United Nations to recognize and further a movement among the different nations to support and actively participate in fostering transnational efforts to create and establish a world-wide system of graphic symbols.

Up to the present, the demand for new symbols has come from groups operating within limited fields—professional groups, highway, railroad, and airline officials,

●

Conference, Aspen, Colorado, 1959. Quoted from *Print* magazine.

and hotel men. Impressive as such groups are, they are not enough. What would be gained if railroad officials were to accept one "international" symbol for one concept, let us say, a "First Aid Station," shipping lines another, and highway authorities a third? It is obvious that some kind of top coordinating agency is needed, be it a governmental one or a private one. This would mean, in many countries, the creation of a new public authority or the expansion of the function of private organizations such as the American Standards Association and the International Standards Organization.

The preceding pages should also have made it clear that the scope of the task goes far beyond the competence of those who need symbols for a specific field. Neither engineers nor designers alone should be permitted to have the final say on symbols. The task requires the combined efforts of psychologists, linguists, educators, anthropologists, sociologists, lawyers, engineers, designers, and many others. The need is so important that we cannot afford to take hasty and inadequate measures, but we should not delay in undertaking this essential task.

TO THE BUS

REFRESHMENTS

BAGGAGE LOCKERS

STOP

Symbols proposed by Paul Arthur & Associates, Ltd. to the Canadian Corporation for the 1967 World Exhibition. Designers: Gerard Doerrié and Harry Boller.

HENRY DREYFUSS

CASE STUDY: SYMBOLS FOR INDUSTRIAL USE

This is a case study of the development of symbols such as the one shown here meaning ENGAGE. This work is being carried out by the industrial design office of a large manufacturer of industrial and farm equipment. ● Foreign markets are expanding and an immediate need exists for a set of practically applied and readily understood symbols, which can be used on all equipment irrespective of its ultimate destination. These symbols will promote greater operator safety through increased recognition and reduced learning time. They will also avoid the cost and confusion of identifying controls in each of the respective languages.

The industrial designer's position qualifies him well for this task. He is familiar with company policy and with its equipment. Furthermore, he can detach himself from the problem and take a more objective view than can company employees. The designer can promote the "customers'" viewpoint and apply a keen sense of graphic design and knowledge of application techniques.

The first step—undertaken by the research staff—was to list all items requiring symbols. This included those controls, indicators, accessories, and maintenance and safety instructions which normally would be "captioned," or identified with words.

The designer then sketched a very preliminary design for each item. With these symbols as reference, research was undertaken to acquaint the designer with similar existing symbols from a variety of other disciplines. This research included reviewing books on symbols, magazine and newspaper articles, both foreign and domestic trade association documents and periodicals, and generally being aware of all items which incorporate symbols. Inquiries were made to the International Organization for Standardization. All pertinent publications of the American Standards Association, as well as other national standardizing bodies, were reviewed. The related symbols were then studied in relationship to their meaning and graphic portrayal.

●

Deere and Company, Moline, Illinois; staff member, Paul Clifton, is largely responsible for the compilation of the material contained in this article.

ingranare	ITALIAN
eingreifen	GERMAN
engranar	SPANISH
engrener	FRENCH
bekapcsolni	HUNGARIAN
koble ind	DANISH
koppla in	SWEDISH
‏לקשׁר‎	HEBREW
Cцeплять	RUSSIAN
Συμπλέκειν	GREEK
‏قبض‎	ARABIC
फसाना	HINDI
接喞	CHINESE
噛合わせる	JAPANESE

ENGAGE. That is what this symbol and all the words next to it mean: "engage" in the sense of mechanical interlock or meshing of gears. Although all the words may not be understood universally, it is intended that the symbol will.

From this analysis of existing symbols, several basic conclusions were drawn:

1. Most symbols can be divided into two major categories based on the type and degree of their graphic portrayal.

Pictographs. These look very much like the item, or depict qualities generally associated with the item. They are more easily recognized because some prior association already exists.

A fuel pump is almost universally accepted as a designation for liquid FUEL (gasoline, diesel fuel, etc.).

In reference to speed control, the hare is FAST while the tortoise is SLOW.

Abstractions. The initial derivation of these is obscure, but the symbol becomes meaningful through education.

This symbol means STOP; perhaps a simplified push button.

INCREASE or ADD. The Renaissance calculator Tartaglia used the first letter of the Italian *più* ("plus") to signify adding. Today's plus sign is a shorthand form of the Latin *et* ("and").

2. There is no need to invent another symbol if one which has become acceptable through use already exists. The basic concept remains intact although slight graphic changes may be made for clarity.

The United Nations has adopted this symbol meaning PARKING. It applies equally well to the PARK position on the gearshift quadrant of a vehicle.

A proposed symbol for an automotive CHOKE control (U.S. Army Human Engineering Laboratories, Aberdeen Proving Ground, Maryland).

A proposed symbol for an automotive THROTTLE control (U.S. Army Human Engineering Laboratories, Aberdeen Proving Ground, Maryland).

A commonly used symbol on imported cars to designate WINDSHIELD WIPER.

A symbol used on machine tools to denote ENGAGEMENT (International Organization for Standardization Recommendation).

3. New symbols should neither conflict with existing ones nor have any undesirable or erroneous associations.

This is a Nordic symbol in mythology meaning DEATH. It is no longer in common usage, thus there is little chance of conflict.

In current applications the arrow indicates DIRECTION or MOVEMENT.

4. A symbol is most meaningful within its own context or frame of reference.

Although it may look like a water paddle-wheel or windmill, it signifies the platform REEL of a harvesting combine.

To a farmer operating a combine, this is the control which adjusts the cutting PLATFORM HEIGHT.

Each symbol was further refined to reflect the proper operator-machine-symbol relationship. This refinement was based on several considerations:

1. *Consistency.* Certain basic elements, both objective and nonobjective, began to repeat themselves among the various symbols.

Objective elements: tangible objects like transmission, engine, tractor, and combine.

ENGINE is represented by a simplified outline of cylinder and crankcase.

TRANSMISSION is depicted by a gear.

TRACTOR, shown in plan view silhouette.

COMBINE, shown in side view silhouette.

Nonobjective elements: intangible qualities like temperature, movement, adjustment or measure, and direction.

Once a graphic representation has been designed or adapted for these elements, it should be applied consistently wherever required. As these elements reappear in different combinations, their symbolic association is reinforced and operator recognition is increased.

TEMPERATURE is symbolized by a thermometer.

All these symbols relate to the ENGINE: Engine R.P.M.; Engine Oil Pressure; Engine Water Temperature.

ROTATIONAL MOTION is shown as a curved arrow.
LINEAR MOTION as a straight arrow.

These relate to the TRANSMISSION: Transmission Oil Pressure and Transmission Oil Temperature.

ADJUSTMENT or MEASUREMENT are implied by use of the "dimension line" symbol.

These indicate ADJUSTMENT: Reel Height; Platform Height.

UP and DOWN are relative and must be shown with some reference.

The direction of MOVEMENT—up and down—applies to the Loader Boom.

2. *Operator's intelligence and familiarity*. It is assumed that the operator would have reasonable intelligence and an average amount of general mechanical knowledge, coupled with some degree of familiarity with the operations of agricultural and industrial equipment.

3. *Frequency of use or exposure*. During the normal use cycle, the operator would use some controls more than others. Controls used quite often could be identified by relatively "abstract" symbols since the frequency of use would continuously reinforce the symbolic association or reference.

The lightning bolt represents AMMETER or GENERATOR.

Location of the dot in reference to the darkened area determines UP and DOWN.

VOLUME is indicated by the amount of darkened area in a circular form.

More pictographic symbols would be applied to infrequently used controls because the strong pictorial association reduces learning time and increases operator retention.

TOW. This represents a position on the gearshift quadrant used when the tractor is towed by another vehicle.

EMERGENCY BRAKE is symbolized by the addition of a handle to the standard BRAKE symbol.

4. *Identification*. One of the main functions of a symbol is to identify the item and explain the "effect" when the control is actuated.

LIGHTS. All running lights are identified with the same basic symbol. The light "rays" and use of "P" differentiate among High Beam, Low Beam, and Parking.

5. *Directional action.* By design, the direction a control moves in corresponds, in most instances, directly to the movement of the actuated mechanism. Therefore, when a symbol conveys action, it is the *resultant* action of the mechanism.

The arrow indicates ENGAGE and DISENGAGE as relative to the open-sided square form.

6. *Proximity.* The design of a symbol is influenced by its proximity to the item which it identifies. If the symbol is on or immediately adjacent to the item, it can be "abstract," since the actual item reinforces the symbolic association.

ADD OIL. On an oil dipstick, this mark is the point at which oil is added.

But, if a control is quite remote from mechanism it actuates, the symbol should be more pictographic.

ENGINE OIL PRESSURE

TRANSMISSION OIL PRESSURE

The graphic form of a symbol is almost as important as its content. This form is determined by the graphic design elements, the techniques of reproduction, and conditions of application. Graphic considerations include: simplicity and clarity of design; consistent weight and relation of line; use of light and dark areas; general proportions—legibility at reduced sizes.

Reproduction techniques commonly employed on farm and industrial equipment include: casting in the component (firing order or engine block); unfilled stamping (oil-level marks on "dip-stick"); color filled or hot stamping (on knobs and radiator caps); separate printed decals or name plates (on combine control consoles). Each symbol is designed so that it will still maintain its basic character when reproduced by any of the preceding techniques.

Application is determined by the control's location and environment: symbols on an instrument dial, for instance, *must* be legible through a dirty glass. Colors may be introduced if the application and reproduction technique permit. Viewing distance determines size.

This case study represents only a beginning. Now, each proposed design will be applied to its respective piece of equipment and put to practical and extensive field tests. Some symbols may evolve in form (as the alphabet has), while entirely new ones may have to be added. If these symbols are successful in meeting the original requirements, many of them may form the nucleus of a symbol language, which then could be applied to other fields of communication, transportation, and manufacturing.

ABRAHAM H. MASLOW

ISOMORPHIC INTERRELATIONSHIPS BETWEEN KNOWER AND KNOWN

My general thesis is that many of the communication difficulties between persons are the by-product of communication barriers *within* the person; and that communication between the person and the world, to and fro, depends largely on their isomorphism (*i.e.,* similarity of structure or form); that the world can communicate to a person only that of which he is worthy, that which he deserves or is "up to"; that to a large extent, he can receive from the world, and give to the world, only that which he himself is. As Georg Lichtenberg said of a certain book, "Such works are like mirrors; if an ape peeps in, no apostle will look out."

For this reason, the study of the "innards" of the personality is one necessary base for the understanding of what he can communicate to the world, and what the world is able to communicate to him. This truth is intuitively known to every therapist, every artist, every teacher, but it should be made more explicit.

Of course I take communication here in the very broadest sense. I include all the processes of perception and of learning, and all the forms of art and of creation. And I include primary-process cognition (archaic, mythological, metaphorical, poetic cognition) as well as verbal, rational, secondary-process communication. I want to speak of what we are blind and deaf to as well as what gets through to us; of what we express dumbly and unconsciously as well as what we can verbalize or structure clearly.

A main consequence of this general thesis—that difficulties with the outer parallel difficulties within the inner—is that we should expect communication with the outer world to improve along with improvement in the development of the personality, along with its integration and wholeness, and along with freedom from civil war among the various portions of the personality, *i.e.,* perception of reality should improve. One then becomes more perceptive in the sense implied by Nietzsche when he says that one must have earned for oneself the distinction necessary to understand him.

SPLITS WITHIN THE PERSONALITY

First of all, what do I mean by failure of internal communication? Ultimately the simplest example is that of dissociation of the personality, of which the most dramatic and most usually known form is the multiple personality. I have examined as many of these cases as I could find in the literature, and a few I had access to myself, along with the less dramatic fugues and amnesias. They seem to me to fall into a general pattern which I can express as a tentative general theory, which will be of use to us in our present task because it tells something about the splits in *all* of us.

In every case I know, the "normal" or presenting personality has been a shy or quiet or reserved person, most often a female, rather conventional and controlled, rather submissive and even self-abnegating, unaggressive and "good," tending to be mousy, and easily exploited. In every case I know of, the "personality" that broke through into consciousness and into control of the person was the very opposite, impulsive rather than controlled, self-indulgent rather than self-abnegating, bold and brassy rather than shy, flouting the conventions, eager for a good time, aggressive and demanding, immature.

This is, of course, a split that we can see in *all* of us in a less extreme form. This is the inward battle between impulse and control, between individual demands and the demands of society, between immaturity and maturity, between irresponsible pleasure and responsibility. To the extent that we succeed in being *simultaneously* the mischievous, childish rascal *and* the sober, responsible, impulse-controlling citizen, to that extent are we less split and more integrated. This, by the way, is the ideal therapeutic goal for multiple personalities: to retain both or all three personalities, but in a graceful fusion or integration under conscious or preconscious control.

Each of these multiple personalities communicates with the world, to and fro, in a different way. They talk differently, write differently, indulge themselves differently, make love differently, select different friends. In one case I had contact with, "the willful child" personality had a big, sprawling, child's handwriting, vocabulary, and misspelling; the "self-abnegating, exploitable" personality had a mousy, conventional, good-schoolgirl handwriting. One "personality" read and studied books. The other could not, being too impatient and uninterested. How different would have been their art productions had we thought to get them.

In the rest of us, too, those portions of our selves which are rejected and relegated to unconscious existence can and inevitably *do* break through into open effects upon our communication, both intake and output, affecting our perceptions as well as our actions. This is easily enough demonstrated by projective tests on one side and art expression on the other.

The projective test shows how the world looks to us, or better said, it shows how we organize the world, what we can take out of it, what we can let it tell us, what we choose to see, and what we choose *not* to listen to or see.

Something similar is true on our expressive side. We express what we are.[1] To the extent that we are split, our expressions and communications are split, partial, onesided. To the extent that we are integrated, whole, unified, spontaneous, and fully functioning, to that extent are our expressions and communications complete, unique and idiosyncratic, alive and creative rather than inhibited, conventionalized, and artificial, honest rather than phony. Clinical experience shows this for pictorial and verbal art expressions, and for expressive movements in general, and probably also for dance, athletic, and other total bodily expressions. This is true not only for the communicative effects that we *mean* to have upon other people; it seems also to be true for the effects we do not mean to have.

Those portions of ourselves that we reject and repress (out of fear or shame) do not go out of existence. They do not die, but rather go underground. Whatever effects these underground portions of our human nature may thereafter have upon our communications tend either to be unnoticed by ourselves or else to be felt as if they were not part of us, *e.g.*, "I don't know what made me say such a thing." "I don't know what came over me."

To me this phenomenon means that expression is not alone a cultural thing; it is also a biological phenomenon. We *must* talk about the instinctoid elements in human nature, those intrinsic aspects of human nature which culture cannot kill but only repress, and which continue to affect our expression—even though in a sneaky way—in spite of all that culture can do. Culture is only a necessary cause of human nature, not a sufficient cause. But so also is our biology only a necessary cause and not a sufficient cause of human nature. It is true that only in a culture can we learn a spoken language. But it is just as true that in that same cultural environment a chimpanzee will *not* learn to speak. I say this because it is my vague impression that communication is studied too exclusively at the sociological level and not enough at the biological level.

Pursuing this same theme, of the ways in which splits within the personality contaminate our communications to the world and from the world, I turn to several well-known pathological examples. I cite them also because they seem to be exceptions to the general rule that the healthy and integrated person tends to be a superior perceiver and expresser. There is both clinical and experimental evidence in large quantity for this generalization; for instance, the work of H. J. Eysenck and his colleagues. And yet, there are exceptions that force us to be cautious.

The schizophrenic is one in whom the controls and defenses are collapsing or have collapsed. The person then tends to slip into his private inner world, and his contact with other people and with the natural world tends to be destroyed. But this involves also some destruction of the communications to and from the world. Fear of the world cuts communication with it. So also can inner impulses and voices become so loud as to confuse reality-testing. But it is also true that the schizophrenic patient sometimes shows a selective superiority. Because he is so involved with forbidden impulses and with primary-process cognition, he is reported occasionally to be extraordinarily acute in interpreting the dreams of others or in ferreting out the buried impulses of others, for instance, concealed homosexual impulses.

It can also work the other way about. Some of the best therapists with schizophrenics were schizophrenics themselves. And here and there we see a report that former patients can make exceptionally good and understanding ward attendants. This works on about the same principle as Alcoholics Anonymous. Some of my psychiatrist friends are now seeking this participant understanding by having an experience of being transiently psychotic with LSD or mescalin. One way of improving communication with a Y is to *be* a Y.

In this area we can learn much also from the psychopathic personality, especially the "charming" type. They can be described briefly as having no conscience, no guilt, no shame, no love for other people, no inhibitions, and few controls, so that they pretty well do what they want to do. They tend to become forgers, swindlers, prostitutes, polygamists, and to make their living by their wits rather than by hard work. These people, because of their own lacks, are generally unable to understand in others the pangs of conscience, regret, unselfish love, compassion, pity, guilt, shame, or embarrassment. What you are not, you cannot perceive or understand. It cannot communicate itself to you. And since what you are does sooner or later communicate itself, eventually the psychopath is seen as cold, horrible, and frightening, even though at first he seems so delightfully carefree, gay, and unneurotic.

Again we have an instance in which sickness, though it involves a *general* cutting of communications, also involves, in specialized areas, a greater acuteness and skill. The psychopath is extraordinarily acute at discovering the psychopathic element in *us*, however carefully we conceal it. He can spot and play upon the swindler in us, the forger, the thief, the liar, the faker, the phony, and can ordinarily make a living out of this skill. He says "You can't con an honest man," and seems very confident of his ability to detect any "larceny in the soul." (Of course, this implies that he can detect the *absence* of larceny, which means in turn that the character becomes visible in mien and demeanor, at least to the intensely interested observer, *i.e.*, it communicates itself to those who can understand it and identify with it.)

MASCULINITY AND FEMININITY

The close relationship between intra- and inter-personal communication is seen with especial clarity in the relations between masculinity and femininity. Notice that I do not say "between the sexes," because my point is that the relations *between* the sexes are very largely determined by the relation between masculinity and femininity *within* each person, male or female.

The most extreme example I can think of is the male paranoid who very frequently has passive homosexual yearnings, in a word, a wish to be raped and injured by the strong man. This impulse is totally horrifying and unacceptable to him, and he struggles to repress it. A main technique that he uses (projection) helps him to deny his yearning and to split it off from himself, and at the same time permits him to think about and talk about and be preoccupied with the fascinating subject. It is the *other* man who wants to rape him, not he who wishes to be raped. And so there is a suspiciousness in these patients which can express itself in the most pathetically obvious ways, *e.g.*, they will not let anyone get behind them, they will keep their backs to the wall, etc.

This is not so crazy as it sounds. Men throughout history have regarded women as temptresses, because they—the men—were tempted by them. Men tend to become soft and tender, unselfish and gentle when they love a woman. If they happen to live in a culture in which these are nonmasculine traits, then they get angry at women for weakening them (castrating them), and they invent Samson and Delilah myths to show how horrible women are. They project malevolent intentions. They blame the mirror for what it reflects.

Women, especially "advanced" and educated women in the USA, are frequently fighting against their own very deep tendencies to dependency, passivity, and submissiveness (because this unconsciously means to them a giving up of selfhood or personhood). It is then easy for such a woman to see men as would-be dominators and rapists and to treat them as such, frequently by dominating *them*.

For such reasons and others, too, men and women in most cultures and in most eras have misunderstood each other, have not been truly friendly with each other. It can be said in our present context that their intercommunications have been and are still bad. Usually one sex has dominated the other. Sometimes they manage to get along by cutting off the women's world from the men's, and making a complete division of labor, with concepts of masculine and feminine character that are very wide apart, with no overlapping. This makes for peace of a certain sort but certainly not for friendship and mutual understanding. What do the psychologists have to suggest about the improvement of understanding between the sexes? The psychological solution stated with especial clarity by the Jungians but also generally agreed upon is as follows: the antagonism between the sexes is largely a projection of the unconscious struggle *within* the person, between his or her masculine and feminine components. To make peace between the sexes, make peace within the person.

The man who is fighting within himself all the qualities he and his culture define as feminine will fight these same qualities in the external world, especially if his culture values maleness more than femaleness, as is so often the case. If it be emotionality, or illogic, or dependency, or love for colors, or tenderness with babies, he will be afraid of these in himself and fight them and try to be the opposite. And he will tend to fight them in the external world too by rejecting them, by relegating them to women entirely, etc. Homosexual men who solicit or accost are very frequently brutally beaten up by the men they approach, most likely because of the fears they arouse by being tempting. And this conclusion is certainly fortified by the fact that the beating up often comes *after* the homosexual act.

What we see here is an extreme dichotomizing, either/or, Aristotelian thinking of the sort that Goldstein, Adler, Korzybski, *et al.*, considered so dangerous. My psychologist's way of saying the same thing is "dichotomizing means pathologizing; and pathologizing means dichotomizing." The man who thinks you can be *either* a man, *all* man, *or* a woman, and *nothing but* a woman, is doomed to struggle with himself, and to eternal estrangement from women. To the extent that he learns the facts of psychological "bisexuality," and becomes aware of the arbitrariness of either/or definitions and the pathogenic nature of the process of dichotomizing, to the degree that he discovers that differences can fuse and be structured with each other, and need not be exclusive and mutually antagonistic, to that extent will he be a more integrated person, able to accept and enjoy the "feminine" within himself (the "Anima," as Jung calls it). If he can make peace with his female inside, he can make peace with the females outside, understand them better, be less ambivalent about them, and even admire them more as he realizes how superior their femaleness is to his own much weaker version. You can certainly communicate better with a friend who is appreciated and understood than you can with a feared, resented, and mysterious enemy. To make friends with some portion of the outside world, it is well to make friends with that part of it which is within yourself.

I do not wish to imply here that one process necessarily comes before the other. They are parallel and it can start the other way about, *i.e.,* accepting X in the outside world can help achieve acceptance of that same X in the inside world.

PRIMARY- AND SECONDARY-PROCESS COGNITION

My final example of intra-personal split which parallels split with the world is the dichotomizing of conscious and unconscious cognitive processes, or to use Freud's later terminology, of primary process and secondary process. Unconscious thinking, perceiving, or communication is archaic (in Jung's sense), mythological, poetic, metaphorical, preverbal, often concrete rather than conceptualized. It is characteristic of our night and day dreams, of our imagination, of revery, of an essential aspect of all art, of the first stages of creative production, of free association, etc. It is generally stigmatized by most well-adjusted, sane, sober adults in the West as childish, crazy, senseless, wild. It is thus threatening to their adult adjustment to the outer world, regarded as incompatible with it and therefore often repudiated. This means it cannot be communicated with, and cannot be used.

This repudiation of the inner psychic world in favor of the external world of common-sense "reality" is stronger in those who *must* deal successfully with the outer world primarily. Also, the tougher the environment is, the stronger the repudiation of the inner world must be, and the more dangerous it is to a "successful" adjustment. Thus the fear of poetic feeling, of fantasy, of dreaminess, of emotional thinking, is stronger in men than in women, in adults than in children, in engineers than in artists.

Observe also that we have here another example of the profound Western tendency, or perhaps general human tendency to dichotomize, to think that between alternatives or differences, one must choose *either* one *or* the other, and that this involves repudiation of the not-chosen, as if one couldn't have both.

And again we have an instance of the generalization that what we are blind and deaf to within ourselves, we are also blind and deaf to in the outer world, whether it be playfulness, poetic feeling, aesthetic sensitivity, primary creativity, or the like.

This example is especially important for another reason, namely that it seems to me that reconciling this dichotomy may be *the* best place for educators to begin in the task of resolving *all* dichotomies. That is, it may be a good and practicable starting point for teaching humanity to stop thinking in a dichotomous way in favor of thinking in an integrative way.

This is one aspect of the great frontal attack upon an overconfident and isolated rationalism, verbalism, and scientism that is gathering force. The general semanticists, the existentialists, the phenomenologists, the Freudians, the Zen Buddhists, the mystics, the Gestalt therapists, the Humanistic psychologists, the Jungians, the self-actualization psychologists, the Rogerians, the Bergsonians, the "creative" educationists, and many others, are all helping to point out the limits of language, of abstract thought, of orthodox science. These have been conceived as controllers of the dark, dangerous, and evil human depths. But now as we learn steadily that these depths are not only the wellsprings of neuroses, but also of health, joy, and creativeness, we begin to speak of the *healthy* unconscious, of healthy regression, healthy instincts, healthy non-rationality, and healthy intuition. We begin also to desire the salvaging of these capacities for ourselves.

The general theoretical answer seems to lie in the direction of integration and away from splitting and repressing. Of course all these movements which I have mentioned can too easily themselves become splitting forces. Anti-rationalism, anti-abstractionism, anti-science, anti-intellectualism are also splits. Properly defined and conceived, intellect is one of our greatest, most powerful integrating forces.

AUTONOMY AND HOMONOMY

Another paradox that faces us as we try to understand the relations between inner and outer, between self and world is the very complex interrelation between autonomy and homonomy. We can easily agree with Angyal[2] that there are within us these two general directions or needs, one toward selfishness and one toward unselfishness. The trend toward autonomy, taken by itself, leads us toward self-sufficiency, toward strength over against the world, toward fuller and fuller development of our own inner unique Self out of its own laws, its own inner dynamics, autochthonous laws of the psyche rather than of the environment. These psychic laws are different from, separate from, and even opposed to the laws of the nonpsychic worlds of the external reality. This quest for identity, or search for self (individuation, self-actualization) has certainly been made familiar to us by the growth and self-actualization psychologists, not to mention the existentialists, and the theologians of many schools.

But we are also aware of the equally strong tendency, seemingly contradictory, toward giving up the self, toward submerging ourselves in the not-self, toward giving up will, freedom, self-sufficiency, self-control, autonomy. In its sick forms this results in the wild romanticism of blood, earth, and instinct, in masochism, in contempt for the human being, in the search for values either *outside* the human being altogether or else in his lowest animal nature, both of which rest on contempt for the human being.

Elsewhere I have made the differentiation between the high homonomy and the low homonomy.[3] Here I should like to differentiate the high autonomy from the low autonomy. I wish then to show how these differentiations can help us to understand the isomorphism between inner and outer, and thereby lay a theoretical base for improvement of communication between the personality and the world.

The autonomy and strength which is found in emotionally secure people is different from the autonomy and strength of insecure people.[4] Very broadly, and without too much inaccuracy, we can say that insecure autonomy and strength is a strengthening of the personality as *over against* the world, in an either/or dichotomy in which they are not only quite separate but also mutually exclusive, as if they were *enemies*. We might call this selfish autonomy and strength. In a world in which one is either hammer or anvil, these are the hammers. In the monkeys in which I first studied the different qualities of strength, this was called autocratic or fascistic dominance. In the college students who were later studied it was called insecure high-dominance.[5]

Secure high-dominance was another matter altogether. Here there was affection for the world and for others, big-brotherly responsibility and a feeling of trust in and identification with the world rather than of antagonism and fear toward it. The superior strength of these individuals was therefore used for enjoyment, for love, and for helping others.

On various grounds we can now find it possible to speak of these differentiations as between psychologically healthy and unhealthy autonomy, and between psychologically healthy and unhealthy homonomy. We find also that this differentiation enables us to see that they are interrelated rather than opposed to each other; for as the person grows healthier and more authentic, the high autonomy and the high homonomy grow together, appear together and tend finally to fuse and to become structured into a higher unity which includes them both. The dichotomy between autonomy and homonomy, between selfishness and unselfishness, between the self and non-self, between the pure psyche and outer reality, now tends to disappear, and can be seen as a by-product of immaturity and of incomplete development.

While this transcendence of dichotomy can be seen as a usual thing in self-actualizing persons, it can *also* be seen in most of the rest of us in our most acute moments of integration within the self, and between self and the world. In the highest love between man and woman, or parent and child, as the person reaches the ultimates of strength, of self-esteem, of individuality, so also does he simultaneously merge with the other, lose self-consciousness and more or less transcend the self and selfishness. The same can happen in the creative moment, in the profound aesthetic experience, in the insight experience, in giving birth to a child, in dancing, in athletic experiences, and others which I have generalized as peak-experiences.[6] In all of these peak-experiences it becomes impossible to differentiate sharply between the self and the not-self. As the person becomes integrated so does his world. As he feels good, so does the world look good. And so on.

Observe first of all that this is an empirical statement and not a philosophical or theological one. Anyone can repeat these findings. I am definitely speaking of human experiences and not of supernatural ones.

Secondly, observe that this implies a disagreement with various theological statements which imply that transcending the limits of self means spurning or repudiating, or *losing* the self or the individuality. In the peak-experiences of ordinary people and in self-actualizing people as well, these are end-products of the development of greater and greater autonomy, of the achievement of identity; and they are the products of self-transcendence, not of self-obliteration.

Thirdly, observe that they are transient experiences, and not permanent ones. If this is a going into another world, then there is always a coming back to the ordinary world.

FULL-FUNCTIONING, SPONTANEITY, B-COGNITION

We begin to know something in a scientific way about the more integrated personality as it affects receiving and emitting communications. For instance, the many studies by Carl Rogers[7] and his collaborators indicate that as the person improves in psychotherapy, he becomes more integrated in various ways, more "open to experience" (more efficiently perceiving), and more "fully functioning" (more honestly expressive). This is our main body of experimental research, but there are also many clinical and theoretical writers who parallel and support these general conclusions at every point.

My own pilot explorations (not exact enough to be called researches in the contemporary sense) come to the same conclusions from another angle, *i.e.*, the direct exploration of the relatively healthy personality. First of all, these explorations support the finding that integration is one defining aspect of psychological health. Secondly, they support the conclusion that healthy people are more spontaneous and more expressive, that they emit behavior more easily, more totally, more honestly. Thirdly, they support the conclusion that healthy people perceive better (themselves, other people, all of reality) although, as I have indicated, this is not a *uniform* superiority. A current story has the psychotic saying, "2 plus 2 equals 5" while the neurotic says, "2 plus 2 equals 4, but I can't *stand* it!" I might add that the valueless person—a new kind of illness—says, "2 plus 2 equals 4. So what!" And the healthier person says in effect, "2 plus 2 equals 4. How interesting!"

Or to put it another way, Joseph Bossom and I have recently published an experiment[8] in which we found that secure people tended to see photographed faces as more warm than did insecure perceivers. The question remains for future research, however, as to whether this is a projection of kindness, or of naïveté, or more efficient perception. What is called for is an experiment in which the faces perceived have *known* levels of warmth or coolness. Then, we may ask, are the secure perceivers who perceive or attribute more warmth right or wrong? Or are they right for warm faces and wrong for cool faces? Do they see what they want to see? Do they want to like what they see?

A last word about what I call B-cognition (cognition of Being). This seems to me to be the purest and most efficient kind of perception of reality (although this remains to be tested experimentally). It is the truer and more veridical perception of the percept because most detached, most objective, least contaminated by the wishes, fears, and needs of the perceiver. It is noninterfering, nondemanding, most accepting. In B-cognition, dichotomies tend to fuse, categorizing tends to disappear and the percept is seen as unique.

Self-actualizing people tend more to this kind of perceiving. But I have been able to get reports of this kind of perception in practically *all* the people I have questioned, in the highest, happiest, most perfect moments of their lives (peak-experiences). Now, my point is this: Careful questioning shows that as the percept gets more individual, more unified and integrated, more enjoyable, more rich, so also does the perceiving individual get more alive, more integrated, more unified, more rich, more healthy for the moment. They happen simultaneously and can be set off on either side, *i.e.*, the more whole the percept (the world) becomes, the more whole the person becomes. And also, the more whole the person becomes, the more whole becomes the world. It is a dynamic interrelation, a mutual causation. The meaning of a message clearly depends not alone on its content, but also on the extent to which the personality is able to respond to it. The "higher" meaning is perceptible only to the "higher" person. The taller he is, the more he can see.

As Emerson said, "What we are, that only can we see." But we must now add that what we see tends in turn to make us what it is and what we are. The communication relationship between the person and the world is a dynamic one of mutual forming and lifting-lowering of each other, a process that we may call "reciprocal isomorphism." A higher order of persons can understand a higher order of knowledge; but also a higher order of environment tends to lift the level of the person, just as a lower order of environment tends to lower it. They make each other more like each other. These notions are also applicable to the interrelations between persons, and should help us to understand how persons help to form each other.

1. A. H. Maslow, *Motivation and Personality*, New York, Harper and Row (1954).
2. A. Angyal, *Foundations for a Science of Personality*, Cambridge, Mass., Commonwealth Fund (1941).
3. A. H. Maslow, *Towards a Psychology of Being*, Princeton, N.J., Van Nostrand (1962).
4. A. H. Maslow, *Motivation . . .* , Chapter 3.
5. *Ibid.*

6. A. H. Maslow, *Toward a Psychology . . . .*
7. C. Rogers, *On Becoming a Person*, Boston, Houghton Mifflin (1961).
8. J. Bossom and A. H. Maslow, "Security of Judges as a Factor in Impressions of Warmth in Others," in *The Journal of Abnormal and Social Psychology*, 55 (1957), pp. 147–148.

CHARLES MORRIS AND FRANK SCIADINI

PAINTINGS, WAYS TO LIVE, AND VALUES

It is not the fashion today to look at modern works of visual art as signs, nor to attempt to relate them to the values of their makers and their perceivers. Such works are often thought of simply as the results of manipulation of some medium, producing novel combinations of elements much as the chemist now synthesizes daily in his laboratory many compounds which probably never before existed in the universe. They are not thought of as signs or symbols of anything. And, while it must be admitted that "values" are involved in the fact that their makers preserve or exhibit some such works and not others, and that their perceivers prefer some such works to others, it is often felt that such considerations are of little importance, or at least so complex that nothing can be said about them. The contrary thesis would be that all works of visual art are in some sense signs, and signs of the very values in terms of which they are preserved and preferred, and that such matters can be clarified by experimental procedures. In this paper we do not wish to argue that the contrary thesis is true in all cases, and so we deliberately leave out of consideration the significant contemporary idioms of such abstract painters as Mondrian, Kandinsky, Pollock, and others. We choose for consideration paintings which are clearly representational. And our main purpose is not to show in detail the relation of such paintings as signs to the values of their makers and perceivers, but to show how experimental methods may be applied to such complex problems. What follows is intended as a modest contribution to experimental aesthetics.

It is plausible to suppose that persons like those signs which signify things they like. Thus if we like the violent sea we may like paintings which portray for us a violent sea.

Similarly, it seems natural that persons would favor signs which portray ways of life which accord with their own favored way of living. If we like to live peacefully and quietly we might be expected to favor paintings which portray quiet and peaceful persons or situations.

And, finally, it is often held that a person's appraisal (or evaluation) of something as good or bad is closely linked to his own liking or disliking of what is being evaluated.

Some evidence was given in *Varieties of Human Value*● that these relations do obtain as tendencies. Nevertheless it was noted there that the relations do not invariably hold. Thus the correlation of liking something and evaluating it as good or bad was not always exact. Paintings liked by Chinese subjects did not to any great degree portray the qualities stressed in the ways to live which they favored. Some of the walls of Tibetan Buddhist monasteries are covered with paintings of violent and lustful actions—symbols not of what the monks like or praise, but of the qualities of the world with which they have to cope and repudiate. The relation between signs and values, while generally positive, is complicated, and much effort will be required to unravel the situation. The study here reported is one attempt to work on these problems experimentally.

Two groups of students at the University of Florida were used as subjects. Group A was composed of 68 students in a general course in psychology. They were mainly sophomores and juniors. There were 40 men and 28 women. Group B was composed of 38 students taking a course in art, and a good number of them were art majors. Some were graduate students, and the women were approximately twice as numerous as the men. We were interested in the similarities and differences of these two groups.

These students were given a number of tasks. They were to indicate by a number from 7 to 1 how much they liked each of five possible Ways to Live; how much they liked each of five Paintings; how good or bad as paintings they thought these Paintings were (Group A but not Group B also evaluated the five Ways to Live in terms of degree of goodness); and how the Paintings were described in terms of a number of Osgood semantic-differential scales (Group A but not Group B also rated the five Ways to Live on these scales).

In *Varieties of Human Value* analysis had disclosed five dimensions of value common to the thirteen Ways to Live there studied, and in the present study the five Ways chosen were those highest on the five value dimen-

●

Charles Morris, *Varieties of Human Value,* Chicago (1956), Chapters 7, 8.

sions. The relation of the Ways to the value dimensions is as follows:

Way 1 Social restraint and self-control
Way 2 Withdrawal and self-sufficiency
Way 8 Self-indulgence (or sensuous enjoyment)
Way 9 Receptivity and sympathetic concern
Way 12 Enjoyment and progress in action

The statements of the five Ways to Live that were chosen are as follows:

Way 1: In this "design for living" the individual actively participates in the social life of his community, not to change it primarily, but to understand, appreciate, and preserve the best that man has attained. Excessive desires should be avoided and moderation sought. One wants the good things of life but in an orderly way. Life is to have clarity, balance, refinement, control. Vulgarity, great enthusiasm, irrational behavior, impatience, indulgence are to be avoided. Friendship is to be esteemed but not easy intimacy with many people. Life is to have discipline, intelligibility, good manners, predictability. Social changes are to be made slowly and carefully, so that what has been achieved in human culture is not lost. The individual should be active physically and socially, but not in a hectic or radical way. Restraint and intelligence should give order to an active life.

Way 2: The individual should for the most part "go it alone," assuring himself of privacy in living quarters, having much time to himself, attempting to control his own life. One should stress self-sufficiency, reflection, and meditation, knowledge of himself. The direction of interest should be away from intimate associations with social groups, and away from the physical manipulation of objects or attempts at control of the physical environment. One should aim to simplify one's external life, to moderate those desires whose satisfaction is dependent upon physical and social forces outside of oneself, and to concentrate attention upon the refinement, clarification, and self-direction of one's self. Not much can be done or is to be gained by "living outwardly." One must avoid dependence upon persons or things; the center of life should be found within oneself.

Way 8: Enjoyment should be the keynote of life. Not the hectic search for intense and exciting pleasures, but the enjoyment of the simple and easily obtainable pleasures: the pleasures of just existing, of savory food, of comfortable surroundings, of talking with friends, of rest and relaxation. A home that is warm and comfortable, chairs and a bed that are soft, a kitchen well-stocked with food, a door open to the entrance of friends —this is the place to live. Body at ease, relaxed, calm in its movements, not hurried, breath slow, willing to nod and to rest, grateful to the world that is its food—so should the body be. Driving ambition and the fanaticism of ascetic ideals are the signs of discontented people who have lost the capacity to float in the stream of simple, carefree, wholesome enjoyment.

Way 9: Receptivity should be the keynote of life. The good things of life come of their own accord, and come unsought. They cannot be found in the indulgence of the sensuous desires of the body. They cannot be gathered by participation in the turmoil of social life. They cannot be given to others by attempts to be helpful. They cannot be garnered by hard thinking. Rather do they come unsought when the bars of the self are down. When the self has ceased to make demands and waits in quiet receptivity, it becomes open to the powers which nourish it and work through it; and sustained by those powers, it knows joy and peace. To sit alone under the trees and the sky, open to nature's voices, calm and receptive, then can the wisdom from without come within.

Way 12: The use of the body's energy is the secret of a rewarding life. The hands need material to make into something: lumber and stone for building, food to harvest, clay to mold. The muscles are alive to joy only in action, in climbing, running, skiing and the like. Life finds its zest in overcoming, dominating, conquering some obstacle. It is the active deed which is satisfying, the deed adequate to the present, the daring and adventuresome deed. Not in cautious foresight, not in relaxed ease does life attain completion. Outward energetic action, the excitement of power in the tangible present —this is the way to live.

The authors then selected five Paintings which they thought "matched" in value each of the five selected Ways to Live, *i.e.*, which signified and exemplified the corresponding value. Not only the representational content was considered, but also certain formal elements such as the colors, lines, and shapes employed. Hence the method used could be applied to nonrepresentational paintings, though such works were not considered here. The Paintings selected were the following:

Painting 1: Seurat, *La Grande Jatte.*

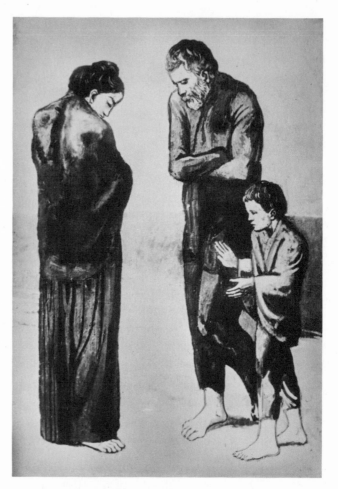

Painting 2: Picasso, *The Tragedy.*

Painting 8: Brueghel, *The Peasant Wedding.*

Painting 9: Constable, *Wivenhoe Park, Essex.*

Painting 12: Géricault, *Chasseur Officer, Charging.*

The students looked at a Painting (or read a Way to Live) and then put a check mark on one of the seven blanks of the Osgood semantic-differential scale, to indicate how *smooth* or *rough, vibrant* or *still* the object was. An Osgood semantic-differential scale is illustrated in the following manner:

smooth —— —— —— —— —— —— —— rough

In addition to the *good-bad* scale (the evaluative scale), the following scales were used, tapping the major connotative meaning dimensions of Osgood's work: •

smooth-rough	colorful-colorless
vibrant-still	hard-soft
active-passive	strong-weak
stable-changeable	violent-gentle

Each of the Paintings and Ways were rated on all the scales. By the use of these scales (except for the *good-bad* scale) the subjects "described" the Paintings (and in the case of Group A, the Ways).

The first clear result is that both Group A and Group B agree strongly on the *description* of the Paintings in terms of the Osgood scales. Thus Group A puts the Paintings in terms of *smooth-rough* in this order: 9, 1, 8, 2, 12, and Group B puts them in the same order. The women in Group A strongly agree with the men in this group. The agreement between the two groups with respect to the other descriptive scales is always high and in many cases exact.

Next, with respect to Group A the description of the Paintings in terms of the scales matches closely the description of the corresponding Ways in terms of the scales. (The only significant difference is that Painting 9 was felt to be much more *stable* and somewhat *smoother* than Way 9.) Thus the Paintings rated in terms of the *vibrant-still* scale were put by Group A in this order: 12, 8, 1, 2, 9, and Group B gave them the

•

Charles E. Osgood, George J. Suci, and Percy H. Tannenbaum, *The Measurement of Meaning,* Urbana (1957).

same order. Group A described the Ways in the same order with respect to the scales. The results were similar for all of the other scales (excluding the *good-bad*), though the order was not exactly identical in all cases. This result confirms the authors' belief that the Paintings did to a considerable degree match the Ways to Live they were selected to match.

What, however, is the relation of liking a Painting or Way to its *evaluation* as good or bad? Here many problems arise. Some of the empirical results are as follows:

Order of Liking of the Ways to Live:

Group A	12	8	1	9	2
Group B	12	2	8	1	9

Order of Liking of the Paintings:

Group A	9	12	8	2	1
Group B	12	2	1	8	9

Order of Evaluations ("Goodness"):

Ways:	Group A	12	8	1	9	2
Paintings:	Group A	9	12	8	1	2
	Group B	9	1	2	8	12

Group A likes and evaluates the Ways in the same order (12, 8, 1, 9, 2), and likes and evaluates the Paintings in practically the same order (9, 12, 8, 2, 1 versus 9, 12, 8, 1, 2). But Painting 9 is liked much more than the Way 9 which the authors expected to correspond with it.

With Group B a different situation appears. While the Paintings and Ways are liked in almost the same order (12, 2, 1, 8, 9 versus 12, 2, 8, 1, 9), the order of the evaluation (9, 1, 2, 8, 12) is practically the reverse of the liking for the Paintings.

The direction of the difference between Groups A and B is suggestive. It seems from this material that the less-trained persons in the arts do not distinguish between liking a painting and its evaluation as a painting, and that the more trained persons have formed standards of evaluations which need not correspond to their liking—indeed they may even tend to discount their likings as a standard for their evaluations. But this raises a problem, for in *Varieties of Human Value* evidence was given that persons especially interested in art agreed more in their likings and evaluations of paintings than did those not so interested. So here we have what seems to be a contradiction, and only further data and deeper analysis can clarify the situation.

Further, for both Groups A and B, all the Ways are liked in practically the same order regardless of which Painting is rated a 7 or a 6; and the Paintings are liked in practically the same order regardless of which Way is rated a 7 or a 6. This means that though both Groups A and B liked the Paintings in the same order in which they liked what we took to be the matching Ways, and though they described by the Osgood scales almost the same order for the Ways and the Paintings we took to be the corresponding ones, the study failed to exhibit a close relation between liking a given Way and liking a given Painting. The most that can be said is that in general the subjects liked Paintings portraying certain values in the same order that they liked Ways thought by the authors to portray those values. This is true of both Groups A and B.

As for evaluation, while Group A liked the Paintings in almost the same order in which it appraised them as good or bad, the likings of the Paintings by Group B is markedly different from their appraisals.

This means that for Group B (the more artistically trained group) other considerations were operating than the ones which guided the authors' matching of Paintings and Ways, or the characteristics noted in the descriptive semantic scales. Group B liked Paintings 1 and 2 more than did Group A. These are more "modern" paintings and this may cause them to be favored by the more trained group. This might also account for the fact that Painting 9, which is more realistic and naturalistic, is liked best by Group A and least by Group B. But whatever characteristics of the Ways and the Paintings are operating in the difference of likings and evaluations in Group B, they are evidently not caught by the instruments used in this study. Some of the differences may be due to the composition of the two groups, such as differences of temperament, or the larger proportion of women in Group B; thus the Picasso used here is liked more by women, and the same was found in *Varieties of Human Value* for a similar Picasso painting. This may have a bearing on the higher liking and evaluation given to Painting 2 in Group B.

Hence the three problems raised earlier in this paper—the relation of liking signs and liking what they signify, the relation of the values embodied in specific Paintings to the values embodied in specific Ways to Live, and the relation of liking and evaluating paintings—still remain largely unsettled. But it is hoped that the methods and techniques used here, when more refined and extended, suggest some possibilities for obtaining emperical knowledge on this borderline of science and aesthetics.

A few methodological points may be noted. It might be well to use a number of Paintings for each Way to Live, differing as much as possible in all characteristics other than the values they are thought to portray. For a sign may signify a value that is liked and yet not be liked as much as another sign signifying that value, since the signs have characteristics of their own in addition to what they signify. These characteristics are particularly important for the aesthetic perception of an object. *Varieties of Human Value* used many more paintings, and this may be relevant to some of the differences between that study and this one.

The whole attempt to match Paintings and Ways to Live in advance may be inadvisable. For as this study shows, those who do the matching will be selecting certain characteristics which they agree on, but which may not be the sole, or even the most important, characteristics for those who evaluate or express liking for a Painting or a Way. *Varieties of Human Value* did not attempt matching in advance. This may account for some of the differences between the results given there and in this study.

In conclusion, it seems that paintings, at least insofar as they are signs, have some relations to the values and modes of life of those who perceive them. But the relations are complex, and their exact nature is still a problem for an experimental study of art.

TOUCHE AND ECRITURE

A new element, essential for the proper critical appreciation of a picture, has made itself felt in the course of the last hundred years, and now—after considerations of absolute artistic quality—has taken its place beside such constant elements as technique and material, composition, color, period and style, motif, etc. It is the visible evidence of the painter's handiwork—what the French call his *écriture*—his handwriting.

Touche is a notion often met with also in literature. Both *touche* and *écriture* indicate aspects of the same phenomenon, but there is an important difference in their significance. *Touche* refers particularly to that which is personal and individual in the painter's brushwork, without inclusion of any formative element of style. With *touche* we can speak of style only in a subjective sense, in the sense in which it occurs in Buffon's dictum: *"Le style est l'homme même."* This saying does not mean that the character of the artist is reflected in the style of his work. It means that even if the work exhibits objective style elements, the mode of expressing them remains the artist's personal offering in which his own peculiar talent and originality make themselves known.

The idea expressed by *écriture,* however, does include objective style elements, which take us back to the origins of the artist's handwriting and enable us to grasp its essence and importance. The artist's handwriting has proved itself to be an indispensable means of critical research into matters of style, for it is at one and the same time a manifestation of his personality and a clue to his traditional affiliations. It is firsthand evidence of the artist's way of working. It is the most personal act of all artistic expression, inimitable in its subtlety, and therefore of primary importance in the attribution of the painter's work.

Henri Focillon in the chapter on "Forms in the Realm of Matter," of his study, *The Life of Forms in Art,*● lays the greatest emphasis on the painter's mode of material expression as an element in the formation of style. "Touch . . . represents a single moment, in which the tool awakens form in the substance, and it represents permanence, since because of it form has structure and durability. The touch does, to be sure, conceal what it has done: it becomes hidden and quiescent. But, underneath any hard and fast continuity, as, for example, a glaze in painting, we must and we can always detect it. Then it is that a work of art regains its precious living quality . . . A value, a tone, do not depend alone upon the properties and the relationships of the elements composing them, but upon the way in which they are placed, that is, "touched." Because of this, a painting is not the same thing as a painted barn door or wagon. Touch is structure. It imposes upon the form of the animate being or the object its own form, which is not merely value and color, but also (in no matter what minute proportions) weight, density, and motion."

Every work of art aspires to be something that never was before and never can happen again. As a matter of fact, each one represents a whole complex of relationships, and of these the relationship to tradition is for the moment our principal concern. The beginnings of the artist's handwriting lie at the point where his personality finds its contact with tradition. The history of art is written by personalities, not by "isms" or schools. Every artist builds on those who went before him or on those living and working in his own day. He builds his own world, taking to himself and working upon every sort of material that may further the attainment of his creative purpose. That is the essence of learning. The mere statement of influences and derivations (a practice of late much abused) can never take us to the root of the matter, especially in our days of sensation-seeking individualism, straining after new effects and personal advertisement, and obeying the call of the art market rather than the voice of art itself. Our judgment goes to the root of the matter only when it becomes clear to us why the artist took over certain elements of style, how he absorbed them and through what alchemy he made them his own. Originality consciously sought is mere straining after effect. Real originality lies hidden in the personality of the artist. The truth of the matter is well expressed in the saying: "It isn't what is painted or how it is painted that matters; what matters is who paints it."

● Quoted from second edition, New York, Wittenborn (1948) p. 39; first edition, New Haven, Yale University (1942).

In other times the schools played a greater role than they do in our own. The school then meant the technique of a certain master to be painfully acquired. With its help, good painting should follow as a matter of course, and certainly in many cases it did: take Giotto's revolutionary conception of painting (as against Byzantine formalism) and the school that grew out of it; Leonardo's *sfumato* technique; van Eyck's new oil-color technique and the brilliant color it brought with it; Titian's rejection of the Flemish innovations and their brilliant color in favor of the total harmony of the picture, etc. Today, however, the idea of a school is rather repellent: witness the followers of Picasso, Matisse, Bonnard, and Dalì, who took over the cast-off props of Cubism, Fauvism, Surrealism and Impressionism after the curtain had dropped on the play.

Here we should make a sharp distinction between the notion of *écriture* and that of technique. The practical, the technical procedure of the artist, the totality of his tradesman's routine, and the way in which form is brought to life in the material, are two different things. Here again arises the question of personality. In the last resort technique is purely personal and is born of an inner necessity. It may be the technique of an old master, Rubens, for example, who in most cases spread over a gesso-priming a coat of streaky light gray, leaving traces of flat broad brush-strokes. Over this he sketched in light ochre tones, beginning with the shadows. The half tones, which should be cool, he laid in with strong gray, and over this he built up the form in a medium of balsam or spirit varnish. He strengthened the drawing and the shadows with tones of dark ochre and laid over the light planes half-covering tones to give a cool effect against the warm ochres; after which he reinforced the colors of the lighter planes, placing the highlights with a loaded touch. Finally came his strong colors laid on over superimposed cool and warm glazes. On the other hand, the technique may be that of exclusively direct painting, as in much modern work, which dispenses with so many of the old masters' effects in order to achieve others. The important thing is that the artist shall have realized his aim with his summary conception of form and the swift execution of his picture, just as Rubens realized his in works of carnation-like fusion and luminosity. In Rembrandt's words: "The picture is finished when the artist has said what he wanted to say."

THE TRANSITION FROM CONVENTIONALLY HISTORIC TO MODERN HANDWRITING

Delacroix, who held the view that the artist's handwriting should remain as visible as possible, made the following entry in his diary in 1857: ". . . even on the smoothest painting the trace of the brush is visible from near . . . The painter's handwriting serves the purpose of expressing more clearly and in a suitable way the various planes of objects. Strong broad strokes bring them into the foreground; gentler touches allow them to recede . . . Handwriting lends transparence to the tone according to its density . . ." This is one of the first and one of the weightiest passages on *écriture* in the literature of art. There were, of course, pictures of earlier masters wherein the handwriting was clearly visible, but in general the handwriting of the painter was not accorded any great importance. Pictures were smooth, often polished, and revealed little trace of the final coat of paint which completed the careful underpainting. A striking exception is Franz Hals with his spontaneous direct method of painting. By implication his conception was impressionistic, and in his emphasis on certain details and in his light key of color he anticipates Manet. Another forerunner of the moderns is Velásquez, with his light key of color and his painting of air (for example, his *Villa Medici*, Prado Museum).

Mention of atmospheric painting brings us at once to the Dutch (for example, van Goyen), who influenced Bonington and Constable who, in their turn, were decisive factors in the development of the Barbizon school. Watteau might also be mentioned in this connection. In the heavily loaded later work of Rembrandt, the handwriting of the master is plainly visible. El Greco's dramatic summary technique had the same importance for modern French painting as had Titian's subdued, broken color, preferred by the master to the lighter scale as serving the total color harmony of his picture. The Japanese woodcut with its use of contour and its far-reaching simplification also had an important part to play.

Towards the end of the Renaissance, in the later pictures of Titian and Veronese, the painter's handwriting is plainly visible. It was thus in the Baroque period, when the subjective moment in artistic creation was most strongly emphasized, that the painter's handwriting began to assert itself. This development was interrupted by the classicist intermezzo of David and Ingres, but returned, together with vivid color, in the romantic painting of Delacroix.

The work of Delacroix, Théodore Rousseau and Courbet is modern in character in spite of the imitative historical-stylistic element to be found in it. In the first half of the nineteenth century, modeling and color are bound together in the function of handwriting. Later, the accent is rather on plane and color—on the well-defined tract of color. The line goes from Corot through Daubigny, Sisley, and Renoir to Bonnard; and to these may be added Seurat, Toulouse-Lautrec and van Gogh, whose handwriting includes the devices of cross-hatching and line. The outline as a stylistic element in the organization of the picture comes in with Daumier. After him, we meet with it frequently in modern painting as, for example, in the work of Manet, Matisse, Gauguin and Picasso. Here the blue outlines of Cézanne call for reference. In general the contour cuts into and limits the plane. Daumier's outline, which came perhaps from the graphic side of him, is nevertheless purely pictorial when he paints. There is an interesting phenomenon to be observed in the practice of Derain. He paints a form in depth with light and shadow, and cuts suddenly into the painting with a broad, nervous line which threatens to destroy his modeling—a symptom, no doubt, of his restless search for style.

For another group the three-dimensional is of prime importance. Starting from Daumier we can trace this line of development, after a temporary pause, through Cézanne and Derain to Picasso, to Braque, to the New Realism and to Surrealism. After Constable, the work of the brush was displayed in a bold hand, but at the beginning of the century it became more subdued. Up to the time of Constable the painter's handwriting served mainly in the interpretation of plastic values. After Constable's discovery of broken color tones, its aid was invoked for the purposes of color. With Constable, too, began the modern practice of disintegrating the color of material into facets, strokes, or dots.

Together with the handwriting of the brush, the work of the palette knife should be noted. This tool has often been used to further the subsequent work of the brush, or for the direct application of color to pro-

duce a desired impasto. Further devices worth mentioning are the cutting into the loaded material with the butt-end of the brush, and the work of the hard brush in the compact color, etc. In all this, it is extremely important to observe how the handwriting of every painter shows essential differences within the line of his own artistic development. We can not here dwell at length upon this aspect of the matter. The aspects of our material that we are able to treat in this study must be taken as indications, and in very large measure as reference to the illustrations. In this connection it would have been ideal to have been able to reproduce the brush strokes in their natural size so as to convey a complete picture of the paint textures. Unfortunately we have not been able to do this.

Eugène Delacroix is a Romantic, but from the point of view of form, a Realist. The realist side of Delacroix comes very strongly into the foreground in his North African pictures, but it is a modern Realism with hitherto unknown contractions and a summary conception of form. The Delacroix illustrated here shows a detail of a sketch and for that reason is particularly suitable for our purpose, since the large finished paintings of Delacroix are executed in a more conventional manner. His painting is composed of several layers of paint. The first layer is applied rather thinly and with a brush stroke going with the form lengthwise. A constant striving after three-dimensional effect is expressed in it. (Delacroix's diary, 1852: "The painter must lay in his figure like a sculptor working in clay or marble.") Then come light accents on the dry underpainting; these also follow the form but are laid on with a smaller brush. An axiom of Delacroix: *"S'il faut ébaucher avec un balai, il faut terminer avec une aiguille."* ("If it is necessary to rough cast with a broom, it is necessary to finish off with a needle.") For this reason the handwriting of Delacroix lies principally on the surface, where the forms are broken with contrasting values. The whole procedure is traditional—color, light, and modeling as it might be with Veronese, or in the placing of the highlights as it might be with Rubens. The form is Baroque, expansive, but he writes in finer characters than the Baroque painters and his form is more intensively analyzed. Perhaps it was this that led Julius Meier-Graefe to allude to Delacroix's demoniacal capacity for making the picture surface vibrate, and Elie Faure to speak of his flying handwriting. All modern painters, and not only the Impressionists, have their roots in Delacroix. (Cézanne: "We painters all spring from him.") So it may be said that the handwriting of the modern painter goes back to the Baroque through the intermediary of Delacroix.

Fig. 1. Eugène Delacroix. *Lion and Tiger.*
Detail of lion's head.

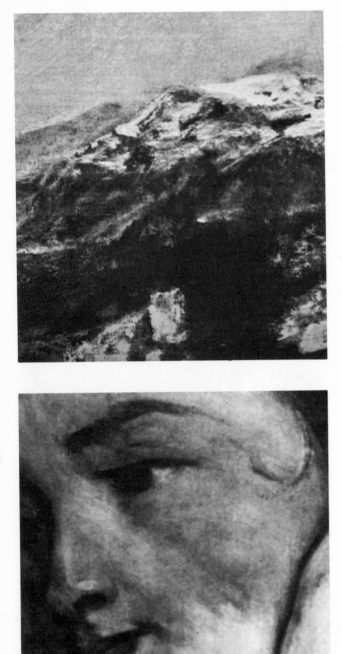

THE REALISTS AND PLEINAIRISTS

The museum conception of art was broken up by the Realists and Pleinairists. They felt that the older art had a deadening effect. The old technique of glazing robbed painting of light and air. They went back to nature and made the discovery that a picture could not be painted out-of-doors with the methods of the studio. The face of nature is constantly changing, so they were forced to simplify and to stress only the most important. In their eager search for new motifs the Realists and Pleinairists even discovered nature. Older art, with a few exceptions such as Breughel and others, had no use for nature, or regarded nature merely as a backdrop or a décor. In spite of their out-of-door practice, however, the Barbizon school never ventured to paint light; hence their forest interiors and their *paysages intimes*. From the point of view of handwriting, even Théodore Rousseau goes back to the Baroque. Allowing for his own personal variations, his conception is the same as that of Delacroix. Rousseau lays on the lighter passages with a softer, broader brush; his loaded light accents are less precise, as can be seen here in a detail from *After The Storm*. Gustave Courbet, the founder of programmatical Realism, owes a great deal to the Baroque. He makes use of a red ground, though not the red bole pigment of the Baroque painters. *Girls on the Banks of the Seine* marks the transition in Courbet's painting from the light and shadow period to the color painting of his later work. Color and lighting are Baroque. Compare this painting of Courbet to the work of Rubens or Jordaens. Courbet strives after realistic flesh tones and for this was called *"faiseur de la chair"* by Emile Zola. Cézanne said of him that he was a navvy but that his handwriting was that of a classic. And Alexandre Gabriel Decamps observed: "Courbet is clever. His painting is heavy-fisted but he brings something fine into it. It is good broad painting, and there's tenderness in it too."

Fig. 2. Théodore Rousseau. *After the Storm*. Detail from upper part of painting.

Fig. 3. Gustave Courbet. Study for *Girls on the Banks of the Seine*. Detail from center of the study.

154

IMPRESSIONISM AND POST-IMPRESSIONISM

Jean Baptiste Camille Corot studied Dutch landscape painting, Claude Lorrain, and Rembrandt, but he had an entirely new approach to nature. In those pictures whose *lumière crépuscule* (Baudelaire) conveys to the beholder a mood of so much beauty, color has begun to play an independent part as the vehicle of lyrical expression. While Delacroix still models, Corot hardly ever follows the form. His brush strokes travel in one direction—the horizontal. Square and round touches are laid on with a fine brush, often one over the other, giving an impression that the picture was painted in layers. The brushwork is extremely sensitive; the color compact. Often he paints with a fluid opaque material. His scale of color is made up of fine grays, and yet he can be reckoned, from the point of view of technique, the first systematic Impressionist.

Charles François Daubigny is fundamentally freer than Corot. His art is an expression of artistic mobility and is served by a swift brushwork eager to seize and hold the fugitive impression. His verve and feeling for the dramatic are of a piece with his temperament. All are there to be read in his nervous and clamant brushwork. He renders the characteristic shapes of the landscape with big broad strokes. Constable's device of broken color is used by Daubigny to break up his space into flat planes. The color is often pressed heavily into the grain of the canvas with the palette knife; or it may be violently thrown on the canvas. The paint varies in thickness, from heavy loading to fluently painted tone values. But whether he paints with a dry or a fluid material, Daubigny is always hot on the chase after the impression.

Fig. 4. Jean Baptiste Camille Corot. *The Boatman of Mortefontaine*. Detail of center. Frick Collection, New York.

Fig. 5. Charles François Daubigny. *Kerity le Vareck*. Detail of center.

6

7

The Impressionists took over the handwriting of Daubigny, and with it they completely revolutionized the color structure of the picture. They accepted Constable's principle of the division of color and carried it to its logical conclusion. New bright color! Every color was admissible with the exception of black—though Manet loved it. Everything was transformed into color, even the darks. Their point of view was naturalistic, but it led them not to naturalism but to abstraction in color. Edouard Manet found his own way from pre-Impressionist painting through Impressionism, and with his broad powerful brushwork and the dynamic force of the Goya *touche,* forged for himself his personal synthetic style without sacrifice of modeling. The principles of the old masters and those of the Impressionists both live in Manet.

Claude Monet is the first orthodox Impressionist. Starting from Jongkind and Boudin and together with Pissarro, he laid the style foundation upon which Sisley built. Here we should mention Turner, whose painting of light was so much admired by Monet and Pissarro in the seventies of the last century. Pissarro, Monet and Sisley are the authentic Impressionists. The others often reckoned in their number (Cézanne, Manet, Renoir, Degas, Toulouse-Lautrec) are Impressionists only in as far as they were confronted with the same problem. Their solution of it brought them to different results.

Fig. 6. Edouard Manet. *Portrait of Emile Zola,* 1868. Detail from center of foreground.

Fig. 7. Edouard Manet. *The Bar at the Folies Bergères,* 1881. Detail.

Fig. 8. Alfred Sisley. *Bridge at Sèvres.* Detail from center.

Fig. 9. Auguste Renoir. *The Lovers.* Detail of woman's head.

Alfred Sisley's handwriting is typically Impressionist. The principal theme of his work is to express light as color, and this leads him to dissolve all objects in light and atmosphere. His brush dances over the canvas with the greatest assurance, leaving clearly defined strokes behind it. He uses a small brush and often follows the forms with it. His touch is more sensitive and less bold than that of Daubigny, not so glittering as that of Monet. (The dazzling surfaces of Impressionism are due to the disintegrating effect of light on color.) Sisley's touch is more vital than that of Pissarro; his system of broken color is more complicated; his scale of values is more differentiated; he works with greater assurance. He lays his color on with varied density and conveys through it an impression of humidity. This he arrives at by superimposing different values of the same color, one upon the other, so that a darker value lying upon a lighter is absorbed by it.

8

In Auguste Renoir one sees how a completely new approach to the problem of light and color can be linked technically with the old masters. Renoir's motif was first drawn on the canvas with pencil, and upon this he painted with light colors, seeming to produce his picture out of a fog. He never dwelt long upon any one passage, but laid glaze upon glaze until his picture achieved its enamel-like finish. There is never a hard touch to break the roundness of his forms. He begins to paint his glowing flesh tones with black and white and a trace of red, then feels for the surrounding tones that give them their effect; but he takes great care that the surrounding tones shall not come so near that they cramp the flesh (Max Doerner). It will be clear from the detail illustrated that Renoir's handwriting is not typically Impressionist. Light, it is true, plays the principal part. The color loses its weight in light and seems to be breathed on the canvas, the grain of which in many cases remains visible. The brushwork is hardly visible except around the eyes, nose and mouth where he draws lightly with the brush. It is in connection with Renoir's technique that Meier-Graefe alludes to the artist's early years as a painter of porcelain. The canvas is more heavily loaded around the face, so as to bring the transparencies of the flesh into greater relief. The impasto passages show impulsive, masterly brushwork.

9

Pierre Bonnard demands consideration as the last of the Impressionists to arrive at an expressive synthesis. He won his way to a personal conception of color but he added nothing essentially new to Impressionist technique. His diffuse, vibrating brush stroke lays on warm rich tones saturated with light. At first, he painted with a somewhat restricted palette; only later did he paint in direct sunlight. With thin glazes or with heavy impasto, *à la prima* or with an underpainting: Bonnard makes use of any and every means to secure the result aimed at. A conscious part of his artistic practice is the cutting down of his picture, which he often undertakes after completion of the painting, thus following Degas and in company with Vuillard.

Fig. 10. Pierre Bonnard. *The Breakfast Room*, 1930–1931. Detail. Museum of Modern Art, New York.

Fig. 11. Georges Seurat. *The Harbor at Honfleur*. Detail.

Pointillism seems a depersonalized method of painting compared with the individually temperamental handiwork of the Impressionists, but only relatively so when one compares the touch of Georges Seurat with that of the less important Paul Signac. A system of scientific, objective discipline designed to eliminate all accidental effects gives Seurat's works their architectural character. Covered with confetti-like dots, all of the same size, arranged in tones which find their relationship only in the eye of the beholder, the Seurat painting conveys a singularly transparent impression. This is value painting carried out with almost mechanical precision.

"I follow no system in painting." Vincent van Gogh wrote to his brother. "I hammer away at the canvas with irregular strokes and let it all stay as it is—here and there impasto, raw canvas in places, unfinished corners. Brutalities!" His handwriting was all of a piece with his attitude towards nature—dramatic, uninhibited, following a biological process and a cosmic rhythm. If he wanted to render the power and solidity of the earth he never hesitated "to squeeze roots and trunks directly from the tubes and then model them into place with the brush." Van Gogh's handwriting is a personal expression of utmost intensity. Its rhythm is that of heartbeats which become ever wilder as his mortal sickness grows upon him. Here painting and handwriting are one. And here, at the same time, that impressionist handwriting which began with Franz Hals receives its final expression. Our reproduction shows a small fragment of a field of corn from the painter's later Arles period. It well expresses the vehemence and impatience of van Gogh's temperament.

Fig. 12. Vincent van Gogh. *Landscape*. Detail.

Fig. 13. Henri de Toulouse-Lautrec. *At the Moulin Rouge: Waltzers*. Detail from the right background of the painting.

Henri de Toulouse-Lautrec is one of the first of the Post-Impressionist masters. He lays his paint on with an easy virtuosity of brush stroke stylistically related to that of Degas. His handwriting is more visible on the contours of his forms; elsewhere it tends to lose itself. Light does not play the dominant part here that it plays in Impressionist painting. Hence the more precise form rendered with a small brush following the light and shadow. The outlines are continuous at times, and at others they are intermittent as the brush point strays from the canvas. Compared with the vibrating form of Renoir, that of Toulouse-Lautrec is concise and hard. He often combines different media—oil, tempera, crayon—on scratched surfaces, a technique later adopted by Max Ernst and others.

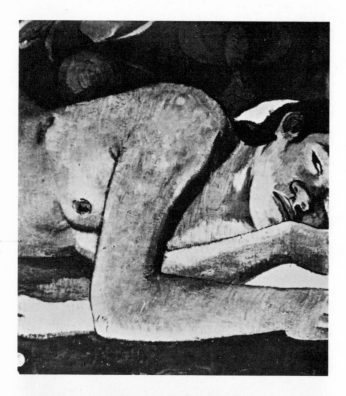

Paul Gauguin's Tahiti pictures are decorative in construction, often resembling tapestry with woven brush strokes. Gauguin began to paint with Impressionist broken color, but as early as his Brittany period he developed a severely formal picture construction, wherein flatly painted planes of color contrast strongly with each other. His broad brush stroke does not always follow the form. He often delimits his forms with a thin outline. The ornamental is strongly marked in Gauguin's work, displaying itself in the juxtaposition of tracts of vivid color. He seldom loads, but works with thin color. The rough texture of his canvas often forms part of his pictorial effect. Compared with the demoniacal tempo of van Gogh, the brushwork of Gauguin is quiet, aristocratic and controlled.

There is a realist attitude in the earliest pictures of Henri Matisse, with an impressionistic handwriting which reminds one of Edvard Munch. In his Neo-Impressionist period Matisse painted rather in the manner of Signac, with broad touches of pure color. It was after this that he attained the typical Matisse style which we recognize in our illustration, and which in its fused softness and confident sweeping brushwork in thin color calls to mind the work of Manet, in his *Olympia* for instance. Only for a short period did Matisse load his canvas, and then he made frequent use of the painting knife. Quite early in his career he began to use outline as a structural form element and here his draftsman's brushwork is easy to read. In many of his later pictures there is hardly a brush stroke to be seen. The tracts of radiant color are laid on quite flat, and the contours are drawn with independent graphic intention. It often seems that the pictures of Matisse have an underpainting, but this is not the case. He is likely, however, to change the color scale of his picture entirely in the course of the work and this may easily leave traces of the previous painting.

Fig. 14. Paul Gauguin. *Nevermore*. Detail from right side.

Fig. 15. Henri Matisse. *The Arm*, 1938. Detail.

THE PLASTIC, THE CUBIST, AND THE SURREALIST PAINTING

In critical studies on the history of art the view is often expressed that artists should not be classified under "isms." Grouping them together under general notions can, of course, only have reference to certain theoretical principles, and these concern only certain personalities. The individual artist develops out of them according to the irrational law of individuation. Honoré Daumier is an outstanding example of the impossibility of classification. According to his generation he should be classified as belonging to the historical style, but a work like the third version of his picture *The Family at the Barricades,* of which we see here a detail, flatly contradicts such a classification. Daumier, who may be termed a self-taught genius, finished this picture with an aquarelle-like wash of color over an impasto, whereas the old masters followed the opposite practice of finishing by loading the lights. In the under layer the brush follows the form, as with Delacroix, except that Daumier divides the principal mass into planes of different value. Light makes form in Daumier's pictures. There is always a strong central lighting which brings the planes of light and shadow sharply against one another. Instead of highlights, Daumier draws outlines around the forms with the narrow side of the brush. These contours reinforce the plastic impression in spite of the fact that their general function is the presentation of a flat plane. In other pictures, such as *The Burden,* the heavy impasto appears on top, worked upon with long, linear brush strokes. The form is brought into relief with parallel cross-hatching, a practice which found no imitators among his immediate successors. A similar sort of workmanship is first seen again, perhaps, in Cézanne's unfinished portrait of J. Gasquet.

Fig. 16. Honoré Daumier. *The Family at the Barricades.* Detail of head of man from center of the painting.

Paul Cézanne is a milestone in the development of modern art, and at the same time its lawgiver. Drawing upon Daumier and Delacroix, his earlier work exhibits an extremely violent handwriting visible in thick oily paint. Later his color became thin and very bright. He worked a long while on a picture, often leaving it and coming back to it again. Hence the use of fluid color dissolved in turpentine. In his landscapes the brushwork goes in strokes of different direction, so that several strokes in nuances of the same color go to make up a larger color tract which then takes its place alongside neighboring tones. One of his favorite devices was to enlist the cooperation of the white canvas, particularly on the contours, to reinforce the harmony of the colored surfaces. With the years, his scale of color became ever more differentiated. Cézanne strove after plastic depth. This is particularly noticeable in his still lifes, although the objects, compared with those of Chardin or Courbet, are modeled in planes. Shadow as such is unknown to him. The Plein-airism in his *Bathing Women* is associated with a strong rhythmical impulse. This is borne out in the brushwork of regular strokes in the masses laid on with a fine brush and reinforced with outlines. Cézanne was not a great draftsman. Hence his constant struggle with form. He often spoke of his difficulty in realizing his vision. His portraits are often unfinished, hands and clothes being merely indicated, and that was not because he willed it so. He knew, however, how to turn his weakness into strength. He wanted to render nature more vividly, to represent an apple like a real material fruit and not like a ball. Thus he sought after something more complete than Impressionism had to give—something in the sense of the absolute permanent art of the past. With this aim he tried to yoke together the newer, more primitive approach to the object with the values of the Venetian masters or of Poussin. He looked

Fig. 17. Paul Cézanne. *Fruit*. Detail from center of painting.

upon himself as a modern primitive painter. The whole artistic development of Cézanne was one of constant seeking and devotion seldom met with even in the history of art. The portrait of J. Gasquet, already mentioned, shows that the graphic element of Daumier has been eliminated. The impressionistic fleck performs the same function for Cézanne that the plane does for Daumier. His mode of applying color proceeds from the heavier to the lighter material with the use of the broad brush. His tones and their application become more sublimated. The detail of one of his earlier still lifes of fruit reproduced here shows how countless superimposed layers of thin color produce an effect of impasto. The fruit is formed from within outward, following the process of ripening.

André Derain also experienced the urge to turn to the old masters, though in a manner different from Cézanne. He is, in spite of Picasso's witticism (*"Derain, guide des musées"*), a real artistic personality, and one in whose character there is a certain vein of tragedy. Derain began to paint in an impressionistic way but with his own personal note. Later, like all the others, he fell under the influence of Cézanne and painted with a smooth surface and fluid material. He often made use of earth colors. His gothic period which lasted ten years and includes such works as *Saturday*, 1911–1914, and *The Last Supper*, 1913, is artistically important. After the first world war came a new realistic phase when he painted rather in the sense of Corot, but with elements derived from the Renaissance artists and the French Primitives. Derain paints with a smooth surface and with the illusion of depth. His out-of-door landscapes are painted direct and in one sitting. Those painted in the studio are more intensively studied. His heads and figures, often extremely simplified, are painted in planes with broad brushes and confident strokes of the brush.

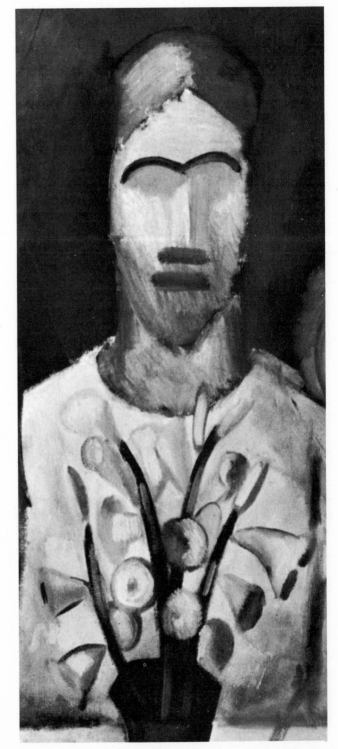

Fig. 18. André Derain. *The Last Supper*, 1913. Detail of Christ. Art Institute of Chicago, Chicago. Gift of Mrs. Frank R. Lillie.

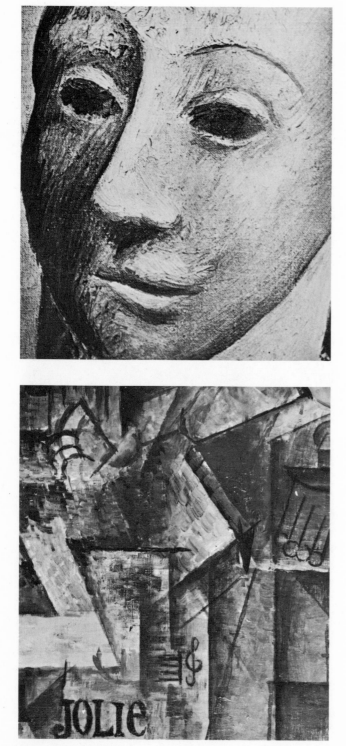

Cézanne's principles of plastic construction were taken up by Pablo Picasso, as can be seen here in a detail from *The Seated Women*, painted about 1906, that is to say, before the proclamation of analytic Cubism. But there is here another element, that of Negro plastic art. The vehemence of the brush stroke is typical of Picasso's passionate painter's temperament.

If we now compare this detail from *The Seated Women* with one of his Cubist still lifes, the extreme versatility of his painter's handiwork becomes evident. Picasso is Cubism; but he is more than that: he is the history of art in person. There can be no better example of the truth that the artist's handwriting and his search for style are one. There is no art period, no important artist, no phenomenon in the world of artistic creation that has not left its trace in the encyclopedic work of Picasso. The work of lunatics, children's drawings, Russian ikons, Assyrian reliefs, Catalonian and Pompeian frescoes, miniatures, handiwork of the artist-craftsman: all are grist for his mill. The same endless variety is displayed in his painter's handwriting and handling of color. Picasso is a great skeptic—a relativist of genius. He deeply mistrusts the taste of his own age and rebels against its judgments. Therefore he seeks and finds beauty in the productions of all times and all places. He has a most highly developed sense of form, which accounts for his preserving a classic element in almost all his work. To make an exhaustive count of all his creative periods—his blue period, his circus, Negro and Cézanne periods, the periods of analytic and synthetic Cubism, his Ingres, pink Tanagra, and graphic periods—and to show how the style of each period was mirrored in its handwriting, would far outrun the framework of this study.

From a technical standpoint the contribution of Cubism to art is the application of the methods of monumental art to the art of the easel painting. Big surfaces look dead unless they give the realistic luster and construction of the object. For this reason the Cubists, Braque and Picasso, enlivened their color by using a thick underpainting of tempera, on which they

Fig. 19. Pablo Picasso. *Sitting Woman,* about 1906. Detail.

Fig. 20. Pablo Picasso. *Ma Jolie,* 1911–1912. Detail.
Museum of Modern Art, New York. Lillie P. Bliss Bequest.

strewed sand or powdered cork. Another technical device was the use of real objects, such as scraps of wallpaper, bits of newspaper, etc.: the collage. This device had already been used but was renewed, particularly by Braque, with happy artistic results. Occasionally, in order to avoid monotony and give an effect of spontaneity, an impressionistic touch appears in Cubist still lifes, together with a rather more objective handling of color. The Cubist revolution in form consisted in representing things not as they appear to us optically, but objectively, in multi-vision in foreshortenings, in hieroglyphics of experience.

Georges Braque, a onetime handworker, was a technician of great virtuosity whose typical excellence is the precise harmony of his color tones. In the synthetic period, about 1922–1923, Braque no longer decomposed his forms into their elements, but sought to bring them together in larger constructions. His color in this period was often applied in two layers, the lower of which was black. Grapes, for example, he painted with an opaque green and drew the outlines in the color of the ground, creating a plastic effect by the depth of space given with the black tone. (Note in this connection the dark grounds of the Venetians.) The charm of the touch gets lost in this process, but is compensated for by the use of sand. The plastic effect is completed with highlights which seem at times to be scratched out with the butt-end of the brush.

Surrealism fixes its attention principally on the dream, in which we spend a third of our lives. It is theoretically hostile to the idealistic conception of the dream and to the positivist conception that the dream is merely a product of the previous meal. It reaffirms the analytical method of Freud with its insistence on the motives of wish, anxiety, association, and reality. This attitude dictates the motifs and technique of the Surrealist picture, which seeks to represent everything with the utmost objectivity so as to secure the desired fantastic effect. And evidently this effect is intensified when the individual objects are set forth in an artificial airless space in the most unexpected relations to each

Fig. 21. Pablo Picasso. *Still Life*, 1937. Detail.

Fig. 22. Georges Braque. *Still Life with Grapes*. Detail. The Phillips Collection, Washington, D.C.

other. If, for example, a tree grows out of a matchbox the beholder is not impressed unless both objects are realistically represented. The consequence is that, technically, Surrealist painting is uninteresting from the point of view of this study. It is a smooth, academic, almost banal way of using the painter's material.

Salvador Dalì is the orthodox representative of this school. As symbols of his Surrealist art have cropped up in all countries, we can speak of a Surrealist school, but not so easily of the true spirit of Surrealism, the aim of which is to bring a province of the subconscious mind into the orbit of pictorial representation.

André Masson is not a typical Surrealist. In point of form he belongs to Cubism, a judgment which his methods of painting figures and surfaces confirm. His figures remind one of Picasso's, but are penetrated with a singularly fantastic, bizarre, baroque spirit. (A human being grows out of a tree, etc.) He personifies the dead through the living. But there is something spontaneous about his work. It exhibits improvisation and intensity, qualities otherwise lacking in Surrealism. They manifest themselves also in the handwriting of his pictures. He often paints direct, without retouch.

The art of Giorgio De Chirico is classic in character. His pictorial conception is plastic, the facture of his pictures smooth. His early work gave a diffuse, washed-out impression. Later it became linear. In his paintings of horses and gladiators, his conceptions resemble those of Pompeian frescoes and antique vase-painting. Architecture, museum objects and monuments are the motifs he uses to express his metaphysical skepticism, his yearning after old tradition and also a certain irony at the expense of the academicians. This is the equipment of his pictorial philosophy. He, too, assigns to dead things the functions of life. A tailor's dummy figures as a human being, and a biscuit as the live unconscious reality. Through the fine recession of the color tones in the severe perspectives of his pictures, suggesting antique scenes, De Chirico succeeds in conveying a mystical atmosphere.

Joan Miró can be counted among the Surrealists during the years 1920–1924 and yet he too, from the point of view of form, belongs to Cubism. He uses the

Fig. 23. André Masson. *Storm,* 1938. Detail.

Fig. 24. Joan Miró. *Portrait I,* 1938. Detail.

166

Cubist space of flat planes instead of the space of perceived reality, and he paints flatly with no element of illusion. Generally the pictures of this period are smoothly painted. Only later did he develop into the master of naïvism.

That the handwriting of all these painters gives none of the effects of the Impressionists is due to their guiding pictorial principles. The same holds good for the techniques exhibited in the mechanistic–abstract work of Ferdinand Léger, the Constructivist work of Piet Mondrian, etc.

THE PRIMITIVE AND THE NAÏVE

Among the tendencies of modern art the Primitive and the Naïve figure relatively large. Negro art, the magic art of the South Seas, Gauguin's primitivism, the rediscovery of the French and Italian Primitives and of the decorative elements in ancient popular art, have all had their influence on this development. The *douanier* Henri Rousseau is genuinely naïve. In a certain sense Utrillo and often Chagall display naïvistic leanings. There is no consistent handwriting to be found in the work of Chagall, for the reason that he strains without inhibitions after the effect he desires. Comparing his handwriting with that of Cézanne's mature period, it might be said that the one is that of a gypsy fiddler and the other that of a violin virtuoso. Chagall laboriously paints red roses with heavy material on a white raised ground, but he smears in the surrounding space with a wash of thin, characterless paint. Utrillo is a product of Impressionism.

Henri Rousseau was self-taught, and an admirer of the old masters in the Louvre and of Persian and Indian miniatures. In his pictorial expression he is forthright and primitive, though here and there is an accent that recalls the old masters. His handwriting as seen in the illustration is a sort of drawing with large or small brushes, and follows an inner vision rather than nature. Rousseau's painting invites comparison with works of the Trecentists: like those of the Italian Primitives his paintings are epic narratives, and everything represented tends to turn to the beholder. He is not a direct painter: his work is painstakingly executed

Fig. 25. Henri Rousseau. *Self-Portrait*. Detail.

and often reveals the presence of several layers of color. His form is always compact and clear, and, particularly in such later pieces as *The Snake Charmer*, the color is laid on with so smooth a finish that all trace of brushwork entirely disappears. There are other pictures of his, painted probably directly from nature and destined to serve as studies for his finished work, that are almost Fauvist in their handling.

In summary we can say that, together with the sensuous discoveries of Impressionism in color, light, and air, with the intellectual contribution of Cubism in respect to the absolute values of planes, of space and of the multiple aspects of objects, with Surrealist symbolism, and with the Primitives' conception of the picture and naïve pleasure in painting—together with all these, the visible handwriting of the painter is an acquisition that has enriched modern painting with much rhythmic and psychological interest. But just because this element seems so arbitrary, it demands of the painter a masterly command of pictorial craftsmanship. Without this it can be no more than an eloquent testimony to his lack of technical accomplishment.

WERNER SCHMALENBACH

THE PROBLEM OF REALITY IN MID-CENTURY PAINTING

The term "mid-century art" is used to designate the painting of the period from the armistice year 1945 until the writing of this article in 1961. No one likes to give a war credit for being a dividing line between two phases of culture. But it cannot be denied that postwar art as a whole is different from art before 1939. The eternal pessimists as to things contemporary, who look favorably upon the present only when it has become a tried and tested past, often complain that postwar artists have not produced anything essentially new, and that the current generation is living off the dividends of that "heroic" generation, who, between 1900 and 1925, ushered in and created the modern age. Yet there is certainly no such an effete perpetuation of traditions, as a cursory glance in any of today's art periodicals will tell you. It is true, however, that the postwar generation had no cause to rebel demonstratively against its elders. In an earlier day, it had certainly been more necessary to revolt against the art of the academies than to struggle after 1945 against Picasso, Kandinsky, Klee, and the others. Thus, not only the style of art per se had changed, but the style of artistic behavior as well. Nowadays, no more revolutions are being staged. The era of programs and manifestoes, of artists on barricades, is over. Art has lost its ideological character, so very pronounced between the two great wars.

The ante-bellum heritage for a postwar world at ease, the heritage that was enthusiastically accepted after 1945, is called—very generally—"abstract art." What had once been a new gospel became an almost natural legacy. Of course, there were, and still are, significant exceptions and important dissenting voices; and obviously, the more strength this art gains, the more discontent it provokes. But just the same, the overwhelming majority of the most important artists in our time are non-objective. This has nothing to do with dogmatic convictions. Nor is this a postulate. It is a *fait accompli*. Formerly, when it was necessary to acquire authority and legitimacy for non-objective art, things were different. It was a matter of struggling for something new, *i.e.*, of drawing up a program. Today, abstract art is no longer a matter of artistic decision, but merely a framework in which utterly diverging decisions can be made. The generalization "abstract art" is consequently as inane as the lumping together of all other art under the heading "objective." The artistic possibilities covered by this title, *faute de mieux*, are

as numerous as in other art. They constitute an enormous scale of countless adumbrations reaching from Piet Mondrian at one end to Jackson Pollock at the other.

Among the public and some critics the claim is still being made that abstract art is on the decline, that it is in crisis. This crisis is simply a projection into abstract art of an old wish which has gained new publicity. And this wish has given birth to the belief that abstract art really is coming to an end.

The fact is that abstract art is presently undergoing an emphatic transformation actually taking place on its periphery, that is, where the problem of reality exists. By those who do not understand, the artists are asked to stop playing their abstract "games" and to strive more intensively for "reality." As if this desire for reality did not exist as a matter of course for the best artists! Abstract art feels this desire, too, but will not be satisfied with the mere recognition of objects: objectivity is not quite reality, and recognition is not quite cognition. Even abstract art contains a genuine claim to reality. Indeed, the desire to incorporate and to master reality is a decisive and characteristic postwar feature of abstract art and has transformed abstract art without making it obsolete. Any close observer of contemporary art cannot help but notice that no matter how the artists may be working, theirs is an intensive striving for reality. In fact, the "engaged" observer, himself trying to understand contemporary art, will most likely be asking not merely for a new concept of form, but for a new reality as well. It appears that the mastering of reality has become a fundamental and existential problem of art since 1945.

However, in 1945, the motto of art was by no means "reality"; such a shibboleth would have been misunderstood at the time and suspected of constituting an escape from "modern art." The watchword was *liberation;* and the area in which it proved effective was artistic style, the totality of artistic possibilities. It was abstract art that benefited from the forces liberated thanks to the end of war and tyranny. Abstract art had its great day. But this long-awaited liberation had to keep on having an effect: it had to transform the style of abstract art, as it was understood at the time, toward greater freedom. A renunciation of the object did not suffice, even though many painters had to make this decision for themselves anew. Abstract art had to throw off its own shackles—the domination of the ruler and the compass. It had to speak the language of liberty. Thus, soon after 1945, various and diverging forces were to be seen in non-objective art, whereas before the war, hardly anyone would have guessed that they even existed. The geometric conception, one of many, encompassed only a small area, appearing more and more historical and attracting few artists. For many painters at this time, "geometry" was merely a point of departure or a transitional phase leading to a completely different approach.

Every country has painters who have remained true to the fundamental idea of concrete art à la Mondrian: Alberto Magnelli, Auguste Herbin, Fritz Glarner, Victor Pasmore, Victor Vasarely, Richard Mortensen, to name only a few. In an age when art has decided to throw off all fetters of form, they render homage to that radical artistic absolutism which has been formulated most extremely in Malevich's *Black Square* and in Mondrian's gospel of the right angle. The method of further artistic asceticism, of a further reduction of the formal means, was not feasible; the only possibility was that of a greater differentiation. Despite all their submission to strict, "objective" formal laws, these artists give form and color far greater leeway. And it is the leeway itself, rather than the principle, which is expanded. This means above all that the plane is no longer an absolute, plastic medium. Space, movement, light—further dimensions of reality—are drawn into the formal exercises, but the distinction between the work of art and reality is not effaced. These dimensions are thought of solely in mathematical or physical terms, *i.e.,* purely formal and abstract terms. Spatial composition, lighting effects, kinetic phenomena—sometimes in conjunction with new technical material—are problems with which groups of vanguard artists of the younger generation are experimenting everywhere. Their creations have had some exciting visual effects, all the more so as new ideas of form have joined them—for example, the infinite repetition of invariable microforms. Through such practices, the painters operating in the tradition of concrete art arrive at extreme concepts of form, with the picture eventually turning into a mere pattern: an "absolute picture" like Malevich's *Black Square,* whose blackness is replaced to a certain extent by the uniform texture. Surprisingly enough, this extreme point is the meeting place of painting bound by strict laws, and certain phenomena of "non-formal" art. Indeed certain traits are common to both trends of mid-century art: uniformly painted or structured planes, on which nothing happens; patterns in which it makes no difference whether the grid consists of geometric lines or non-formal strokes. Diametrically opposed poles are suddenly close to one another, each proving that the other is a mode of expression for our age.

It is significant that the English artist Ben Nicholson, the most sovereign representative of painting in the spirit of geometry, remains outside this province of experimenters, albeit rooted in that great purist movement comprising everyone from Juan Gris, Fernand Léger, the Purists, to the Constructivists and artists of the Bauhaus and *de Stijl.* He administers this legacy in the freest and therefore most legitimate fashion. Though believing in the dignity of geometry, he does not raise it to the status of an absolute law, but instead draws it back into the realm of human and artistic relativity. Nicholson's line, though based on laws, is more of what medieval scribes called a *ductus* than a line. His colors are not only meant to fill out the planes, but are used to patina the surface in a very subtle and cultivated way. Moreover, Nicholson commits a sacrilege against the spirit of abstraction by admitting, as a matter of course, objective forms into his art, which, nevertheless, remains rigidly formal and essentially abstract. With his many drawings showing landscapes and architecture, which he gives the full status of a picture, he has forced his way out of the limitations of concrete art. If the abolition of the barriers between nature and abstraction is a sign of mid-century art, then Ben Nicholson's works exemplify this —in fact, all the more impressively, as their universe is really that of geometric abstraction.

As said above, after 1945 abstract painting decided to burst the confines of geometry. Painting as such had been silenced by concrete art, and now with the liberation of the pictorial means it regained its old rights. This is specifically true for the central, temperate zone of mid-century painting, with its most important representatives in France. Painting itself has always been the aim of French artists. Anyone surveying the continuity of French painting through the centuries will be aware of this specifically painterly constant. There is some suspicion that fine craftsmanship neglects more pro-

(*Above*) Jean Bazaine, born 1904. *Pierre*, 1955. 120.5 x 60.5 cm. Kunstsammlung Nordheim-Westfalen, Düsseldorf.

(*Below*) Maria Elena Vieira da Silva, born 1908. *Le Métro aérien*, 1955. 162 x 220 cm. Kunstsammlung Nordheim-Westfalen, Düsseldorf.

(*Opposite*) Nicolas de Staël, 1914–1955. *Figure au Bord de la Mer,* 1952. 161.5 x 129.5 cm. Kunstsammlung Nordheim-Westfalen, Düsseldorf.

found human and intellectual expression, but French painters parry this with their basic conviction that painting is *eo ipso* human expression. Form is identical for them with emotion, it is emotion. This basic conviction was consistent with abstract art, but only when the latter discarded its ruler and its compass and adopted the "free" brush. Only then could French notions on art be assimilated in abstract art, which hitherto had had alien status in Paris and had not yet been naturalized.

When the curtain was raised in European countries after the war, the general feeling about painters such as Jean Bazaine, Alfred Manessier, and the much older Roger Bissière—to name only the most important—was, that for the first time, abstract art was thriving on French soil. Now the tradition of French painting was leading organically and without any programmatic radicalism to the ultimate consequence of abstraction, and vice versa, now abstract art was being organically incorporated into the tradition of French painting.

The first exhibition of a representative group of these young painters was held in Paris in 1941, with the characteristic title, *Vingt Peintres de Tradition Française.* Paris was at this time still under German occupation, but French painting quietly went its own way and soon elicited a world-wide response. This was what Chardin or Corot, Braque or Matisse, or Bonnard—whom these young painters held in such great esteem—had meant by *peinture.*

The liberation of form for the sake of the free development of painting itself spontaneously made the abstract idiom a conveyer of human, intellectual, and poetic expression: pure and precious color *eo ipso* brought intellectual expression into the canvas. It is thus no coincidence that in this area of French painting, Paul Klee had a greater influence in France than anyone prior to him. But it was not only reality of subjective feeling that entered into abstract paintings. Instinctively, yet very consciously, these artists thought of their works as an equivalent of nature, for them the source of all inspiration. This manifested itself in many ways. Space was expressed with rich painterly means. Nature's light burst effulgently out of the colors: the ultimate consequence of Delaunay's Orphist doctrine concerning the identity of color and light. Though not representing anything, most of the works of these painters are landscapes. They are "full of nature": the many colors of nature, its light, movement, rhythms, and atmosphere constitute the essence of many of these works. The forces, frozen in form and color, are forces of nature. One is even tempted to compare some of Jean Bazaine's late works with Claude Monet's *Nymphéas*.

We must therefore repeat, and with great justification, that although the barrier between nature and abstraction was once erected with resoluteness and intolerance, it was done away with in mid-century art. Yet this did not mean the abolition of non-objective painting, but rather its enrichment and expansion as well as an incomparably greater reality.

French painting is a model representative of this phase of contemporary art: it occupies a national position within international art, even though it may have elicited response and gained followers far beyond the borders of France, and it has earned itself the title of the School of Paris, albeit completely different artists claim a place in it. Indeed, artists of other nations—all artists who combine a highly developed painterly quality with a sense of the nature symbolism of form and color—have been approaching this same conception of painting, even if these non-French painters have different origins and cannot be easily included in the French tradition.

Within the School of Paris itself there are two very special cases: the Portuguese-born Vieira da Silva, and the Russian-born Nicolas de Staël.

Vieira da Silva is not a product of the French *peinture* tradition but rather of Surrealism, which in her case—as in that of many other contemporary artists—led to abstraction. She began to overcome the noticeable Surrealist component of her earlier paintings by opening the magic perspectives of her hallucinatory interiors and making an enormous non-perspective, undefined space the locale and desire of her imagination. She started drawing dream-like city panoramas and enchanted architecture in the expanse of her canvases. Mysterious cities emerged like mirages out of the ether only to vanish again. These were and were not cities, mere patterns of lines, of very fine, tremulous antennae quivering with an almost inaudible music of the spheres. Finally, in her more recent works, the "real" apparition is hidden by the equally real lyricism of mute lines. Lines, strokes of color, are the direct and sole trace of sensitivity.

Nicolas de Staël followed the course of the majority of artists in his generation—but in the opposite direc-

tion: he turned more and more to the object. Yet it was not so much the object as the conflict between reality and abstraction—the basic motif of twentieth-century art—that dramatically and tragically became the theme of his painting. In the short time allotted to his creative activity, he again and again returned to the starting point of his skepticism and thus, since painting was his existence, to the starting point of his own self. At every step of the way, the power of his questions was equal to the power and validity of his answers: an artist, constantly searching for something, and constantly finding it. The capture of reality was indispensable for his art, in his early abstract works and in his later objective paintings alike. With his extraordinary mastery of color and form, seen in his brilliant canvases done around 1951, he was able to come to grips with visible reality. After the memorable experience of a nocturnal soccer game in the Parisian stadium, Parc des Princes, in 1952, visible reality—figures, landscapes, still lifes—came forth in his painting, and he produced works of breath-taking power. Indeed, he yielded more and more to the irresistible call of reality and

Hans Hartung, born 1904. *Painting*, 1951.
Galerie Louis Carré, Paris.

Pierre Soulages, born 1919. *8 décembre 1959*. 201.5 x 162 cm.
Kunstsammlung Nordheim-Westfalen, Düsseldorf.

made an attempt (seemingly traditional and devoid of problems, yet extraordinary after such intense questioning) to capture visible reality with traditional painterly means. By virtue of his eminent artistry, he intervened in his own "copying" and in the best works of the final months of his life, he transformed the things he painted into apparitions. A wonderful outsider of mid-century art, who, though seemingly turning his back on this period and eventually departing from it by his own hand in 1955, was one of its foremost representatives.

Whenever in the course of history expressive desires decisively influenced art, this meant that fixed modes were discarded in favor of a dynamic idiom of expression imperiling form. Such a development took place with truly elemental power after 1945, when forces which had been held back far too long were suddenly released. This liberation form was at first limited to a very few isolated artists. But then it seemed as if a dike had burst which hitherto had been protecting the continent of art against an unknown and dangerous ocean. Throughout all the countries of the free world an art of unrestrained form and uninhibited expression was spreading. After a few years this movement was being headed by young American painting, which for the first time in the history of art had a decisive voice. The American contribution became a new national position within international art, in sharp contrast to the French position.

What crystallized, at least for non-objective painting, was a new conception of form in general. In this sector of present-day art, form is no longer a discrete, isolated entity, but an active and dynamic occurrence. Form is the immediate trace left by the movement of expression signing its own name, so to speak, and is conceived of as pure handwriting, as script, as an expressive gesture, as a psychograph. The character of form is determined not by its definitive appearance, but by its execution. The essence of form is action. This is expressed in the slogans with which the movement established itself after 1950 and which are fraught with all the disadvantages of slogans: "Abstract Expressionism," "Action Painting," *"peinture de geste."* The most unfortunate of these slogans, "Tachism," is already obsolescent for artists and critics alike. The name *"art informel"* or "non-formal art" goes beyond this area to that art whose decisive component is "matter" and which will be discussed below.

Before the war and right after 1945, concrete art was the artistic conviction of Hans Hartung, a German who had become a French citizen. But at his own risk he parried geometric abstraction with the wonderful alternative of his emotional, expressive script; and not merely his own handwriting, but script per se, script as a principle. Painting was turned into writing, or better, scribbling on the picture surface. From a historical point of view, this artist was perpetuating the tradition of Kandinsky's early Expressionist "Improvisations" of the *Blaue Reiter* period, of which there were no followers between the wars. At the same time Hartung was seconded by the plastic gestures of the painter Joan Miró and the sculptor Julio Gonzalez. Of all the forms of non-objective art to emerge after the war, this was the most electrifying. It soon became evident that Hartung was one of the artists who had not only given his epoch a new mode of seeing, but had also gone so far as to inaugurate a whole new vision. Yet he was by no means intent on proclaiming a new way or breaking out of the School of Paris. He, too, aimed at clear formal order and a painterly quality. Like many important creators of great trends, he had not been after the results of what he had begun. In the course of later years the painterly component in his work gained so decidedly over the eruptive qualities, and the objectivity over the subjectivity, that the painters of the following generation, though honoring him as a great pioneer, limit their veneration to his work before 1950.

What has been said of Hartung applies also to Pierre Soulages, many years his junior. He was twenty-five when the war ended, and his art developed only during the following decade into the impressive power it has become today. For him too, every form derives its character from the art which engendered it. But Soulages wards off the danger of a lack of formal restraint with his architectural intellect and the hedonistic cultivation of *la belle matière*. He holds the painting as such to be sacrosanct.

This current, soon to become the mainstream of contemporary art, includes Nicolas de Staël's marvelous works: expressive and abstract paintings of somber excitement, with vehement palette-knife thrusts releasing the artist's entire passionate energy, which, a few years later, is pent up in those "form-blocks" painted with broad strokes of the palette knife and constituting his pictorial architecture.

A fissure had opened—the dike burst. While artists such as Hartung, Soulages, and De Staël stayed in the background or moved in completely different directions, a whole generation was fascinated by the adventure of liberated form. Art was threatening to go beyond its own limits. An inherent trait of twentieth-century art is its constant attempt to come into its own in borderline situations, *i.e.*, to define its own character on the very verge of relinquishing it. Mondrian had already very nearly crossed the frontier between art and geometry. And now artists were dangerously verging on chance and arbitrariness. They began wildly splashing paint all over the canvas, even shooting out whole tubes (which Derain had once called "dynamite cartridges"). The watchword was pure energy and pure action.

In art of this ilk, formal control—which we may ask about anxiously—is, so to speak, incorporated in the mechanism of painting and is not so much a stable pole or an Archimedean point regulating the whole process, but rather a part of the action: the artist either "has" form or he hasn't. There is no other protection against formlessness. The considerable danger inherent in chance and arbitrariness can be overcome in only one way: if chance becomes part of artistic law, and arbitrariness part of artistic intention, as elements of expression, both are thus simultaneously included and nullified. If a very definite form does materialize in many cases, it is because all this is based on an unmistakable passion for form, and because, in spite of everything, the best artists operate with great formal energy and even intellectual discipline. The dangers are obvious; but all art leads a dangerous life. All art acquires specific forms of danger, and most art has gained nothing from being free of any danger.

This is an essentially anti-intellectual art, even though it may be propagated with a great deal of intellectual energy—an art in which man is not a being separated into psychological, intellectual, and physical functions, but an indivisible whole, acting and reacting as a whole, with his heart, his body, and his belly. These artists claim that all such forces are artificially separated by consciousness, and thus it is consciousness (or awareness) which is being discredited. Though highly conscious and wide awake, these artists rely on the subconscious as their strongest propelling force.

The term "Abstract Expressionism," one of several coined for this type of painting, suggests connections with Expressionism (formerly, in international art

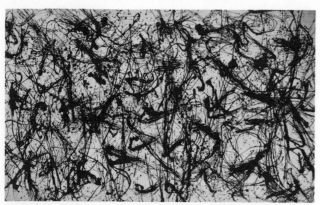

Jackson Pollock, 1912–1956. *Number 32,* 1950. 269 x 457.5 cm.
Kunstsammlung Nordheim-Westfalen, Düsseldorf.

Mark Tobey, born 1890. *Plane of Poverty,* 1960. 186 x 112 cm.
Kunstsammlung Nordheim-Westfalen, Düsseldorf.

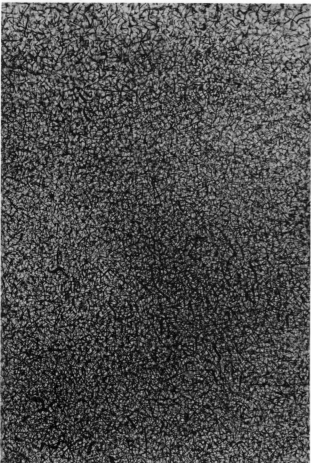

parley, a "German" position), especially with Kandinsky, but also with Klee, who once defined "line" as
energy, and conceived of "form" as formation, as genesis, as something that had once come into being and
was still developing. Hartung is a product of these art
worlds. Yet, a different, later, interwar movement became highly important in this area and in other phases
of present-day art: Surrealism. The Surrealist thesis of
"psychic automatism" could have been coined for today's Action Painters, whose psychological discharges
occur "automatically," even more so than for the Surrealists, for whom the term designated not so much a
manner of painting, as the engendering of pictorial
conceptions and contents from the innermost depths of
the soul. The Surrealists were patient enough to
employ the greatest care and often an almost photographic precision in representing the figures and forma-
tions supposedly evoked by the subconscious. Now for
the first time, in the postwar generation, the automatism entered painting itself. It slipped, as it were, into
the artist's brush, his arms, his muscles. This had little
in common with the Surrealist conception. But it is
significant that many of these painters, before devoting
themselves to pure action, spent some time with Surrealism. Even such "standard representatives" of Surrealism as Joan Miró and André Masson chose the
methods of an abstract pictorial idiom, whose merger
with Surrealism (*e.g.,* Vieira da Silva) is one of the decisive events of postwar art.

It is not possible in such a brief survey to mention,
much less to do justice to, all the artists belonging to
peinture de geste. In America, the list was headed by
Jackson Pollock. He introduced the dripping method
into artistic practice: he swung cans of paint with holes
punctured in the bottoms over his (usually large-sized)
canvases, which were flat on the floor, and let the paints
flow, drip, and splotch. The body played as great a
part as the keenly aware mind. Pictorialness in any
traditional sense was denied. In these paintings there
are no accents, no dominants, no centers of gravity.
The center of gravity is outside the canvas, within the
artist himself. There are no dynamic "signs": the movement of the painting is infinite and devours everything
which could curb it. The picture is a slice of endless
activity.

Action Painting is not limited to the dramatic and

dynamic wielders of unbound form. The term can be applied to any work in which form is conceived of as energy, as something active. The gestures can be very quiet—if you like: "lyrical," "poetic," "musical," and so for a whole field of present-day art the name "Lyrical Abstraction" has been put to use. It might be better to refer to at least some of these artistic creations as "Meditative Abstraction": the process of artistic meditation takes place on the picture surface. This, too, is a process, an action, not expansive, but introverted, and therefore not violent or spectacular, but very quiet. In contrast to the expansiveness of Action Painting, a small format is generally preferred. And first and foremost, these artists use India ink as a medium for setting down their thoughts, evidence that Far Eastern art is exerting an enormous influence here.

Above all, there is Wols, originally a German painter, who died in poverty in 1961. After his death he was acknowledged to be one of the central figures of contemporary art and to have had a great influence on young painters everywhere in the world. He, too, developed via Surrealism, eventually communicating his expressive distress solely by means of chromatic and formal gestures, lines, and strokes. Even though his artistic tenet later became a universal stylistic principle, for him it was an enormous human, intellectual, and artistic necessity, born directly out of personal despair. The martyrdom of his life was continued in the martyrdom of his art, which for the sake of this expressive suffering was far from meditation. His was an Abstract Expressionism bursting with internal and external fury, yet closer to Lyrical Abstraction than the extroverted declamations of the Action Painters. Wols's works do not constitute painting as a pleasure or as an aesthetic bliss, but rather nausea, the *nausée* treated by his friend Jean-Paul Sartre. Every stroke is almost an act, a gesture of suffering, cruelly bursting the colors. Besides the expressive paintings, Wols produced a great number of small, fragile gouaches with their filigree of variegated strokes and lines, in which the artist's sensibilities and sensitivity were woven into the subtlest of miracles: less aggressive or defensive, less self-destructive than in the larger paintings—poetic, lyrical, dream-like formal universes, in which the sufferer's torment is sublimated into incomparable magic.

The American, Mark Tobey, is a past master of lyrical, meditative abstraction. Like Wols and Vieira da

Julius Bissier, born 1893. *22.XI.56.* 15 x 25 cm. Kunstsammlung Nordheim-Westfalen, Düsseldorf.

Sam Francis, born 1923. *Black and Yellow Composition,* 1954. 194.5 x 130 cm. Kunstsammlung Nordheim-Westfalen, Düsseldorf.

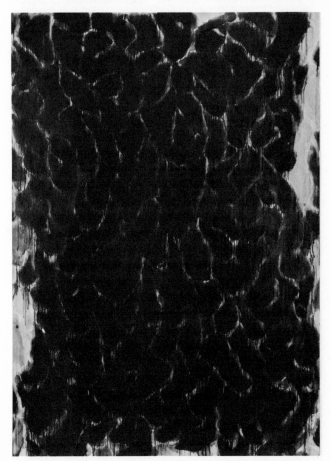

Silva, he loves the chaotic rhythms of a metropolis and introduces a trace of them into the calm of his calligraphic paintings. The loudest noise is transformed into the quietest calm in these microcosms of form and color, these endless accumulations of runes and hieroglyphics, signs and color particles, these incredibly delicate networks of lines, strokes, and points.

Julius Bissier, a German, had already turned to an art of meditatively drawn signs in 1933, at a time when art was far removed from such notions of form. Only twenty-five years later did the world recognize him as one of the most significant painters of the times and also as one of those standing at the beginning of the great mid-century movement. Deeply impressed by Far Eastern art and spirituality, Bissier employed almost exclusively India ink for his sensitive hieroglyphics full of internal mystery. Much later, about 1955, besides the black and white ink drawings, he began working on his great series of "miniatures"—chromatic temperas on canvas—with which he touched the hearts of so many people throughout the world and which were followed a few years later by larger paintings in the same spirit. His, too, is an art of meditative abstraction, which, however, does not develop only from a free pictorial gesture, but leads again and again to small forms having definite outlines and objective associations. The infinite is expressed not by means of itself, not by unlimited formal movements, but by finite forms that always refer to a higher and more universal unity of all life and spirit.

This is an art whose utmost calm is not immobility but the result of introverted activity. In this manner some artists have come to a kind of painting in which "nothing" happens; "everything" is expressed by means of nothing, by means of an absolute vacuum. Naturally, such advances into the void are often little more than programmatically embellished attempts at hiding the fact that there is really nothing there. But occasionally this nothingness is instinct with a great force of experience. Such an idiom is to be found in American painting. Mark Rothko confronts us with large, flag-like paintings containing two or three wide, chromatic planes and nothing else. Barnett Newman divides huge monochrome planes by means of one or two narrow vertical or horizontal stripes. Rhythms of greater vitality are to be found in Clyfford Still's large monochromic pictures with their painterly structures.

Sam Francis, too, at times approaches such "endless" planes of meditation. In France, Ives Klein is the main defender of monochromism. William Scott, an Englishman, paraphrases the notion of an empty, eventless painting with rich, painterly means. Thus, the great artistic liberation movement, which began immediately after the war, has led to a liberation not merely for the sake of form, but from form itself. Klee's statement to the effect that art does not represent what is visible, but renders visible, has been endorsed by almost all modern-day artists. This means that art has reached a point at which, to an extent, it demonstrates only its pure visibility.

In this whole significant realm of dynamic or meditative *peinture de geste* (ranging from Pollock to Hartung, from Soulages to Wols, Tobey, and Bissier) reality has an essential voice—first of all as the artist's life, directly expressed in every gesture, and then, as objective reality. All formal processes occur in space, *ergo* in reality. The fact that painters, especially in the United States, prefer the largest formats is an expression of the desire to traverse the largest space of all: today's space. A further element of reality is the movement many painters "represent" with their abstract means. This movement is a manifestation of vital feelings, and a representation of "objective" movement as well. This is most evident in such artists as K. R. H. Sonderborg, who glorifies a lightning tempo and turns the universe into a setting of breakneck movement; even objective associations arise, such as reminiscences of vehicles: airplanes, rockets, etc.; in other paintings, nuclear explosions. In Bissier's works there are outlines of houses and towers, fruits and receptacles. Last and far from least, the reality, with which such art as Bissier's and Rothko's is instinct, consists in the fact that constantly and ubiquitously the grand context of the world is meant and is tangibly present in all forms.

Form liberation gave impetus to still another art which involved the discovery of new artistic "matter" for painting. This is a wide field of contemporary art, in which countless painters, including some of the leading figures, are working. This area is part of non-formal art, since "form" in the older sense has for the most part been abolished, this time in favor of "formless" matter and structures. And here, too, we have come full circle, for new structures, often in new, mostly technical materials, are sought after by the painters following a modification of Mondrian's principles.

The artists who practice this cult of matter throughout the world have declared war on *peinture* and consider color a cheap preciousness and refinement, generally employed by artists whom they look down upon. For these artists of matter, *la belle matière* is something material, a mass consisting of paint and all sorts of ingredients, a paste of completely different materiality, of more material materiality, and finally, materials completely foreign to painting. Colors are not paints "applied to" the canvas, but merely a characteristic of matter. Consequently, they do not appear as a multiplicity of independent colors, but as a uniform, internally modulated, and structural coloring tending towards the monochromic and even the colorless. Similarly, form is not a plural (forms) occurring on the canvas, but merely a mode of matter, identical with the latter's extension and almost plastic modeling.

The Dadaists once made an attempt to introduce new materials into art. Aside from a few earlier attempts, this was the first step. The Surrealists continued in this direction: a proof of the great importance of Dadaism and Surrealism for mid-century art. Yet these new materials did not signify a discovery of uniform picture-materials. Although the Cubists occasionally added some sand to their paints, thereby indicating a new interest in materials, they put the structures next to one another as autonomous form elements. In the face of present-day art it is difficult to speak of "form elements." From picture to picture, artists are striving for one single element, named "matter." Whenever materials are employed, they normally lose their individual character and are integrated in the basic structure. Thus, to a great extent, the conception of a painting as a paste, a hardened crust, a rind, has emerged and become a leitmotif of mid-century art.

The artist's love of the material element in his trade is as old as art itself. The fact that he derives inspiration from this material element obviously has nothing to do with materialism. All intellectual possibilities are contained in materials, even in those degenerate, decaying, cheap materials on daily view. Artists incorporating such materials into their works offer the notion that marvels are to be found not only in the precious gold grounds of the Middle Ages, but also and perhaps even more readily in what is most common and insignificant. Thus, the intellectual eloquence of matter is the theme of many present-day artists, who again and again are trying to evoke voices from matter. These voices arise as lines, colors, forms —and now and then as human creatures; not superposed on a "neutral" background, but emanating from the matter itself. Whatever formal components occur appear to be not "invented," but rather "discovered" in the pictorial earth. The painter is a geologist and excavator in a world of many secrets. He knows he cannot decipher these secrets: the enigmas are not solved, but painted. In this manner, art, paradoxically enough, has acquired the character of something old, very old, primordial. The solid materials heaped up here appear as old, ancient crusts, showing traces of earlier life, suggesting not so much flourishing life as former life, past, deceased. This geologizing and archaizing of art is already conspicuous in the work of some of the Surrealists, especially Max Ernst, as well as in the work of Paul Klee, who loved to "excavate" for traces of past life, nature's or even history's hidden stock of forms, to be then merely "found" in the imaginary structures.

The important name right after the war (though his full status was generally recognized only much later) was Jean Dubuffet. His extraordinary *oeuvre* is profuse with not only individual works, but new advances in fallow areas, which through Dubuffet's efforts beyond the frontiers of cultivated zones were conquered and made arable for art. Again and again he has yielded to the strangest temptations of materials, techniques, and pictorial conceptions, digging in new places under the spell of the adventure of discovery, and each time extracting a secret from terra incognita.

There should be a catalogue of all the techniques that Dubuffet has employed and introduced into art: this would suffice as a proof of his extraordinary creative activity. Matter is not merely the medium of his art, but the essential subject as well. It is not the chromatic epidermis which is important, but the substantial flesh of the material, its muscles and nerves, its bones and arteries, and its insides. These substances, as such, are something "realer" than the artist's paints and colors; for him, they are immediate nature. The outwardly changing continuum of materiality is the counterpart of the great continuum called nature. Dubuffet takes no pleasure in copying nature. His

Jean Dubuffet, born 1901. *Bronze Landscape,* 1952.
195 x 129.5 cm. Kunstsammlung Nordheim-Westfalen,
Düsseldorf.

great passion is to look for nature in areas where independent and individual forms have not as yet emerged, where nature is merely the general matter that produces shapes, where all living things are stored either as hopes or memories. Dubuffet's art contains matter as the elemental substances of nature with intricate networks of vital veins and arteries and the pulsating forces of germination and growth; and also as a relic of past life, covered with cracks, furrows, and scars. Nature becomes a mythical landscape, a keeper of chthonic mysteries, their veil lifted by artistic genius. At the same time, nature is a symbol of the human soul with all its inscrutability.

Yet, not everything is composed of just structure and texture. Dubuffet yields to a far greater degree to nature and its suggested forms. Frequently a "pure" structure needs very little for an obvious transformation into nature or a landscape. Widely different creatures come into play, haunting the realm of matter,

which gave birth to them. Their substantiality is the same as that of matter: earth and mud, dust and stone; and often these creatures are barely more than accidental modes of primary matter, produced by chance, an unexpected whim of matter. Human creatures, resembling infernal idols, or goblins, gnomes, demons of the nether regions, or real present-day men with moustaches and hats, and yet unrealer, more spectral and ghost-like than the matter into which they will disintegrate. Hosts of creatures with human or animal shapes were domesticated by the artist to populate his abysmal universes. Thus the *oeuvre* of one of the most important mid-century painters is profusely charged with reality.

Many artists throughout the world are operating with new substances and materials. To name but two, Alberto Burri, an Italian, and Antonio Tapies, a Spaniard, have acquired great distinction and significance in mid-century art.

The best representative of a large neo-Dadaist current, with followers all over, Burri is a late, highly individual descendant of Kurt Schwitters. Burri composes his paintings with all sorts of materials, the materials as such never turning into one homogeneous "substance," but always retaining something of their individual character, partaking of the thing fetishism of the Dadaists. Waste products such as pieces of burlap, scorched veneer, plastic foil, or colored cloths are transformed into compositions with a certain classicistic (Italianate) form.

The leading artist of recent Spanish painting is Antonio Tapies. If not limiting himself to paints, he uses a mixture of monochromic paint and such substances as sand and artificial resin, applied to the canvas in a way suggesting a relief. The pictures are either covered with paint or appear, in most cases, as crust, stone, a sandy desert, or as hardened lava. With these materials, the "world" is ruthlessly walled up, hermetically sealed off from the outside and the inside. Any aperture in such a stratum of matter reveals merely another layer underneath; any time the deepest stratum is broken open, as on the crater rim of a form, only the naked canvas comes into view: nothing! Nevertheless, the artist comes to terms with the forces that destroy form and he discovers the strange contours of forms that survive destruction. Tapies, too, loves great voids and is thus akin to certain "meditative" artists discussed above. His void is instinct with reality, not only because of the substance of the materials used, but also because of the magic and solemn reality character of the abstract forms, which either cover the picture surface in huge sweeps or merely occupy a tiny part of it, leaving the rest blank. Everywhere we see reminiscences of banal objects such as doors, walls, carpentry, or technical things, whose striking meaninglessness hints at some deeper meaning. The outcome is a surprising objectification of abstract forms. Thus Tapies offers a new argument in the artistic debate of our immediate present.

Were we to ignore the artists who have adhered to objects and figures, we would be guilty of distorting the picture of mid-century art. Some of the leading present-day artists are not willing to abandon the object for the sake of the autonomous expressivity of color and form. This is ultimately a problem of generation. Today, as in all ages, generations are overlapping one another. Many great figures of yesterday's "modern" period who had no cause to go the way of total abstraction, were, and many still are, working after 1945: James Ensor, Pierre Bonnard, Utrillo, Georges Rouault; the Fauves Matisse, Derain, Vlaminck, and Marquet; the Expressionists Heckel, Schmidt-Rottluff, Kokoschka, Beckmann; the former Cubists Picasso and Braque; Fernand Léger, Feininger, Marc Chagall; the *arte metafisica* painters Carrà, de Chirico, Morandi. As late as the middle of the century, they all represent an art that, according to its external means, is objective and figurative, and now they all have their disciples and imitators.

Within the postwar avant-garde, it was Surrealism more than anything that gave the object a new chance by discovering its magic without rejecting naturalism even to a photographic degree. Max Ernst's art has survived as that of younger Surrealists such as Salvador Dalì, René Magritte, Paul Delvaux, *et al.* After the war, the Surrealist sculptor Alberto Giacometti emerged as a gifted painter, in whose works things and humans are mysteriously caught in networks of magic forces permeating the space about them. Vieira da Silva's early works have already been mentioned. Nor can we leave

Antonio Tapies, born 1923. *Large Gray Painting,* 1955. 195 x 169.5 cm. Kunstsammlung Nordheim-Westfalen, Düsseldorf.

out Surrealist painters such as Matta and Lam, both Latin Americans, Graham Sutherland, an Englishman, or all the younger artists that have joined the tradition of classical Surrealism. Otherwise, as explained above, Surrealism has joined today's non-objective art—that of action and that of matter.

This discussion of mid-century painting should show that the mastery of reality is one of the main mid-century themes, and certainly not only—in fact least of all —in open "objectivity," but in all the different forms of artistic expression and within "purely" non-objective painting. Thus the talk of an artistic return to reality is all the more dubious and inane, as this is already fulfilled in all forms of present-day art. The reality agitating contemporary artists is too general and too complex a notion to be applied exclusively to the world of objects.

AD REINHARDT

ART IN ART IS ART AS ART

The beginning in art is not the beginning.
Creation in art is not creation.
Nature in art is not nature.
Art in nature is not nature.
The nature of art is not nature.
Art in life is not life.
Life in art is not life.

The picture of art is not a picture.
A work of art is not work.
Working in art is not working.
Work in art is work.
Not working in art is working.
Play in art is not play.
Business in art is business.
Art in business is business.
The business of art is not business.

The substance of art is not substance.
The matter of art is not matter.
The subject of art is not the subject.
The object of art is not the object.
The manner of art is not the manner.
Technique in art is technique.
Qualities in art are qualities.

People in art are not people.
Dogs in art are dogs.
Grass in art is not grass.
A sky in art is a sky.
Things in art are not things.

Words in art are words.
Letters in art are letters.
Writing in art is writing.
Messages in art are not messages.
Explanation in art is no explanation.

Knowledge in art is not knowledge.
Learning in art is not learning.
Ignorance in art is ignorance.
Art-schooling is not schooling.
Unlearning in art is learning.
The unschooled in art are unschooled.
Wisdom in art is not wisdom.
Foolishness in art is foolishness.
Consciousness in art is consciousness.
Unconsciousness in art is unconsciousness.

Order in art is not order.
Chaos in art is chaos.
Symmetry in art is not symmetry.
Asymmetry in art is asymmetry.

A square in art is not a square.
A circle in art is a circle.
A triangle in art is a triangle.
A trisection in art is not a trisection.

A color in art is not a color.
Colorlessness in art is not colorlessness.
Blue in art is blue.
Red in art is red.
Yellow in art is yellow.
Dark gray in art is not dark gray.
Matt black in art is not matt black.
Gloss black in art is gloss black.
White in art is white.

A line in art is not a line.
A wiggly line in art is a wiggly line.
A shape in art is a shape.
A blob in art is a blob.
Form in art is not form.
The formlessness of art is not formlessness.
Imagelessness in art is imagelessness.
Non-imagelessness in art is non-imagelessness.

Limits in art are not limits.
No limits in art are limits.
Discipline in art is discipline.
Sameness in art is not sameness.
Variety in art is not variety.
Monotony in art is not monotony.
Balance in art is not balance.
Freedom in art is freedom.

Drawing in art is drawing.
Graphic art is graphic.
A print in art is a print.
A reproduction in art is a reproduction.
Painting in art is not painting.
Plumbing in art is not plumbing.
Carpentry in art is carpentry.
Texture in art is texture.
Figures in art are figures.
Configurations in art are configurations.
Transfigurations in art are not transfigurations.

Simplicity in art is not simplicity.
Less in art is not less.
More in art is not more.
Too little in art is not too little.
Too large in art is too large.
Too much in art is too much.
Junk in art is junk.
Informal art is informal.
Brute art is brute.
Tachist art is Tachist.
Action art is action.
Chuitzbah in art is chuitzbah.
Chance in art is not chance.
Accident in art is not accident.
Spontaneity in art is not spontaneity.
Pushing in art is pushing.
Pulling in art is pulling.
Heroism in art is not heroism.
Hankering in art is hankering.
Hungering in art is hungering.

The perfection of art is not perfection.
The purity of art is not purity.
The idealism of art is not idealism.
The realism of art is not realism.
The corruption of art is corruption.
Compromise in art is compromise.
Food in art is not food.

A collage in art is a collage.
Paste in art is paste.
Paint in art is not paint.
Brushwork in art is brushwork.
Sand, string, plaster in art is
    sand, string, plaster.
Sculpture in art is sculpture.
Architecture in art is not architecture.
Literature in art is literature.
Poetry in art is poetry.
Music in art is not music.
Poetry in art is not poetry.
Sublimity in art is not sublimity.
Rusticity in art is rusticity.

A sign in art is a sign.
A symbol in art is a symbol.
The symbol of art is not a symbol.
The sign of art is not a sign.
The image of art is not an image.

Vision in art is not vision.
The visible in art is visible.
The invisible in art is invisible.
The visibility of art is visible.
The invisibility of art is visible.

The mystery of art is not a mystery.
The unfathomable in art is not unfathomable.
The unknown in art is not the unknown.
The beyond in art is not beyond.
The immediate in art is not the immediate.
The behind in art is not the behind.
The forefront of art is forefront.

The cosmology of art is not cosmology.
The psychology of art is not psychology.
The philosophy of art is not philosophy.
The history of art is not history.
Art in history is not history.
The meaning of art is not meaning.

The morality of art is not morality.
The religion of art is not religion.
The spirituality of art is not spirituality.
Humanism in art is not humanism.
Dehumanism in art is not dehumanism.
Bumpkin-Dionysianism in art is
    Bumpkin-Dionysianism.
The iconology of art is not iconology.
The iconoclasm of art is iconoclasm.

Darkness in art is not darkness.
Light in art is not light.
Space in art is space.
Time in art is not time.
Evolution in art is not evolution.
Progress in art is not progress.

The beginning of art is not the beginning.
The finishing of art is not the finishing.
The furnishing of art is furnishing.
The nothingness of art is not nothingness.
Negation in art is not negation.
The absolute in art is absolute.

Art in art is art.
The end of art is art as art.
The end of art is not the end.

What of the unconscious?

How does one portray this area of experience?

How do we draw what Freud in his spare and lonely life peeled back for us to see?

How do we show the ID, the ego, & the superego? Or how do we formalize related areas of Projections, Angers, Aggressions, Fears . . . or render the nature of "Incompetence"; . . . or draw sensations such as: how chocolate TASTES, or depict how BLINDNESS feels for *you* at the back of your eyes as they fail you.

In short, how does one elucidate in clear & understandable terms which other humans can comprehend the sensations of our beings & the new areas of experience which have been brought to the surface by Freud and his German & French predecessors? For the subjective sensations have become as real for us in the twentieth century as the objective object was to Renaissance Man; they are part of Western man's verbalizations . . . but how does one make the images of sensation?

The ancient symbols which man once drew from his unconscious . . . the serpent, the fish, the butterfly, the mandala . . . to name a few . . . and made into an accepted (unconsciously) and understandable sign language . . . no longer suffice. Since Freud such symbols seem too static to express *our* experiences & not immediate enough to convey the passions, & fears & loves of our beings and our times.

We require new means to make our sensations visible and, more important, *felt*. Precisely that! To show how things FEEL!

For fun let us take as an example the bibulous excesses of the evening & then observe the following day when all "the evils and glories of last night are gone except for their effects" and trace them to the externals of the next dusk.

Partygoer

The foolish laughter

Cantankerous or *by now difficult*

Final collapse

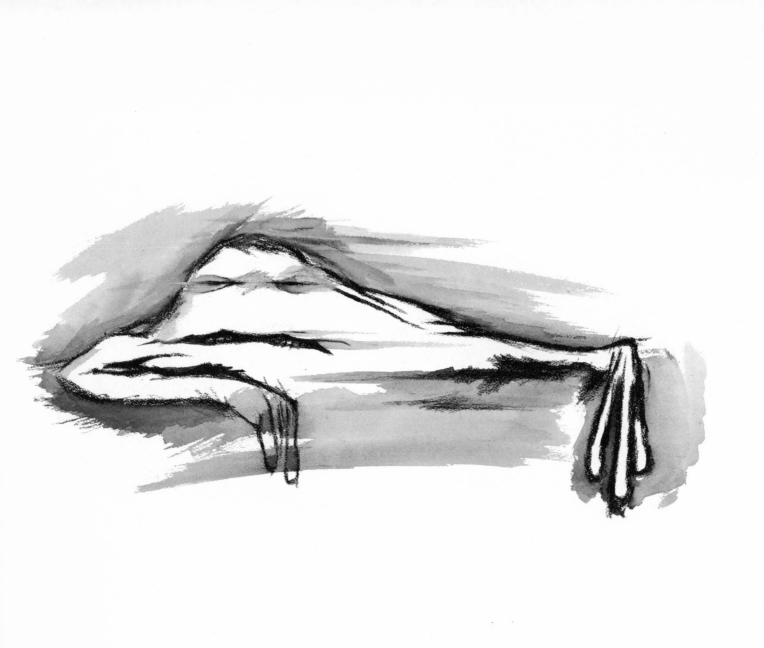

Awakening

Slow emergence

Into the day

Full realization of the prospect

Nausea

The inhuman state

The bloodshot eyes

The inexcusable breath

The state

The brain is split-level

. . . or *lightly large*

. . . or *strangely open at the top*

The Puritanical remorse begins

Feeble soul

The attempted recovery by black coffee

...*which oddly enough works!*

You start to brighten ... or *you brighten!*

Perhaps a drink?

Yes!

My entry into the world of film was through a side door in the cellar: I designed a motion picture title. A graphic and industrial designer heretofore, dealing with reasonably stabile entities, I now found myself confronted with a flickering, moving, elusive series of images that somehow had to add up to a communication. Always an ardent movie-goer, I now found the ultimate justification for my addiction . . . since my frequent visits to the theater now fell under the heading of "professional observations." As I went along, slipping, sliding, and grasping for handholds in this new design medium, some inevitable comparisons between the stabile and the moving image occurred to me.

Film credits had always intrigued me. A motion picture is such a complex cooperative undertaking, that it is only in recent times that I have discovered what all those designations really mean. It is generally recognized that the film-going public is interested mainly in the leading actors and actresses and a very few well-known craftsmen. However, in spite of all efforts to control the situation, the list of credits on films grows larger each year.

Since trade requirements understandably demand these extensive credits, it seemed desirable that this usually rather dull interlude should be converted into a positive introduction to the film. Normally, the running of the title is a period during which patrons leave their seats for popcorn, make small talk with their neighbors, or simply explore their seat for long-range comfort. Thus, when the film itself begins, there is usually an initial "cold" period. However, titles can be sufficiently provocative and entertaining to induce the audience to sit down and *look*, because something is really happening on screen. I believe at this moment it is possible to project a symbolic foretaste of what is to come, and to create a receptive atmosphere that will enable the film to begin on a higher level of audience rapport.

While the title of a film is a rather small appendage to the large organism that is the film, I soon discovered it contains, in miniature, many of the procedures and problems that are characteristic of the body of the film. As I became more involved with the visual aspects of the production as a whole, I began to link the basic time-motion factor of film to other areas of my experience, and some interesting differences and similarities between film and graphic expression, such as painting, became apparent.

We tend to think of movement and time-span as the unique attributes of film. Yet these qualities are common to both painting and film. If we should examine, let us say, a Rubens painting, we would see that it has a built-in time-motion factor. When a painting surface has objects placed upon it, a sequence in time must be assigned to these objects. We see them sequentially, albeit with infinitesimal time duration between each step. The eye, we are told, has the capacity to absorb in one Gestalt an average of four or five objects, depending upon the differences or similarities between the objects, and upon their positioning. When the points of perception in a painting are increased to ten, twenty, or thirty (as is frequently the case in a Rubens), it becomes necessary to organize these points of perception into a rhythmic sequence which enables them to be seen in a larger, simpler relationship, and still allow each to express itself individually. This is one of the exciting aspects of much of post-Giotto painting. These great, sweeping rhythms and patterns, formed of many diverse elements, course in and out of the painting space; as a result, the viewer, upon entering the painting, has a motion and time experience.

The positing of the similarities between the two forms almost simultaneously poses the differences between them. For while the spectator acts upon the painting, film acts upon the spectator. The painting receives its life through the immersion of the viewer, while film imposes its life on the viewer. Film lives at its own pace, on its own terms, and the viewer receives rather than imparts movement.

Anatomy of a Murder. Title design by Saul Bass. Otto Preminger—Columbia Pictures. Black and white film.

The credits for this film grew out of the symbol designed for use in the general advertising and promotion of the film—a segmented figure. Working closely within the framework of a fine, contemporary jazz score by Duke Ellington, the staccato and fragmented character of the title was developed. The various pieces of the figure quickly form its total configuration and then there ensues a playful handling of its various elements . . . arms, legs, head, body and hands . . . all in counterpoint with the appearance of the various credits . . . until, finally, a pair of hands appear with quick, successive jumps forward, obliterating and blackening the screen. At this point the first scene of the film fades in.

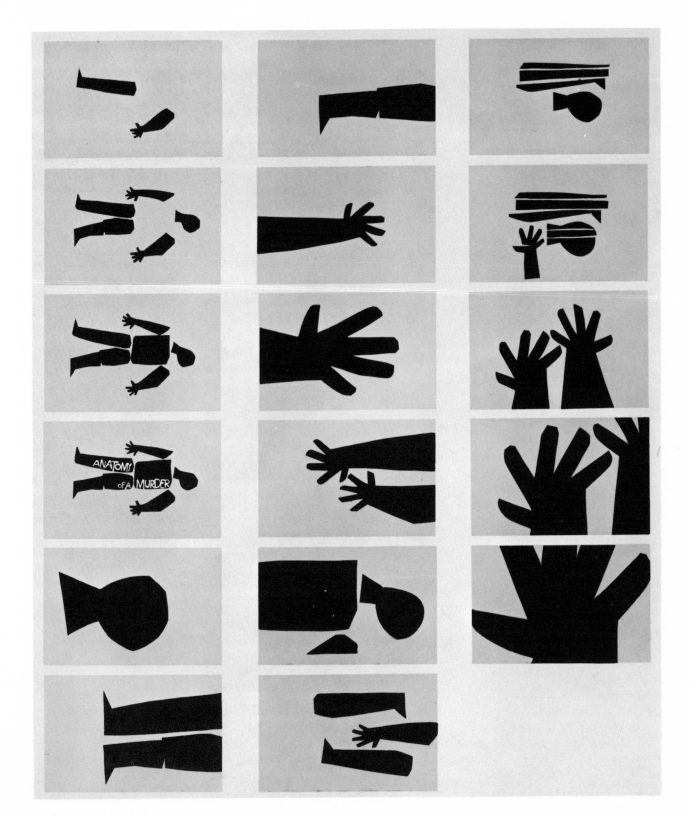

The Man with the Golden Arm. Title design by Saul Bass.
Otto Preminger—Columbia Pictures. Black and white film.

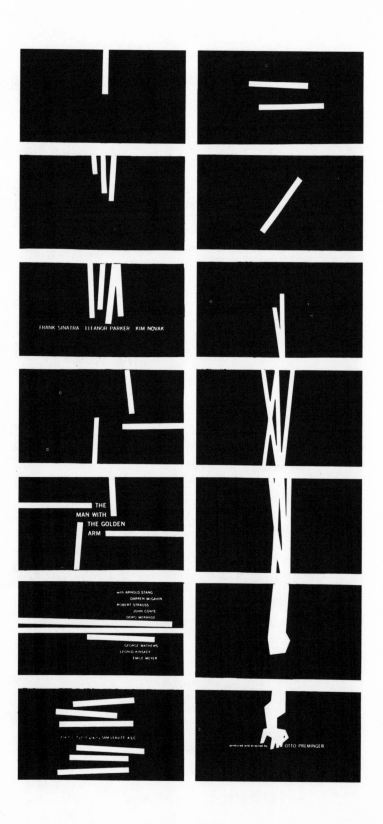

Storm Center. Title design by Saul Bass.
Julian Blaustein—Columbia Pictures. Black and white film.

This film has as its theme book censorship in the library of
a small American town. The story revolves mainly about the
librarian and one of the school children in the community.

Olin Mathieson Corporate Presentation. One minute opening designed by Saul Bass for the Olin Mathieson sponsored television series *Small World*. These images are intended to indicate the range of activities of Olin Mathieson as expressed in its five divisions: 1. Pharmaceuticals; 2. Winchester-Western (sporting arms); 3. Chemicals; 4. Energy-Fuels; 5. Packaging. Appropriate filmic symbols are used that relate to the materials produced by each of these divisions.

Profiles in Courage. Opening for a television anthology designed by Saul Bass. Music by Nelson Riddle. This anthology is based on the Pulitzer Prize-winning book by the late President John F. Kennedy. It consists of dramatizations of moments in American history when individual political leaders, acting on their beliefs, took positions involving great moral courage.

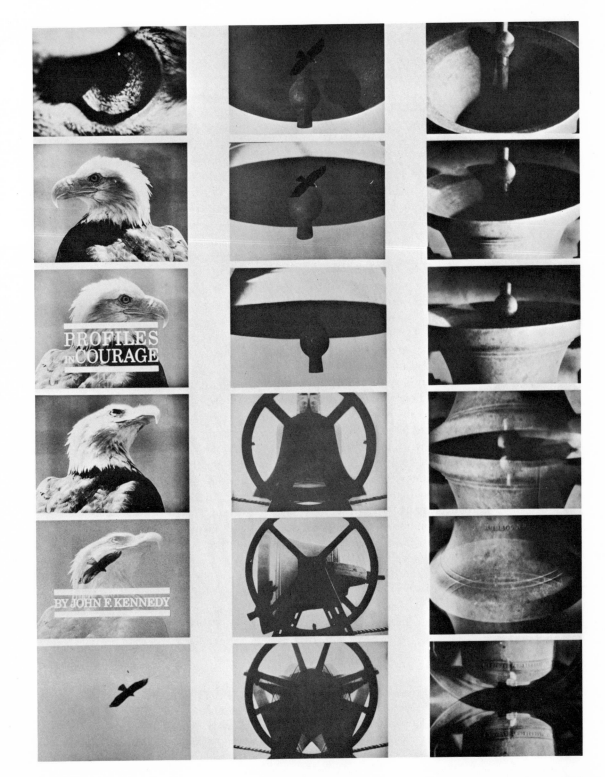

In the mid-winter of 1772, in the desolate Canadian tundra, Samuel Hearne and his native companions saw the track of a strange snowshoe. They followed it to a little hut where they discovered a young woman sitting alone. She told of her capture by a hostile band, the murder of her parents, husband, and infant, and of her escape nearly seven months ago. Living alone, without seeing a human face, she supported herself by snaring small game.

"It is scarcely possible to conceive," observed Hearne, "that a person in her forlorn situation could be so composed as to contrive, or execute, anything not absolutely essential to her existence. Nevertheless, all her clothing, besides being calculated for real service, showed great taste, and no little variety of ornament. The materials, though rude, were very curiously wrought, and so judiciously placed as to make the whole of her garb have a very pleasing, though rather romantic appearance."

From northern Scandinavia, across the tundra and taiga of Siberia, Alaska, and Canada, to the ice-bound coast of East Greenland, men have lived for thousands of years. It is a hard land. The earth never thaws. It is snow-covered most of the year. Nothing grows. The mystery is not that men should be tossed by chance into this desolate waste; it is, rather, that within this prison of ice and wind they are able to draw from themselves images powerful enough to deny their nothingness.

Nowhere is life more difficult than in the Arctic, yet when life there is reduced to its barest essentials, art and poetry turn out to be among those essentials. Art to the Eskimo is far more than an object: it is an act of seeing and expressing life's values; it is a ritual of exploration by which patterns of nature, and of human nature, are revealed by man.

As the carver holds the unworked ivory lightly in his hand, turning it this way and that, he whispers, "Who are you? Who hides there?" And then: "Ah, Seal!" He rarely sets out to carve, say, a seal, but picks up the ivory, examines it to find its hidden form and, if that is not immediately apparent, carves aimlessly until he sees it, humming or chanting as he works. Then he brings it out: seal, hidden, emerges. It was always there: He did not create it. He released it: he helped it step forth.

I watched one white man, seeking souvenirs, commission a carving of a seal but receive instead a carving of a walrus. Another, who wanted a chess set, though his explicit instructions were clearly understood, received a set in which each pawn was different. *Ahmi*, "it cannot be known in advance" what lies in the ivory.

Eskimos have no real equivalents to our words "create" or "make," which presuppose imposition of the self on matter. The closest Eskimo term means "to work on," which also involves an act of will, but one which is restrained. The carver never attempts to force the ivory into uncharacteristic forms, but responds to the material as it tries to be itself, and thus the carving is continually modified as the ivory has its say.

This is the Eskimo attitude toward not only ivory, but toward all things, especially people: parent toward child, husband toward wife. Where we think of art as possession, and possession to us means control, means to do with as we like, art to them is a way of revealing.

In the Eskimo language, little distinction is made between nouns and verbs, but rather all words are forms of the verb "to be," which is itself lacking in Eskimo. That is, all words proclaim in themselves their own existence. Eskimo is not a nominal language; it does not simply name things which already exist, but rather brings both things and actions (nouns and verbs) into being as it goes along. This idea is reflected in the practice of naming a child at birth: when the mother is in labor, an old woman stands around and says as many different eligible names as she can think of. The

Note: Most of the photographs used for this paper were made by Reuben Goldberg. The specimens are the property of the American Museum of Natural History, New York; British Museum, London; Danish National Museum, Copenhagen; Robert H. Lowie Museum, Berkeley; Museum of the American Indian, Heye Foundation, New York; Museum of Anthropology and Ethnology, Leningrad; Museum für Volkerkunde, Hamburg; Bernard Reis Collection; Royal Ontario Museum, Toronto; United States National Museum, Washington, D.C.; University Museum, Cambridge, Mass.

child comes out of the womb when its own name is called. Thus the naming and the giving birth to the new thing are inextricably bound together.

The environment encourages the Eskimo to think in this fashion. To Western minds, the "monotony" of snow, ice, and darkness can often be depressing, even frightening. Nothing in particular stands out; there is no scenery in the sense in which we use the term. But the Eskimos do not see it this way. They are not interested in scenery, but in action, existence. This is true to some extent of many people, but it is almost of necessity true for the Eskimos, for nothing in their world easily defines itself or is separable from the general background. What exists, the Eskimos themselves must struggle to bring into existence. Theirs is a world which has to be conquered with each act and statement, each carving and song. The secret of conquering a world greater than himself is not known to the Eskimo. But his role is not passive. Man is the force that reveals form. He is the force which ultimately cancels nothingness.

Language is the principal tool with which the Eskimos make the natural world a human world. They use many "words" for snow which permit fine distinctions, not simply because they are much concerned with snow, but because snow takes its form from the actions in which it participates: sledding, falling, igloo-build-

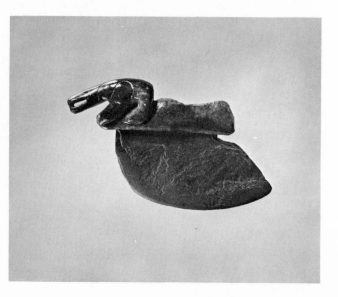

ing, blowing. These distinctions are possible only when experienced in a meaningful context. Different kinds of snow are brought into existence by the Eskimos as they experience their environment and speak; the words do not label something already there. Words, for the Eskimo, are like the knife of the carver: they free the idea, the thing, from the general formlessness of the outside. As a man speaks, not only is his language *in statu nascendi,* but also the very thing about which he is talking. The carver, like the poet, releases form from the bonds of formlessness: he brings it forth into consciousness. He must reveal form in order to protest against a universe that is formless, and the form he reveals should be beautiful.

Since that form participates in a real situation, the carving is generally utilitarian. One very characteristic Eskimo expression means "What is that for?" It is most frequently used by an Eskimo when he finds some object and stands looking down at it. It does not mean "What can I use that for?" but rather something closer to "What is it intended to be used for?" That portion of the antler, the shape of which so perfectly fits the hand and gives a natural strength as well, becomes, with slight modification, a chisel handle. Form and function, revealed together, are inseparable. Add a few lines of dots or tiny rings or just incisions, rhythmically arranged to bring out the form, and it is finished.

Here, then, is a world of chaos and chance, a meaningless whirl of cold and white. Man alone can give meaning to this—its form does not come ready-made.

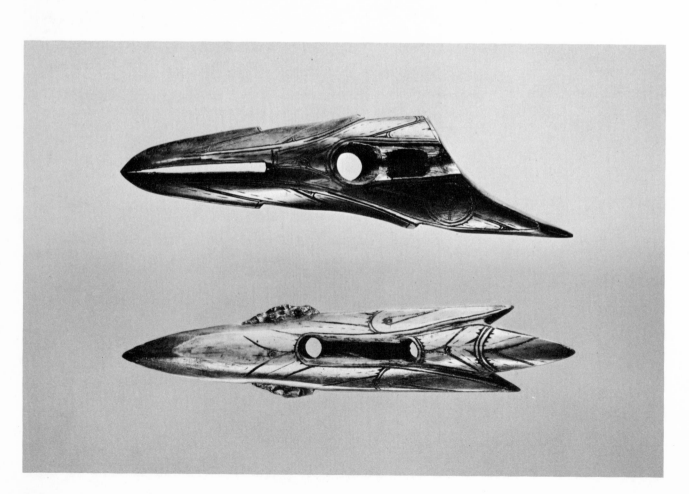

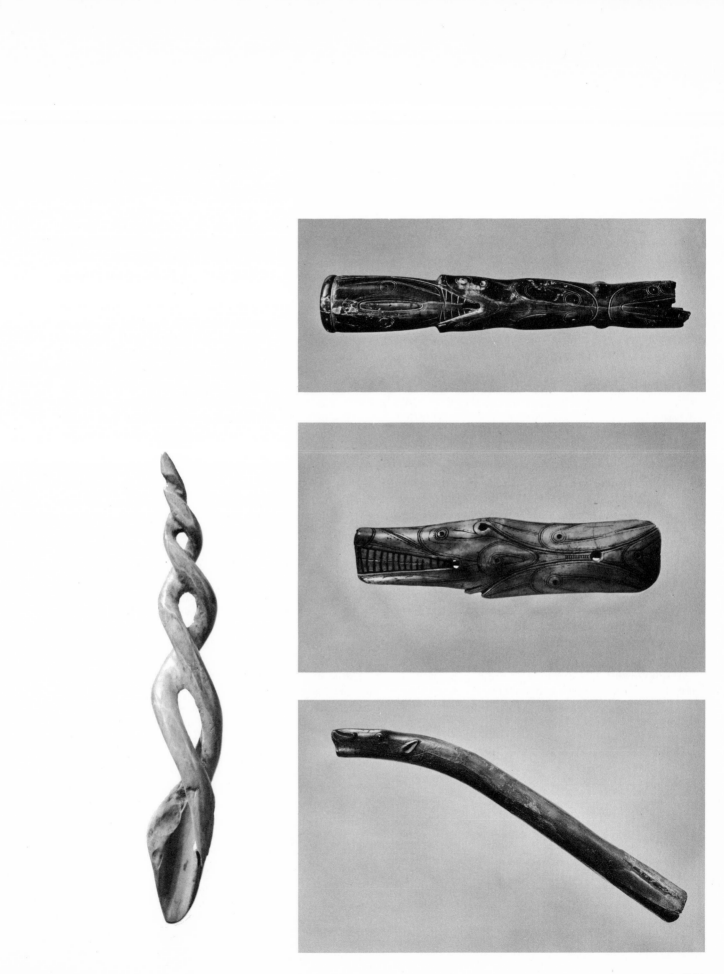

When spring comes and igloos melt, the old habitation sites are littered with waste, including beautifully designed tools and tiny ivory carvings, not deliberately thrown away, but, with even greater indifference, just lost. Eskimos are interested in the artistic act, not in the product of that activity.

A carving, like a song, is not a thing; it is an action. When you feel a song within you, you sing it; when you sense a form emerging from the ivory, you release it. The Eskimo word "to make poetry" is the word "to breathe"; both are derivatives of *anerca*, the soul, that which is eternal, the breath of life. A poem is words infused with breath or spirit: "Let me breathe of it," says the poem-maker and then begins: "One has put his poem in order on the threshold of his tongue."

There is no separation of prose and poetry; all Eskimo speech has a musical quality and for heightened emotional expressions the speaker moves easily into song. Eskimos often talk and sing to themselves. To them, thinking and speaking are one: there is no purely inner experience. Members of our culture who are indifferent to literacy also do this: the lone child talking to his toys, the drunk, the angry man who walks away mumbling, the senile, the insane. Momentarily or permanently, all have reverted to an earlier, perhaps more basic philosophy, in which individualism plays little part and thought is conceived of as an external experience.

To the Eskimo, all thought is "outside." "If thoughts were *in* a mind, how could they *do* anything?"

Ohnainewk asked. Thought, Eskimos believe, is everything outside of man, especially natural forces. But thought cannot exist without man. It makes itself known to man: it speaks first and man in turn gives it shape and expression.

The old question, "What is the silent igloo-sitter thinking?", misses the point. Early ethnologists believed he was in a self-induced trance; Freudians said he was suppressing his anxieties. Both assumed there was an inner dialogue. But inner dialogue, far from being universal, is largely the product of literacy. It belongs to literate man whose mind is a never ending clock which his will cannot stop, sleep cannot still, madness only makes go faster, and death alone silences. I do not believe the silent Eskimo with his impassive, tribal face is thinking anything. He is just not "with it" and "it" in this case is generally hunting, which he loves above all else.

I have seen silent, gentle, slow-moving Eskimos, suddenly caught up in the hunt, accomplish astonishing feats of skill and daring. Yet there was consistency here. They were the same. They simply allowed the world to act towards them with complete freedom. They were not passive: they freed this experience from its formless state and gave it expression and beauty. When you feel a song welling up within you, you sing it; when Eskimos feel themselves possessed by the hunt, they commit themselves fully to it.

This sort of electrifying performance always reminded me of slouching new method actors who coast along and then suddenly "get with it," erupting with startling jets of power. The comparison may be legitimate, for postliterate method actors who regard all life as empty dialogue, save those moments when one is fully committed to an external experience, share much with preliterate hunters.

The Eskimo language contains no first-person pronoun, which in English is so important we make "I" upper case, an honor otherwise restricted to gods and kings. Eskimo does provide a suffix to indicate participation of self in experience, but generally Eskimos avoid even this, and use an impersonal pronoun: "One has driven his spear into a walrus." Yet, despite the absence of individualism in our sense, there is often spectacular achievement, and though there is no "I," there is great dignity.

Carvers make no effort to develop personal styles and take no care to be remembered as individuals, but simply disappear, as it were, behind their works. Their goal is not to develop unique art styles, not to present personal views, nor even to bring to fruition biases peculiar to them personally; rather, it is to express to perfection a timeless tradition, breathing into it "the breath of life" so that each form is fresh, though the grammar is never violated.

I recently traveled across Siberia, studying Arctic art. The contrast was remarkable: here was the most completely nonliterate art tradition known, seen against a setting of total literacy. For Soviet Russia is the final, most sterile expression of literacy, with all the worst of the Renaissance and none of the freedom and hope and release of that incredible experiment. Everything is segmental and replaceable—especially people: Napoleon's citizen army at last! Everything visual requires a single point of view—a review position, like Stalin reviewing troops; all painting is in three-dimensional perspective; every plaza is to be viewed from X. One cannot enter into an experience, complete it, modify it, interpret it. All communications: high-definition, exact, with the same meaning for everyone. Dictionaries are popular. Lectures involve learning the correct, single meaning: copy it, memorize it. Da Vinci, yes; Miro, no.

Literacy creates a "middle distance"; it separates observer from observed, actor from action; it leads to single perspective, fixed observation, singleness of tone, and introduces into poetry and music the counterpart of three-dimensional perspective in art, all, of course, artistic expressions of the Western notion of individualism, every element being now related to the unique point of view of the individual at a given moment.

The phonetic alphabet and all its derivatives stress a one-thing-at-a-time analytic awareness in perception. This intensity of analysis is achieved at the price of forcing all else in the field of perception into the subliminal. For twenty-five hundred years literate man lived in what Joyce called "ABCED-mindedness." As a result of this fragmenting of the field of perception and the breaking of movement into static bits, man won a power of applied knowledge and technology unrivaled in human history. The price he paid was existing personally and socially in a state of almost total subliminal awareness.

The Eskimo artist emphasizes all-at-onceness. For him there is no subliminal factor in experience; his mythic forms of explanation explicate all levels of any situation at the same time. Freud makes no sense when applied to him. The carver leaves nothing hidden, suppresses nothing. He employs X-ray techniques, carving an animal with its rib cage open and an inner being exposed, or with ribs and vertebrae etched on its surface; he delights in visual puns that show the many dimensions of a being; he uses multiple perspective, observing an experience with the eyes of many. At the same time, he never expresses thoughts openly, but rather drops slight hints, not to censor or suppress, but rather to force his audience to participate, to join in the creation, to complete. There is freedom in all this; nothing is presented ready-made.

A distinctive mark of Eskimo art is that many of the ivory carvings, generally of sea mammals, will not stand up, but roll clumsily about. Each lacks a single, favored point of view and hence a base. They were never intended to be set in place and viewed, but rather to be worn and handled, turned this way and that. I knew a trader with a fine, showpiece collection of such carvings who solved this problem by lightly filing each piece "on the bottom" to make it stand up, but alas he also made them stationary, something the carver never intended.

The carving lives in the hand as it is moved, spoken to and about. Charm, toggle, ornament move on the clothing of the wearer. Some, especially ones of the Dorset Culture dating from as early as 800 B.C., are so detailed and so accurate we can identify species, even subspecies: a red-throated loon from a common loon. Yet one carving of a ptarmigan is scarcely larger than the head of a match; an ivory bear—running, with claws—is less than three-eighths of an inch high; a carving of a glaucous gull weighs less than one-sixtieth of an ounce. I photographically magnified, 1000–1200 times, a number of these pieces. All shared a quality of sizelessness: each, when blown up to monumental size, suffered no qualitative change of effect, for the artists had reduced each form to its basic essentials. All were produced, of course, without the aid of lenses or steel. Though incredibly minute, they lack the charming fragility of miniatures, and give instead the impression of mature power. Each seems independent, self-contained.

Eskimo tales share this quality. Generally the narrator speaks only of things you can touch and see. He constantly chooses the concrete word, in phrase after phrase, forcing you to touch and see. No speaker so insistently teaches the general through the particular. He has mastery over the definite, detailed, particular, visualized image.

The Eskimo language, being polysynthetic, favors such construction. Phrases are not composed of little words chronologically ordered, but of great, tight conglomerates, like twisted knots, within which concepts are juxtaposed and inseparably fused. Such conglomerates are not verbs or nouns or even words; each is a linguistic expression for an impression forming a unit to the speaker. Thus, "the house is red" in Eskimo is phrased "the-house, looking-like-flowing-blood-it-is"; the sequence may indicate a kind of subordination, but "red" is felt and treated as a substantive. Such parts of speech, though they follow one another, are remarkably independent, with the result that Eskimo is jerky; it does not flow. What we call action, Eskimos see and describe as a pattern of succeeding impressions.

I ran an experiment with a number of Eskimos. I sketched on paper some twenty figures, each oriented in a different direction. Then I asked each individual to point to the seal, the walrus, the bear. Without hesitation, all located the correct figures. But though I had myself made the drawings I found it necessary to turn the paper each time to ascertain the accuracy of their selections.

Igloo walls are often covered with magazine pictures obtained from the trader. These reduce dripping; perhaps they are enjoyed for their colors as well. Some effort is made at vertical rendering but really very little, and the over-all result is haphazard. When the children wanted to imitate me, a sure way to provoke delighted laughter was to mimic my twisting and turning as I tried to look at the *Life Magazine* pictures.

Walrus tusks are carved into aggregates of connected but unrelated figures; some figures face one way, others another. No particular orientation is involved, nor is there a single "theme." Each figure is simply carved as it reveals itself in the ivory.

In handling these tusks I found myself turning them first this way, then that, orienting each figure *in relation to myself*. Eskimos do not do this. They carve a number of figures, each oriented—by our standards—in a different direction, without moving the tusk. Similarly, when handed a photograph, they examine it as it is handed to them, no matter how it is oriented.

The value we place on verticality (it influences even our perception) stems from the strength of literacy in our lives. Children must be taught it. Natives do not know it. And when the mentally ill in our society withdraw from the burdens of literate values, and return to nonvertical, nonlineal codifications, we call them childlike, and even note parallels with primitives. To the lack of verticality can be added multiple perspective, visual puns, X-ray sculpture, absence of background, and correspondence between symbol and size: all examples of non-optical structuring of space.

Few examples illustrate this absence of vertical rendering quite so forcefully as visual puns. Eskimos, of course, do not turn them: delight comes from instantaneous perception of multiple meanings. Poems, too, present simultaneously the variations of a character or the diversities of an immediate experience:

Great grief came over me—
Great grief came over me,
While on the fell above us I was picking berries.
Great grief overcame me
My sun quickly rose over it.
Great grief came over me.
The sea out there off our settlement
Was beautifully quiet—
And the dear, great paddlers
Were leaving out there—
Great grief came over me
While I was picking berries on the fell.

Here berry-picking is not background for grief, nor are departure and grief causally related; they simply occur together: two independent impressions intersecting, each modified, as in translation, when seen through the other.

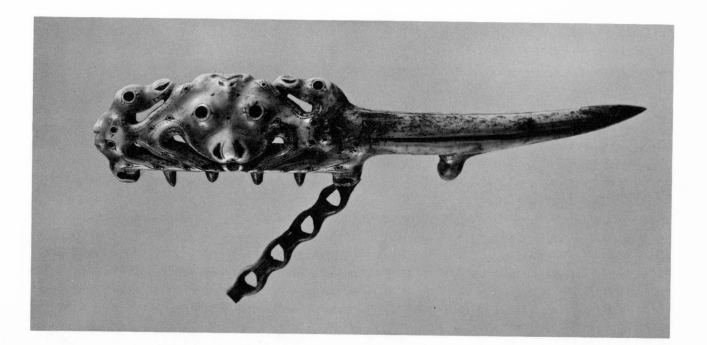

I do not think it accidental that we see the closest parallels with Eskimo art in the work of Paul Klee, for in both there is a structuring of space by sound. Klee said his works owed more to Bach and Mozart than to any of the masters of art. He wanted art "to *sound* like a fairy tale," to be a world where "things fall upward."

Literate man often has difficulty in understanding a purely verbal notion. In *Alice in Wonderland* ". . . the patriotic Archbishop found it advisable."

"Found *what?*" said the Duck.

"Found *it,*" the Mouse replied rather crossly: "Of course you know what 'it' means."

"I know what 'it' means well enough when *I* find a thing," said the Duck: "it's generally a frog, or a worm. The question is, what did the Archbishop find?"

Literate man feels happier when *it* is visible; then he feels he can understand it, judge it, perhaps control it. In his workaday world, space is conceived in terms of that which separates visible objects. "Empty space" suggests a field in which there is nothing *to see*. We call a fume-filled gasoline drum or a gale-swept tundra "empty" because nothing is visible in either case.

The Eskimos do not think this way. One hunter I knew, when assured by a white man that a gasoline drum was "empty," struck a match and peered inside: he bore the scars for life. With them the binding power of the oral tradition is so strong as to make the eye subservient to the ear. They define space more by sound than sight. Where we might say, "Let's see what we can hear," the Eskimo would say, "Let's hear what we can see."

The essential feature of sound is not its location, but that it *be* that it fill space. We say, "The night shall be filled with music," just as the air is filled with fragrance: locality is irrelevant. The concert-goer closes his eyes. Auditory space has no favored focus. It is a sphere without fixed boundaries, space made by the thing itself, not space containing the thing. It is not pictorial space, boxed in, but dynamic, always in flux, creating its own dimensions, moment by moment. It has no fixed boundaries; it is indifferent to background. The eye focuses, pinpoints, abstracts, locating each object in physical space, against a background; the ear favors sound from any direction.

The "wrap-around" aspect of auditory space is shown by the manner in which an Eskimo constructs an igloo. Surrounded by space in all its acoustic non-direction, he does not mould his igloo from the outside looking in, but from the inside working out. Working from the center, he builds a series of concentric circles, tapering upwards conically. When the keystone at the apex has been set in place, Eskimo and structure are one. Only then does he cut a small hole at the base, through which he crawls—in effect, doffing his igloo.

Eskimo carvers do not work within borders. The composite nature of their great mobile masks is a deliberate effort to let each mask assert its own dimensions. The familiar Western notion of enclosed space is foreign to the Eskimo. Both snow igloos and skin tents lack vertical walls and horizontal ceilings; no planes parallel each other and none intersect at ninety

degrees. There are no straight lines, at least none of any length. Rectangles are unknown. Euclidean space is a concept unique to literate man. Eskimos, with a magnificent disregard for environmental determinism, open up rather than enclose space. They must, of course, create sealed-off heat areas, but instead of resorting to boxes, they build complex, many-roomed igloos which have as many dimensions and as much freedom as a cloud.

I know of no examples of Eskimos describing space primarily in visual terms. They do not regard space as static, and therefore measurable: hence they have no formal units of spatial measurement, just as they have no uniform divisions of time. The carver is indifferent to the demands of the optical eye: he lets each piece fill its own space, create its own world, without reference to background or anything external to it. Each carving

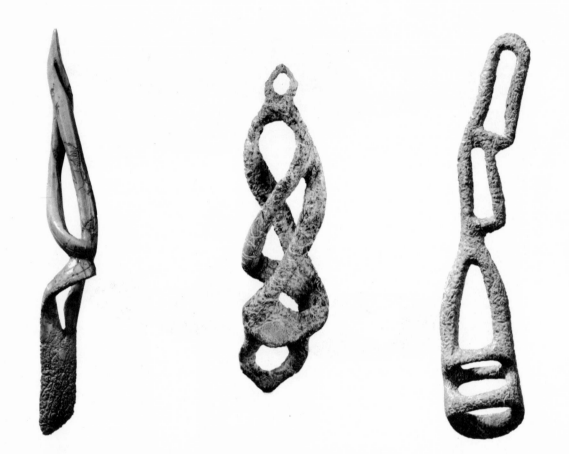

lives in spatial independence. Size and shape, proportions and selection, these are set by the object itself, not forced from without. Like sound, each carving creates its own space, its own identity; it imposes its own assumptions.

In the beginning was the Word, a spoken word, not the visual one of literate man, but a word which, when spoken, revealed form: "And God said, Let there be light: and there was light." "By the word of the Lord were the heavens made, and all the hosts of them by the breath of His mouth." The Eskimo speaker imposes his will diffidently upon unbounded reality. Form is temporary, transient; it exists, as the Eskimo poet says, "on the threshold of my tongue."

In literate society, however, to be real a thing has to be visible. We trust the eye, not the ear. Not since Aristotle assured his *readers* that the sense of sight was "above all others" the one to be trusted, have we accorded to sound the role of dominant sense. "Seeing is

believing." "Believe half of what you see, nothing of what you hear." "The eyes of the Lord preserve knowledge, and he over-throweth the words of the transgressor." Truth, literate man thinks, must be observed by the eye, then judged by the "I." Mysticism, intuition, are bad words among scientists. Most thinking in literate societies is done in terms of *visual* models, even when an auditory one might prove more efficient. We employ spatial metaphor even for such inner psychological states as tendency, duration, intensity. We say "thereafter," not the more logical "thenafter"; "always" means "at all times"; "before" means etymologically "in front of"; we even speak of a "space" or "interval" of time.

To the Eskimo, truth is given through oral tradition, mysticism, intuition, all cognition; not simply by observation and measurement of physical phenomena. To them, the ocularly visible apparition is not nearly as important as the purely auditory one.

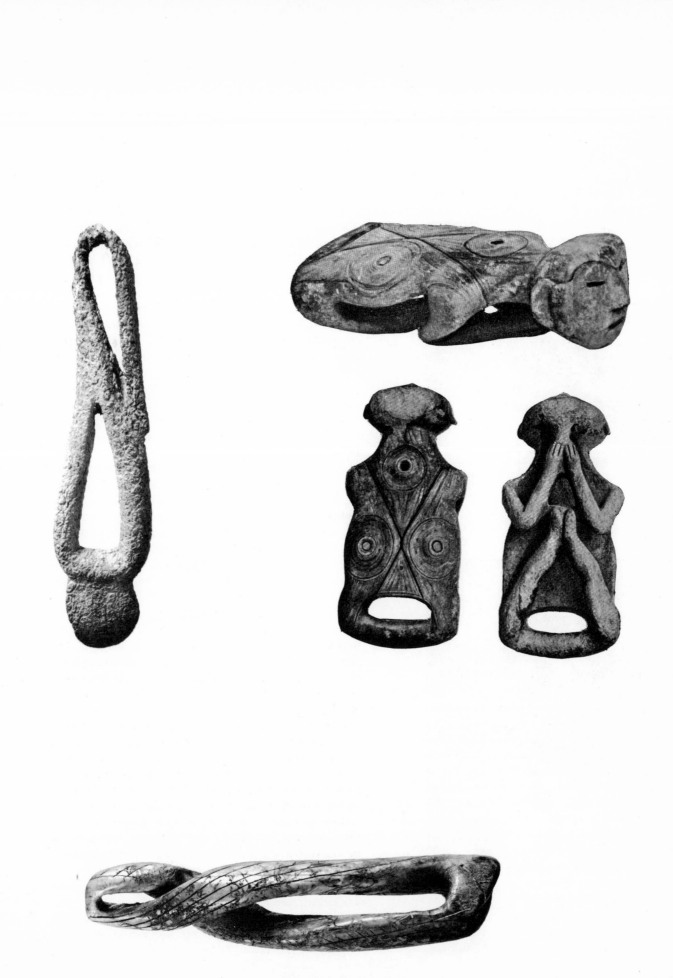

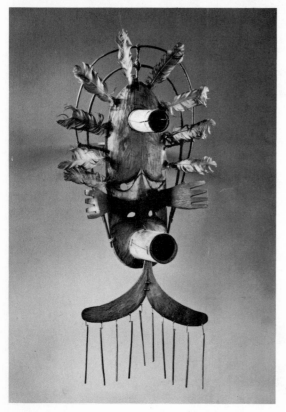

The Eskimo view of self is not as clearly demarcated as ours, and its precise limits often vary according to circumstances. They do not reduce the self to a sharply delimited, consistent, controlling "I." They postulate no personality "structure," but accept the clotted nature of experience—the simultaneity of good and evil, of joy and despair, multiple models within the one, contraries inextricably commingled. Where literate man regards an "alias" as deceiving, representing something other than the "real" self, every Eskimo has several names, each a different facet of himself, for they assert that man's ego is not a thing imprisoned in itself, sternly shut up in boundaries of flesh and time. They say that many of the elements which make it up belong to the world before it and outside it, while the notion that each person is himself and can be no other, is to them impossible, for it leaves out of account all the transitions which bind the individual consciousness to the general. The Eskimo conception of individuality belongs in the same category of conceptions as that of unity and entirety, the whole and the all; and the distinction between spirit in general and individual spirit possesses not nearly so much power over their minds as over ours.

There is a significant difference between Eskimo and Northwest Coast Indian masks. Neither culture is much concerned with change or "becoming," but Northwest Coast artists do emphasize metamorphosis or "coming-to-be." A wolf mask may suddenly open, revealing bear; this springs apart—within is the face of another spirit. Nothing has a definite, invariable shape. Like Echo, the mythical being who successively comes to be all things, the mask is shape-shifting: by a sudden metamorphosis, it is first this, then that. Eskimos, however, emphasize "is"; they depict these elements together, simultaneously, and they accept in the most casual way this blurring of human-animal-spirit forms.

The most interesting Eskimo masks known to me are great composite, mobile puns: the same lines serve to depict Walrus-Caribou-Man; turned slightly, one form may be emphasized, but the others are never lost. There is no need for shape-shifting; all relevant forms are already present. Such a mask expresses the variety and infinite subtlety of personality; its power lies in preserving due proportion between diverse and opposite elements.

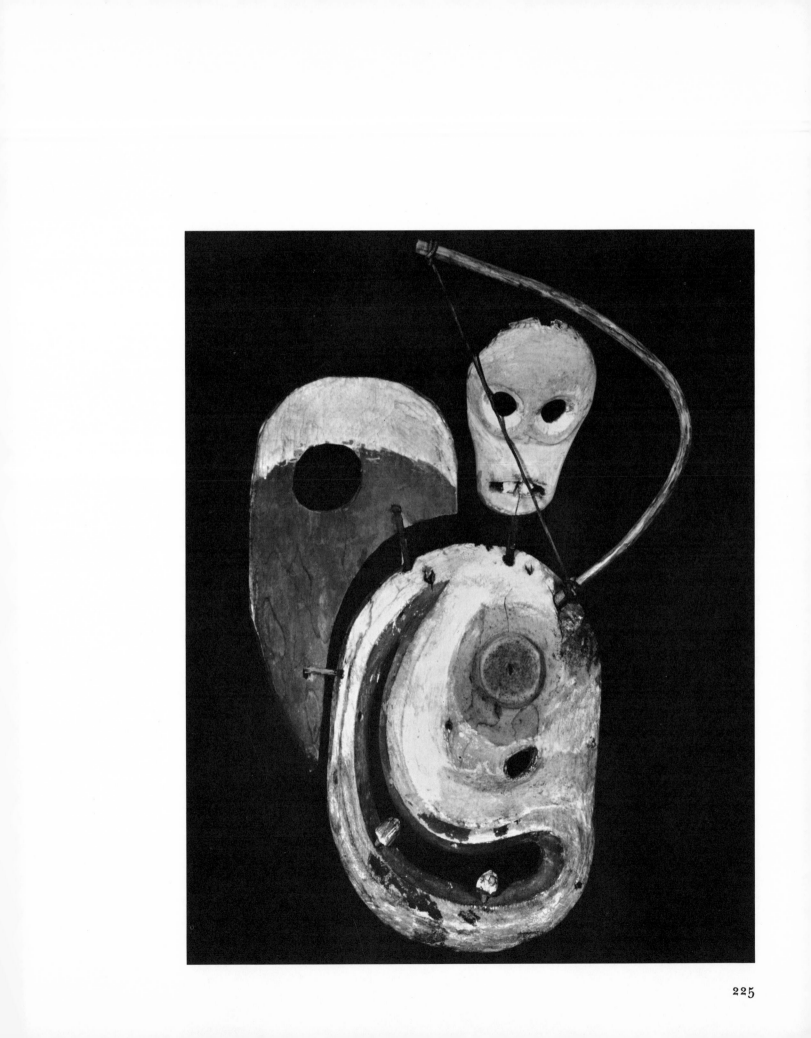

PAUL RIESMAN

THE ESKIMO DISCOVERY OF MAN'S PLACE IN THE UNIVERSE

A good reason for being interested in the Eskimo view of man's place in the universe is that we are not satisfied with our own view. In the first part of this essay I hope to show why this is so.

Many people, notably the Existentialists and many anthropologists, accept the notion that the world men live in is made by men. This means that ultimately each person lives in his own world. A culture, then, can be considered as meanings, or at least paths leading to meaning, which are shared by the participants in that culture. In this context the concept "man-made" does not mean the actual fabrication of the material world, but rather the meaning given by men to the material they find around them. One quality of this material, which will be seen to be very important, is that when it is found by people there is no reason for them to believe that it has purposes other than those which they give it. The material may be indifferent, without any particular purpose, but if it turns out to have a function for human life there is no reason to think that this in some way violates the purpose of the material. There is nothing about a pebble lying on the ground that tells you it is not to be thrown or formed into an arrowhead.

The world of Western man, however, is man-made in another sense. A great proportion of our material world has actually been fabricated by men. For those who live in large cities this may be almost the total visible landscape. That world which is man-made in this sense (I will use the word "fabricated" from now on) is vastly different from the world outside in that almost all of the material lying at hand is recognized as having purposes already. The new individual born into this world finds himself immediately incased in a net of purposeful objects. Very little is available to be freshly made, since so much of the material is made already.

The problems of the artist in such a world symbolize, I believe, the problems which every individual in such a world must face (or refuse to face). The artist has always been a seeker of meaning. In any given medium he has created patterns which both nourish meanings in his life and in some way respond to the nature of the medium as he apprehends it. The material with which the artist works, however, is not limited to the substance out of which he creates his work: it is the whole world in which he lives. The painter's material, for example, is not just the pigments, the canvas, etc., it is also his fantasy and the meanings he sees in his world.

In most of the non-Western world the landscape is dominated by what we may call natural forms: the shapes, pulses, processes of the universe untouched or only slightly embellished by man. The meanings to be found here are infinite, however selective be the artist's vision. The creation of a new art object is never thought of as destroying an old meaning, and very often it is conceived of as the bringing forth, the releasing of a meaning which was latent in the material itself.

In the Western world, on the other hand, the landscape is dominated by "fabricated" forms. These forms have meanings in themselves which were put there by the men who conceived them and made them. Most of us live within terms of the meanings implied by these forms that surround us: we work from nine to five, we trade in last year's model for the new one, we prefer anything to brand "X," we strive for greater efficiency and increased mechanization. In other words, most of us accept our world as a piece of the universe, a fair sample of it. What meanings is the contemporary artist, working with the materials of our civilization, going to find? Obviously there can be no freshness in bringing out meanings which have already been put there by other men. As a consequence the artist must either forget civilization and search entirely within his own self (not that this is possible), or he must actively destroy the meanings of civilization to find within its forms new meanings. We see both of these things being attempted in contemporary art in all media. In some artists we see a wild kind of destructiveness, as in the work of Jackson Pollock, while in others the destruction seems to be pursued in a rational way, as in the work of the Cubists. This tendency seems carried to a logical extreme in the techniques of collage and of sculpture in "junk."

With the destruction of meaning goes the fear that there may be no new meaning. Everyone has this fear, including artists. This may be partly due to the fact that a sudden loss of meaning naturally brings insecurity in its wake. But it suggests something more, too. It suggests that we believe the meaning within whose crystallized forms we live to be the ultimate one. This may help to explain the public's annoyance and protest at the seemingly chaotic outpourings of many modern artists. But to the artist, as is so beautifully revealed in the poetry of Wallace Stevens,[1] the world *is* a chaos—pregnant with meaning. And thus to our contemporary artists civilization itself is a chaos: it must be seen as meaningless before meaning can be found. When it is seen only in terms of the meanings inherited from its makers, we are truly living in illusions, out of touch with the real world.

To the extent that modern man lives completely within his civilization, then, he lives within a sterile dream world. The dreams are not his own dreams—he is afraid to dream his own dreams. Once fabricated, the forms of civilization have no power to grow in their own right and interact with the human beings who live in them. The only things which grow and change in themselves are organisms, whose meanings and purposes are unknown, to be discovered: this means people, other forms of life, and the universe itself in all its aspects. Fabricated objects and meanings do not have this property. Growth is a process which can take place only in some kind of interaction or transaction between two different organisms. Thus man living in civilization stifles his own growth, and if he is sensitive to this, falls into deep despair.

Some people have sought the meaning of life through a scientific investigation of the ultimate nature of the universe. Despite the successive blows which science has given to our feeling of being the center of the universe, many people have continued to have faith that the discovery of the laws of the universe would reveal some vast order in which humans would continue to be significant and even powerful. Two different aspects of science require our attention here: first, some of the theories themselves, and second, the methods used to investigate the universe. These two aspects are related, for some of the most striking developments in theory have dealt with the question of what can be known, and how much of it. The theory of relativity, for example, implies that given two events you cannot determine which of them happened first, and hence it is impossible to say which of them is the cause or effect of the other. Heisenberg's principle of uncertainty places a definite limit to the knowledge we can obtain about any given particle, such as an atom or an electron. The most powerful tool which science has at its disposal for investigation of the universe is measurement and statistical analysis. The result of this is that our knowledge of the universe, at its most precise, consists of numbers: almost everything we know about the universe—from atoms to stars, from cells to societies—can be expressed in terms of equations or probabilities. And yet when we ask of science the question "Why are we here?" or "What is our place in the universe?" the probabilities and equations which we get for answers do not satisfy us.

They do not satisfy us because we feel somehow that the question has not been answered. After all, what we want to know is something quite definite: "Where are we?" The probability that we might be here, yet on the other hand that we might just as well be somewhere else, will not do. Science tells us that our place in the universe is nowhere in particular . . . or anywhere. I think that this is the best that science will ever do for us. No amount of research will effect a qualitative change in that answer. For it is true; it is the correct answer. It has stared us humans in the face throughout our history. Think of all the natural calamities that we know about in history: the comings and goings of the ice age, the volcanic eruptions, the earthquakes, the floods, the droughts: do not these things tell us that the universe does not know that we are here, that whether we exist or not does not matter? Or consider any historical event, such as a war: in a sense the more we investigate it the less we know about it with certainty: the recent proliferation of works on our Civil War, for example, suggests to me that the closest we can come to understanding it is to consider it as something that "just happened" to us, rather than as something we did for such and such reasons.

All that modern science has done in this situation is point out the facts more clearly. Conventional reactions to science, for example, our faith in it, our belief in progress, together with social and technical developments such as I indicated at the beginning of this essay, have made it difficult for people to understand what is going on or what they can do about it. And yet in all times and places human beings have resisted the idea that they are nowhere for no particular reason and for no particular purpose. They have almost always managed to find a somewhere to be, and a reason to be there. The finding of these somewheres is an activity which is crucial to human life, for people seem to go to pieces when events force them to contemplate the ultimate nowhere of their lives. Then they act in ways which the majority of mankind would consider inhuman, ways which they themselves would have considered inhuman from the point of view of somewhere.

So, we turn to the Eskimos to see what their somewhere is like, what they make it out of, and how they make it. First of all, they have certainly not escaped the eternal reminders of the universe that they are nowhere. In fact, on the face of it, they of all people should be most aware that they are nowhere. Civilized men who visit the Eskimos do not know at first what to make of this world. Aside from the obvious dangers of freezing, starving, and being eaten by animals, the landscape itself has a profoundly disturbing psychological impact on some people. For example, the strange winds, whirling storms which continually alter the immediate landscape, although they never vary the constant visual diet of grays and whites, caused Gontran de Poncins, a French anthropologist, to write:

> . . . Indeed nothing up here is settled. . . . The landscape itself changes as if manned by scene shifters. You stare and say to yourself in bewilderment, "Am I mad, or is it this land that is out of its wits?" When you see igloos disappear suddenly before your eyes; when invisible dogs stir beneath the snow under your feet as you walk; when things rise suddenly out of the earth and vanish as if sucked up into the air, it is hard to think of life as normal. You knew very well what this landscape looked like; and where is it? That shack you saw yesterday is today but a roof lying on the surface of the snow. What is this, you wonder? Is it the prelude to Judgment Day? Our globe that we thought a solid turns out to be a mere soap-bubble blown into different shapes by the wind. In this sea of gray your heart quakes, your brain reels. You are enclosed in it like a rat in a box, and someone is there shaking the box with all his furious might. You stand speechless, childish, despairing; and in a moment you fly into a rage, you want to bite and tear the snow with your teeth, to do battle with the storm in hand-to-hand encounter. . . .
>
> Often when I wandered alone in this silence, this infinite solitude, this dead infinity, I wondered if I were dreaming. Who was this man that seemed to be me and that stumbled in rude clothes over the snow, an Eskimo knife in his hand? If this was I, what was I doing here floating like a phantom through this gray air?[2]

Obviously if a person felt like this all the time, he could not possibly live, no matter how well his physical needs were taken care of. But, we may ask, does this unsettling quality of the environment really exist, is it really *there?* Or is this experience entirely the product of an unstable imagination? The Eskimos, to a Western way of seeing, live almost constantly in an extreme situation. To them, perhaps more than any other people, the universe is constantly demonstrating that they are nowhere. Knud Rasmussen, the Danish anthropologist, tried to plumb the Eskimo mind to the very depths on this question. Being part Eskimo himself, he spoke the language fluently. The Eskimos liked him and revealed themselves to him almost as if he were one of them. One day his persistent questioning caused a very unusual and moving episode to take place.

> I once went out to Aua's hunting quarters on the ice outside Lyon Inlet to spend some time with [the people]. For several evenings we had discussed rules of life and taboo customs, without getting beyond a long circumstantial statement of all that was permitted and all that was forbidden. Everyone knew precisely what had to be done in any given situation, but whenever I put my query: "Why?", they could give no answer. They regarded it, and very rightly, as unreasonable that I should require not only an account, but a justification of their religious principles. They had of course no idea that all my questions, now that I had obtained what I wished for, were only intended to make them react in such a manner that they should, excited by my inquisitiveness, be able to give an inspired explanation. Aua had as usual been the spokesman, and as he was still unable to answer my questions, he rose to his feet, and as if seized by a sudden impulse, invited me to go outside with him.

It had been an unusually rough day, and as we had plenty of meat after the successful hunting of the past few days, I had asked my host to stay at home so that we could get some work done together. The brief daylight had given place to the half-light of the afternoon, but as the moon was up, one could still see some distance. Ragged white clouds raced across the sky, and when a gust of wind came tearing over the ground, our eyes and mouths were filled with snow. Aua looked me full in the face, and pointing out over the ice, where the snow was being lashed about in waves by the wind, he said:

"In order to hunt well and live happily, man must have calm weather. Why this constant succession of blizzards and all this needless hardship for men seeking food for themselves and those they care for? Why? Why?"

We had come out just at the time when the men were returning from their watching at the blowholes on the ice; they came in little groups, bowed forward, toiling against the wind, which actually forced them now and again to stop, so fierce were the gusts. Not one of them had a seal in tow; their whole day of painful effort and endurance had been in vain.

I could give no answer to Aua's "Why?", but shook my head in silence. He then led me into Kublo's house, which was close beside our own. The small blubber lamp burned, but with the faintest flame, giving out no heat whatever; a couple of children crouched, shivering, under a skin rug on the bench.

Aua looked at me again, and said: "Why should it be cold and comfortless in here? Kublo has been out hunting all day, and if he had got a seal, as he deserved, his wife would now be sitting laughing beside her lamp, letting it burn full, without fear of having no blubber left for tomorrow. The place would be warm and bright and cheerful, the children would come out from under their rugs and enjoy life. Why should it not be so? Why?"

I made no answer, and he led me out of the house, into a little snow hut where his sister Natseq lived all by herself because she was ill. She looked thin and worn, and was not even interested in our coming. For several days she had suffered from a malignant cough that seemed to come from far down in the lungs, and it looked as if she had not long to live.

A third time Aua looked at me and said: "Why must people be ill and suffer pain? We are all afraid of illness. Here is this old sister of mine; as far as anyone can see she has done no evil; she has lived through a long life and given birth to healthy children, and now she must suffer before her days end. Why? Why?"

This ended his demonstration, and we returned to our house, to resume with the others the interrupted discussion.

"You see," said Aua, "you are equally unable to give any reason when we ask why life is as it is. And so it must be. All our customs come from life and turn towards life; we explain nothing, we believe nothing, but in what I have just shown you lies our answer to all you ask."[3]

A very important idea emerges from this intense episode. This idea is clearly stated when Aua says, "All our customs come from life and turn towards life." It is an idea which is so basic to the Eskimo sense of place in the universe that it is not really an idea at all, but a way of being in relation to life. This way of being is the highest value for the Eskimos. It is not an easy way to be, but it is a necessary condition for being Eskimo.

Perhaps we can begin to learn what it is like to be Eskimo by examining a myth. The myth of Nuliajuk is central to the Eskimo view of the source of life and man's relation to this source. There are many versions of this myth—probably each Eskimo has his own version—and all of them are correct, for the problems encompassed by the myth are too many-faceted to be included in a single telling. The basic events, however, remain constant, and can be told as follows: some Eskimos are out in a boat on the water. Nuliajuk, a girl, is thrown into the water. She tries to climb back on board. The people who threw her in cut off her fingers as she grips the edge of the boat. The joints fall off and become the animals of the sea on which men feed, and Nuliajuk falls back into the water and becomes a sea spirit.

Rasmussen collected two versions of this story from the Netsilik Eskimos: in one the girl is an orphan whom nobody wants, and hence she is thrown into the sea; in the other version she is already the mother of a number of children, and it is her children who throw her into the water, cutting off her fingers as before. Among the Iglulik Eskimos the version which Rasmussen noted made the girl's father the chief agent. Fearing that he would drown in the storm caused by a petrel (the girl's supernatural husband), he threw Nuliajuk into the sea, and, as in the other stories, cut off her finger joints when she tried to climb back into the boat.

When Nuliajuk went to the bottom of the sea, she became the ruler of all those beasts which had been formed from her finger joints as they were chopped off. She is also now believed to rule all the beasts, although it is not explained why this is so. Her power, then, is enormous, for the Eskimos depend upon animals for food, clothing, and fire. In fact, she "became the most feared of all spirits, the most powerful, and the one who more than any other controls the destinies of men."[4]

In the three versions of the myth recounted above, the protagonists are related to each other by three of the most basic kinship ties possible in human society. In the first version the child is an orphan, and therefore there is no relationship between her and the others. In the second version the relationship is that of child to parent, for it is the children who throw their mother into the sea. And in the third the relationship is that of parent to child, for in this story the father kills his daughter. Probably many readers will be familiar with the fact that the Eskimos often abandon their old people when it is no longer possible for them to continue with the group. Infanticide of girl children is also extremely widespread. Rasmussen found in one community that the mothers had killed four-fifths of the girls which they had borne. It should be noted, finally, that the position of an orphan is perhaps the most precarious of any in the community, since unless it is adopted (highly unlikely for a girl) it will support no parents in their old age. One's own kinsmen always take precedence. Thus, the abandonment or killing of people is a normal experience in the life of the Eskimos. The myth of Nuliajuk's abandonment can be seen to be a representation of a certain crucial human situation as the Eskimos see it. But look at the consequences of this abandonment! The abandoned person becomes the most powerful force of what we could call the good and evil with which the Eskimos must contend. She is really the source of life for the Eskimos, and by withholding life she brings death.

By the act of abandoning Nuliajuk the Eskimos have taken upon themselves the responsibility for the fact that the world is the way it is. And this responsibility is not merely a burden from the mythical past, but it is lived out from day to day. In accepting responsibility for their own lives and the lives of others, they also accept responsibility for the universe. They accept this responsibility in spite of the fact that the universe is constantly telling them that they have no responsibility, that they do not belong anywhere in particular. Out of this dialogue, in which the universe tells them that they are nowhere, and in which they assert their place and their responsibility, grows, as we shall see, a beautiful poetic expression.

Although we cannot help but react with feeling to the emotional impact of the Eskimo songs, we shall understand them better if we can grasp something of the Eskimo view of the nature of thought and of the creative process. These two things are inextricably bound together. The most important difference between the Eskimo concept of thought and the Western is that we believe that thought takes place in our heads, while the Eskimos believe that thought is entirely outside man. In fact, the Eskimo word for "thought" is the same as the word for "the outside." It refers to all that is outside man: the air, the weather, the sky, the world, and ultimately the universe itself. From our point of view the logical conclusion to be drawn from these facts would be something like Parmenides' statement, "For it is the same thing to think and to be." In other words, since thought in the Eskimo view is not a product of the mind but actually *is* what exists "outside," then whatever one thinks is so, in fact is so. This is true for the Eskimos, but with very important modifications. How, after all, does thought come into being? How does thought make itself known, as it were, to man? Can thought exist without man? The answer to this last question is "no," for it requires a creative human act for thought, or the universe, to acquire a form that one would call existence. And yet the universe must speak first. It must affect man, move man, so that man may free it from its formless state of latent existence. The universe as chaos is the universe telling man that he is nowhere in particular; when man is moved by this chaos he *experiences* something, an emotion wells up in him. At bottom this emotion is the feeling of being alive, of existing in relationship to the universe, and at this moment a sense of place in the universe, the establishment of a somewhere, begins to emerge.

The singing of a song is both one of the most common and one of the most unfathomable responses of man to the universe. Orpingalik, perhaps the most gifted poet Rasmussen met on his travels among the Eskimos, once tried to put into words what songs were, and how they came into being:

Songs are thoughts, sung out with the breath when people are moved by great forces and ordinary speech no longer suffices.

Man is moved just like the ice floe sailing here and there out in the current. His thoughts are driven by a flowing force when he feels joy, when he feels fear, when he feels sorrow. Thoughts can wash over him like a flood, making his breath come in gasps, and his heart throb. Something, like an abatement in the weather, will keep him thawed up. And then it will happen that we, who always think we are small, will feel still smaller. And we will fear to use words. But it will happen that the words we need will come of themselves. When the words we want to use shoot up of themselves—we get a new song.[5]

It is clear from this beautiful and moving statement that it is through man's emotions that a response to the universe in song arises. The feeling of smallness described by the poet is, I believe, the feeling which develops out of an awareness of the chaos of the universe. It is man's way of listening to the universe tell him that he is nowhere. It may well be the only honest human response to the movements of the universe. And only out of a feeling of smallness before nature can man give a truly creative statement of his place in nature.

When the poet says, "And we will fear to use words," he does not mean that he is afraid of the words themselves. He means that he is in awe of the power of words to bring thought, the universe itself, into existence. He knows that the words must "shoot up of themselves" in some inexplicable fashion from the transaction that is taking place between him and the outside. To impose words of his own invention would be sacrilegious. The spiritually disastrous effects of making up words, rather than allowing them to arise naturally out of emotional experiences, can be seen more clearly in our own civilization than in that of the Eskimos. In James Joyce's story "The Dead," we find an example of this very problem. Gabriel Conroy, the main character, makes his annual speech to his ancient aunts, the hostesses for the family Christmas party. The fine words of the speech are happily applauded by the guests, but since they express no real emotion their hollowness is evident both to the reader and to Gabriel himself. This kind of hollowness is a sense of meaninglessness which arises not through contact with the chaos of the universe, but from just the opposite situation. It arises when for some reason one can no longer respond to the chaos with emotion—the emotion which is the only indication that one is alive and has something to do with the universe.

But the Eskimos *are* moved by their experiences. They are not afraid to experience the feeling of smallness. Perhaps the fact that they are able to be so moved by nature is enough to tell them that they are *in* nature, that they really belong there. The following song by the shaman Uvavnuk, a woman, expresses a great joy at simply being moved by nature, and therefore participating in it.

The great sea
Has sent me adrift,
It moves me as the weed in a great river,
Earth and the great weather
Move me,
Have carried me away
And move my inward parts with joy.[6]

The great joy which the Eskimos take in life is possible because they really love their world. This joy is not a reward for anything, but rather is actually a part of the attitude with which they meet life. Nor is there anything mystical in this joy, no exaltation of the occult. As the following poem shows, what is most important and beautiful in life cannot be separated from the seemingly trivial. Through an all-engrossing concern with the minor problems of everyday life comes awareness of the forces that are active in the universe.

And I think over again
My small adventures
When with a shore wind I drifted out
In my kayak
And I thought I was in danger.
My fears,
Those small ones
That I thought so big,
For all the vital things
I had to get and to reach.

. . . .

And yet, there is only
One great thing,
The only thing:
To live to see in huts and on journeys
The great day that dawns,
And the light that fills the world.[7]

1. See especially his "Connoisseur of Chaos" and "The Sense of the Sleight-of-Hand Man," in *The Collected Poems of Wallace Stevens,*
   New York, Alfred A. Knopf, Inc. (1957).
2. Gontran de Poncins, *Kabloona,* New York, Reynal and Company (1941), pp. 146–148.
3. Knud Rasmussen, *Reports of the Fifth Thule Expedition, 1921–24,* Copenhagen, Gyldendalske Boghandel, Nordisk Forlag, vol. VII, no. 1: *Intellectual Culture of the Iglulik Eskimos* (1929), pp. 54–56.
4. Rasmussen, *Reports . . . ,* vol. VIII, nos. 1–2: *The Netsilik Eskimos, Social Life and Spiritual Culture* (1931), p. 226.
5. Rasmussen, *Reports . . . ,* vol. VIII, nos. 1–2, p. 321.
6. Rasmussen, *Reports . . . ,* vol. VII, no. 1, p. 123.
7. Rasmussen, *Reports . . . ,* vol. IX: *Intellectual Culture of the Copper Eskimos* (1932), p. 53.

Words like *sign, image* and *symbol* are used loosely in much speech and writing, especially perhaps in talking about the arts. In this essay I am not going to keep words in their places by letting them mean what I want them to mean. Instead I have turned, selectively, to authority. The authority is *Webster's Unabridged Dictionary,* second edition, printing of 1957. I use an American lexicon because this is an American book; and I use the second edition for reasons which will be obvious to anyone who knows the subsequent editorial history of this work. In what follows, I plan to respect the following meanings.

An *image* is an imitation, a representation, or the similitude of any thing or person, made perceptible to the senses. There may, then, be visual, tactile, olfactory, or auditory images. The visual and the auditory or verbal are no doubt the strongest of these and they are all I shall be talking about. By extension the image also exists in a mental representation, the revival or imitation of sensible experience, the reproduction of such an experience in the memory or the imagination. Webster does not say whether the experience may have been vicarious. I intend to include such a possibility. I shall exclude illusory appearances, magic, and the special meanings to be found in philosophy or physics. I shall exclude rhetorical meanings such as the introduction, figuratively, of something concrete or abstract to represent something which it strikingly resembles (sleep as an image of death or vice versa). Most of all I shall discard those definitions which move towards even more metaphorical associations such as "she is the image of devotion." And I shall be adamant against any interpretation which can begin to merge with the meaning of *symbol,* that is something that represents or is regarded as representing another thing. The *image* of St. Peter's is the *image* of St. Peter's and nothing more; if it suggests Rome or the Holy Catholic Church the image has become symbolic.

For the purposes of this essay, then, I can in turn discard many of the meanings of *symbol.* I can and will discard its arbitrary usage as a sign, its rare meaning as a maxim, its specialized meanings in logic or psychoanalysis. Here it means only something which stands for or suggests something else. It may do this by reason of relationship, association, convention, even accident. But whatever its history the symbolic interpretation of an image should be in the end spontaneous. El Greco's portrayal of Toledo is merely an *image;* it becomes a *symbol* if you choose to extrapolate it to suggest, for example, the frowning seriousness of medieval Spain; but it will not be a good symbol if it is labored or far-fetched. Delaunay's paintings of the Eiffel Tower are of course images of that tower and little more; they can readily be viewed as symbols of Paris. If the thought of Paris then evokes for you some greater generalization you may or may not be able to find in the painting the trigger for your ultimate symbolic thrust.

An *emblem* is a special kind of symbol. The balance of justice, the scepter of sovereignty, the dove of peace are samples. The emblem has the particular distinguishing characteristic that it must be a *visible* object. Of course after it has been seen it may be reinvoked by words. Here we begin to have a foretaste of the unpleasantness we are going to encounter more severely later on.

The visual and the literary arts are easily confounded. Perhaps it is well that it should be so, though artists, in what seems to me too defensive a posture against the power of words, are always trying to separate them and to use pejorative terms about words and word-mongers. Yet it is often the case in symbolism that the word is indeed more powerful than the sight. *Dove* will almost always suggest peace in words, but doves seen on a telegraph wire may not remind one of peace at all; and when the dove of peace is portrayed she usually needs the prop of an olive branch to be held in her talon or her beak. The "scales of justice" is enough to invoke the symbol; a bas relief of a scale may be too great an abstraction and suggest other symbols; so may the blindfold; together they are visually concrete. Woe to the power of the symbol when the visual abstraction becomes too pure.

So all *emblems* are *symbols* but all *symbols* are not *emblems*. There is the suggestion, also, that many symbols may suggest a more profound or recondite significance than many emblems. But here the woods get pretty thick.

The word *sign* is probably the most often misused. It has a number of respectable technical uses which need not concern us, in theology, philology, music, medicine, mathematics, hunting, or astronomy. These we can lay aside readily. For our purpose we may also forego intimations of grace, of remarkable events, of trace or portent, and the obsolete meaning, as effigy. This brings us down to the symbolic uses and again we can conveniently ignore those attached to heraldic standards, constellations, gestures, highway boards, or ideographic marks in printing. This leaves us with but one definition. A *sign* is a conventional symbol, representing an idea. *Conventional* is the discriminating term, but *idea* is not unimportant. *Signs* cannot be private; if invented they will usually need some gestation before they can attain a minimal consensual acceptance.

To repeat, the *image* is the explicit reminder of a specific thing, the *symbol* the extrapolation of the image to suggest something different (usually something more but occasionally something less; usually something abstract but occasionally concrete like a city or a specific president of the United States, as suggested by split rails, hard cider, the hat of a rough rider, or a beagle's ears). An *emblem* is a particular kind of symbol which must be *visible;* the *sign* is a *conventional* symbol, suggesting wide acceptance. The image may be shared with no one, though some images are shared widely; the symbol is not worth much if it is not shared at least by a group, and private symbols are arrogant and ineffective; the sign must by definition be shared with, indeed accepted and understood by many.

In what follows I shall try to deal with images and symbols and signs which I fancy to be rather generally current and not with any which I may carry around in my secret life. I never think, for example, of the *quais* of Paris without seeing again the two young lovers who bicycled by me on a wonderful gusty autumnal day, dismounted, sat briefly on the parapet for a long embrace, remounted and wheeled away in opposite directions. This recollection may or may not move me to further reflections about Paris or young love or what not. But it would all remain private even though I can be quite sure that others have had comparable visual experiences on the banks of the Seine. I shall talk here on more conventional lines.

I shall also exclude the rich field of speculations opened up, for example, by the work of Kevin Lynch, or at least pass it by lightly. I am not going to try to deal here with the image, symbol, or sign of a particular street corner or neighborhood as it may be seen or construed by a native or an *aficionado.* I shall mention only tangentially that same local detail when somehow it has been projected onto the national, international, historic or contemporary scene, whether it be the Faubourg St. Antoine, or Savile Row. Instead I shall try to grapple with the city as a whole.

It is obvious that symbols require some degree of knowledge before they can clearly be evoked from images. Characteristically the art of the Middle Ages used stories of the Old Testament to prefigure the events of the New; and often combined these with ideas of animal life drawn from Pliny via the *Bestiaries*. The people who looked at them, or at least the people who made them, learned to see in Daniel, Jonah, the pelican piercing its breast, the lioness breathing life into the mouths of her still-born cubs, common symbols of the Resurrection. After one has the knowledge and the continuous experience the association may become automatic—as for example the association of the national flag—and any alternative association becomes impossible to entertain. The cross is a similarly universal symbol—at least in the Christian world—as the fish is not, while figures from the more obscure litanies can make no claim to universality. In the end the source of the symbol may indeed be forgotten or interpreted differently while the symbol goes merrily on.

It is for this reason, I suppose, that verbal symbols are on the whole so much more powerful than visual ones, at least in literate populations. The symbols may have begun with a visual image but often the need for that stimulus has atrophied, and the statement of the symbol may call up no visual recollection whatsoever. This is an embarrassing thing to have to report in a book about vision but I am afraid it is just so. The most powerful and universal symbols that are associated with cities are in fact literary, historical, verbal, and can often be entertained without ever conjuring up a visual image.

This is not to say that the mere mention of the name of some cities will not evoke powerful and positive *images* of the city and to this point I shall return. All I am saying is that the evocation of these images is by no means necessary to establish the strength of the symbol.

Consider for example the symbolic suggestions implied in the very names of some cities. There are symbols of sin, at the high level of Babylon, Tyre, Sidon, Sodom, Gomorrah, or the low level of Las Vegas. There are symbols of Power such as Rome, Thebes, Berlin, Moscow. There are symbols of Holiness or Faith: Banaras, Jerusalem, Mecca, Lourdes. There are symbols of Pleasure: Paris, Vienna; of Decadence: Byzantium. There are symbols of products: Damascus, Toledo, Sheffield, Milwaukee, Hollywood. There are symbolic cities that merely suggest the exotic and the faraway: Samarkand or Timbuktu. There are cities that bear the cross of the symbolic association with one bad man or one unhappy event: Chicago, Ferrara, Dallas. There are cities with heavy symbolic significance because of a single such repeated reference: Samarra of the appointments. Symbolism pours from cities which never existed at all: Atlantis, Xanadu, The City of Brass, Anaurot, The City of Dis. So strong is the verbal power of these associations that, though their symbolic meaning springs to mind as soon as they are mentioned, there may be no visual association at all. Indeed for many of them there cannot be either, because we have never seen them or because nobody has ever seen them. And in all cases the visual image is weaker than the verbal (Blake's conjectural Dis, Debussy's *cathédrale engloutie*).

This seems even more clear when we start talking about the Eternal City, the City of Light, The New Jerusalem, or the Third Rome. Within particular cities, individual urban elements have become immediately symbolic: Threadneedle Street, the Quai d'Orsay, Wall Street, Downing Street, the Vatican, the Kremlin. These are often personified, often made to "say" or to "think" something. One can easily use the Kremlin in this way without ever recalling how it looks.

I shall not belabor these examples further. Obviously many more will spring to mind. The symbols I have been talking about have clearly risen to the status of signs, having a highly conventional, largely consensual use. Indeed the consensual understanding may be so general that many people who would understand the signs clearly would be hard-put to identify the images from which they have sprung, let alone to explain the steps by which they had been transmuted from image to symbol or sign. Even if the original images were visible and powerful they have long ago ceased to be so.

Would one modify this conclusion if he approached the problem from a somewhat different angle? I think not. Let us imagine a game. A group of people are each shown a series of pictures, one for each of a number of host-cities and asked to identify, instantaneously the cities. There are a dozen to fifteen cities in the world for which this would be easy. The image is in fact not only a symbol but also a sign of the city.

The examples are easy to list: Westminster Houses of Parliament, Capitol at Washington, Eiffel Tower, St. Peter's, Piazza San Marco, the Leaning Tower, lower Manhattan Island from the sea, the Taj Mahal, Sugar Loaf and Copacabana, the Pyramids, the Brandenburger Tor, the Acropolis, the Kremlin, Hagia Sophia from the water, the Golden Gate Bridge. There are not many more, however important to locals may be the Bridge of Sydney, The Town Hall of Oslo, The Rathaus of Bremen, Grant Park of Chicago, even the Palazzo Vecchio of Florence, or whatever may be unusual or prized in Little Rock.

A fair first question is whether the process is reversible. If one mentions the name London will the image of Big Ben always spring first to mind? Not necessarily. For some cities the single image is all that can be summoned; for others the images may be multiple. Clearly there will be more images of London for the person who has visited London than for the one who has had to depend on the filters of travel posters, the *National Geographic Magazine,* and the work of a few painters or novelists or poets.

The collection of images naturally comes nearer to establishing the total character of a city than the landmark image, however much the latter may in truth epitomize the city. London *is* more than the Houses of Parliament, Paris than the Exposition, Washington than the Congress or the President of the United States. Perhaps the band of easily evoked images does offer a comment on the versatility and the magnificence of a city. If Washington is more than the Capitol what are the other visual images that come most promptly to mind (remember we are leaving out private images so the Smithsonian Institution, the Hot Shoppes and Rock Creek Park need not apply)? They are the White House, the Washington Monument, the Lincoln Memorial, perhaps the Union Station and the cherry trees. Collectively they are in fact symbols of Government and this may be a serious suggestion of all that Washington amounts to now.

The band of Roman associations is, not surprisingly, wider: the Pincio, The Spanish Steps, the Thermae, the Fora, Imperial and Republican, the Campidoglio, the Colosseum, the Palatine, the Fountains, the Lateran, the Vatican, St. Peter's, the Castle San Angelo, Hadrian's Villa, the Villa d'Este, perhaps Trajan's Column and even Ostia. But curiously they are all imperial symbols in one way or another and Rome remains an Imperial City despite the antics on the Via Veneto or in front of the Hotel Excelsior.

The band of visual London associations may be still wider: the Cenotaph, Trafalgar Square, Nelson's Column, Whitehall, Admiralty Arch, St. James and Buckingham Palaces, the Tower and the Tower Bridge, St. Paul's, the Bank, Hyde Park, Kew Gardens, Piccadilly Circus, Waterloo Station, Covent Garden, Berkeley Square, Belgravia, Sloane Square and perhaps a few more. (Baker Street, The Yard, The Pool, Mme. Tussaud's, Bloomsbury, Hampstead Heath, the British Museum, Sir John Soanes Museum, the Cheshire Cheese, and Simpson's in the Strand begin to fall into the domain of private images.) The characteristic emphasis of the most easily recalled images is surely the suggestion of Empire, the Pax Britannica, and in fact of Queen Victoria, whose shadow falls on the great city in such a charming way, even on the parts which long precede her in time.

It is significant of the versatility of Paris that its images cannot be so neatly packaged. Notre-Dame, The Trocadéro, the Madeleine, The Opéra, the Place de la Concorde, the Place Vendôme, the Palais Royal, the rue de Rivoli, Sacré-Coeur, The Champs Elysées, the Etoile, the Seine banks and bookstalls, the Ste-Chapelle and the Conciergerie, the Panthéon, the Invalides, the Louvre, and the Tuileries offer so rich an array of government, religion, pleasure, commerce, fashion, the simple life, the life of the salon, the life of Les Halles and the life of the Grand Véfour that one knows at once that here he has met metropolis. Other great cities of course entertain such a range of activities but the visual evidences of their existence are somehow less explicit.

Now if each of our game-players were to go through this exercise to its bitter end, running the book for each of the fifteen cities and omitting what was special knowledge or interest or association for a particular player only, they would quickly find that but a few of the fifteen had genuine and powerful multiple designators. They would find little to add to Cairo, Agra, Pisa, even to Istanbul, though of course any individual who knew and loved one of these cities could do better. The point about the additional images would be that they are not commonly evoked, and if symbolic at all they are so only in a private sense, and thus incapable of becoming signs. Is this because fewer people have encountered Istanbul, Edinburgh, Stockholm, Bangkok, Honolulu, Siena, Florence, or Cologne, while so many have encountered London and Paris? It can be only a partial explanation. Great writers or painters have encountered the others and after their visits any city is better known. Is it only an accident that the very names of London, Paris, and Rome (and if we were better educated, no doubt Peking as well), are so evocative of images, symbols, and signs? Again I think the answer has to be no.

Yet all this comes to, perhaps, is that a few cities have been such vital centers over such long periods of time that they have, in truth, impressed at least some of their visual images upon us; that we are familiar with, or at least think we are familiar with, their history; that some of the images have been powerful enough to have become good symbols or even signs of very large abstractive merit, while most cities, even admirable cities like Florence, Isfahan, or Shiraz, offering a good deal of imagery, at best, have to be confined to a restricted symbolism and an even more limited value as signs. Finally it is evident that for the great cities what is literary and what is visual are very hard to disentangle. While few of us can hear their names without immediate recall of one or more visual images, we can never be sure if they are ours or another's, whether we conjecture our own London or the different Londons of Dickens, Thackeray, Boswell, or Pepys; our own Paris or the Paris of Hugo, Balzac, Zola, Villon,

Baudelaire or even lesser writers like Eugène Sue, Henri Murger, Eliot Paul, or Henry Miller. Moreover, to be repetitious, the relation of these visual images—whether personal or vicarious—to the urban symbol or sign, either at the local or the world level, is seldom apparent; if once apparent it is now forgotten, or indeed it may be at best tenuous, or at worst, never existent.

This might help to explain why painters seem to have had so much difficulty with the city as a total thing to observe. The components have naturally attracted their attention: streets and *quais* and rivers and buildings; the life of neighborhoods high and low; the life of special groups; an important urban place as the background for an historical event; a whole city as the background for a Renaissance procession à la Sassetta. But not many of these images have been portents of the whole, much less symbolic through the city. They may have been symbolic of something quite different and unrelated to the city in its own right. Not only has much urban painting not extrapolated to the whole, but much less has it elongated into a symbol or a sign. *The Scream* of Munch is no doubt heavily symbolic and it is apparently heard in an urban context, but the city is hardly, if at all, involved in the extrapolation. It does not seem to matter much for my generalization whether the urban background was as meticulous as that of Canaletto or Bellini or as impressionistic as that of Turner; whether the streets were by Utrillo or Marin; the buildings by Feininger or Vermeer; the life by Breughel, Manet, Renoir, Marsh, Toulouse-Lautrec, Degas, or Seurat. Delaunay's Paris, explained by the Eiffel Tower, ventures a little further. Perhaps, so does Mondrian's *Broadway Boogie-Woogie,* though it does not impress me as a very penetrating comment. Indeed of all the painters of cities it may be that only Turner, Dufy, and especially El Greco came near to the mark of predicting the macroscopic city as symbol; and they did not come very near. The microscopic use of the city as symbol, of course, merely makes the city another source of detail for which no special power or weakness can be claimed.

Was this because the city was too big for them? It is possible, but I think not. Was it because the city did not interest them? Surely the answer to this is "no." Was it because, when all the grain is sifted, the position of the city as *visual* symbol is not very important, however important it may be in literary terms? This is, I suspect, the truth of the matter. The painters did not explore the idea deeply because their intuitions told them that there was not much to probe.

This unhappy conclusion for a chapter in a book on vision leaves me open, of course, to attack on the ground that I have been superficial or that I have been insensitive to the multiple levels of modern criticism. To the first charge I might plead guilty unhappily; to the second guilty joyously. We ought to stop looking for things that are not there. A city may be good to look at and the looking may mean little more. A city may be good to think about and to press into use as a symbol or a sign. But the city which we see and the city which we interpret and the city which we project beyond itself is never the city that is actually there. Ours is more beautiful and simpler and perhaps even more symbolic. That ought to be enough. One can feel sorry for those who are so realistic that they know that there never has been a Xanadu; or those who are so intellectual that they have to transfer every sensuous experience into something that is vastly and drearily meaningful.

ERNESTO N. ROGERS

THE IMAGE: THE ARCHITECT'S INALIENABLE VISION

Nam imago refertur ad prototypum . . . ("Indeed, the idea leads to the prototype . . .") "But the prototype no longer lies in the mind of God, where all enjoy equal opportunity of contemplating it, but in the books and the laws of men, to which only the privileged have access."

I take this acute quotation from Saint Bonaventure and the brief comment from an essay on the Baroque by Ezio Bonfanti because they seem to me appropriate to introduce the subject of this paper. There is no one who fails to realize how diversity in the use of concepts changes their meaning so essentially, that in speaking of the image of perfection on the concrete phenomenological plane—that is, divorced from any transcendental suggestion—we must examine the experience of the concept itself in the environment of new realities.

We can, therefore, affirm that the image is the first step to expressing the perception of the architectural phenomenon, and its rational conquest is concluded through the arduous elaboration of the process itself: the *idea* becomes *reality*.

The image is always, and of necessity, the work of an ordering will. So true is this that any organizing process of Man—either as mover or intermediary—is termed a "formation." This form can be born concretely, almost physically, within the artist, as it was for Leonardo in his machines and in the rough walls of his frescoes, or for Michelangelo in the hard Apennine stone. Even when, as with the artists of the *de Stijl*, one would like to oppose the necessity and regularity of the machine to the "uncertainty of the hand," the human intervention subsists and is revealed, in a historical perspective, as a poetic illusion. The hand that traces the programs of the machine, and, in consequence, the finished product, is always the "fallible" hand of Man. Form remains, in production as well as in observation, something that Man has ordained by conception and, precisely because of this fact, it is realized as an ideal.

Theorizing, that is, a priori stylization, has profoundly changed the mode of composition in architecture, but has not lessened the aesthetic importance and expressive value of the ideal of perfection, which remains the culminating generative act of architectural creation. If one considers a building as a single object, this theory needs no further elucidation. On the contrary, it appears both urgent and ill-defined when one begins to think in terms of urban design or city planning, where the importance of many other indispensable elements can distract from this ideal.

No one would wish to deny the importance of scientific and technical research; yet there is no more dangerous error than the belief that calculations (demography, meteorology, traffic density, or any other physical and historical element of space and time) can, in themselves, give character to a city or a landscape. Only a form that has been considered and expressed can contribute to this process, that is, in the Greek sense, give an imprint, a seal, a specific nature to the subject.

Diverse considerations assist in the conception of an architectural ideal which can be perfected only by means of numerous perspectives. Under normal conditions this ideal may demand a considerable period of time before being fully accepted, but this period must have a certain compactness so that the successive experiences achieve a synthesis in which space absorbs every distinct moment of time. In the case of architecture we are instinctively induced to conclude our observations (without even having exhausted them) after a period in which our attention and emotions have been concentrated on and possessed by the totality of the object.

The ideal of an individual architecture becomes an element distinct in the time and space of experience and, therefore, distinct in the memory. In consequence, it is possible to adopt simplifications which reduce architecture to its stereometry, to the combination of materials of which it is constituted, to its essential structure and color. Our tendency to unify and to simplify can be practiced with relative facility on a well-defined architecture; and the ideal can be close and connected to each of the partial ideals contained in the consciously planned single form. In the case of a town, the period of observation is excessively long, and, most important of all, disconnected. It is, one may say, inextricably involved in the period of life itself. Indubitably architecture can and must be lived, but its ideal of perfection lends itself to a synthetic observation which is frequently illuminating. A city does not exist merely in its emblematic manifestations, its famous monuments, useful though these may be in revealing to us a dimension that the image of a city must offer. There exists a kind of continuous thread which unites the areas of particular note to those of lesser importance. The whole constitutes that entirety of experience which enables us to share in the single and total reality, displayed in its typical form. This process of interpretation is closely connected to the fact that the city, in the majority of cases, is a composite object, and its image absorbs those constituent elements through which we are sensorially capable of defining its specific character.

The many sides which a city reveals lead us, on the other hand, to neglect its general appearance. That immediate conformity between partial elements and the synthetic instant, which can be noted in the case of one distinct building, is lacking in our perception of the city. Our capacity for individual simplification must, in the case of the city, overcome the obstacles presented by a perception inevitably dissipated in discordant and disconnected events.

In the majority of cases, the modern city grows and conforms to rules which, at first sight, give comfort to the dispersive judgment of perception, but there is rarely an orderly design which subordinates the part to the whole. In the modern city diverse and conformistic wills make their presence known. The accusations of harshness and lack of harmony directed against the contemporary city emphasize the difficulty of the average citizen to recognize as something of his own, the city in which he lives.

The rhetoric which surrounds the celebrated places and that unique ideal which so many historical cities, harmonious and complete, yet tend to reveal, influences the negative experience of the contemporary city. But this process must be changed, so that we shall be able to perceive an individual face, even in a city which is deformed, and we shall be able to discern this face even in its most unpleasing features. This does not mean that we shall be obliged to accept them, to abandon all thought of correction, but it reminds us that an ideal does not cease to be such simply because it is unlovable. In this is the reaffirmation of the moment of synthesis when, transcending every meritorious judgment on the quality of the image, fragments joined together by spatial contiguity and human interrelationships are reunited.

It is paradoxical that modern planners, although frequently neglectful of the urban ideal, give so much

Seal of the city of Bruges, 1281.

Francesco di Giorgio. *Ideal Square of a City,* about 1460. Urbino, Galleria delle Marche.

View of the city of Florence, 1602.

El Greco. *View and Plan of the City of Toledo,* about 1609. Toledo, El Greco Museum.

244

importance to the so-called functional reports, expressing them quantitatively and concentrating exclusively on this aspect. They fail to realize how such reports have, in their concrete form, the effect of human connections. They can be gauges of the attention of the citizen, gauges which embrace the entire city, above all from the point of view of the ideal of perfection.

Economic and sociological interrelationships, as facts of life, find their realization visually, and not through the media of abstract diagrams. On the other hand the territorial planning process is now so complex (city-territory; city-region, etc.) as to be capable of provoking any kind of demiurgic conception in the architect, in his role of synthesizer of the diverse fields of activity. In this way the architect has unconsciously come within reach of every kind of assistance: political, economic, sociological, anthropological, and ecological, losing sight of the spatial, morphological, and psychological aspects of planning.

The urban architect seems to have progressively lost faith in his own capacity to respond to the task to which he was called, discouraged by a series of increasingly notable failures encountered in the efforts to construct a city according to a formal, precise, and intentional scheme. In this situation the consequential and controllable formulations of other disciplines have seduced his disillusioned desire for control. Through this extradisciplinary evasion the architect has encountered the planner. But this complex and rather ambiguous figure, however usefully he exerts many synthetic evaluations, ultimately lacks the conviction that the urban ideal is an integral part of the plan. It is rather considered as a decorative complement to the plan, of value, perhaps even necessary, but it can always be added as an afterthought. An initial and binding contribution to the morphological model is denied, because it is not comprehended that only in this way can the plan be made to function authentically, that is, in the spatial conception. Such an architect, at the same time apostate and prevaricator, has certainly not won the trust of those summoned to collaborate with him in the work of planning. His dilettantish digressions in the economic and sociological field, as they cannot substitute his shortcomings in the morphological sphere, are not likely to earn him the esteem of genuine economists and sociologists.

The present-day task of the urban architect, as planner of the shape of the territory, is therefore not to exceed or usurp the other disciplinary limits involved in the planning scheme, but to "sit at the table of general discipline," offering the fundamental contribution of his own new-found competence. In order to further this end, however, in the hope that the themes elaborated by the architect find both listeners and consideration, it is vital that he should use a language in common with that of the other specialists and learn to give weight to his own requirements, in order to align them with those of the other fields of activity. It is necessary, in other words, to discover some instrument to express the importance he attributes to the finest morphological results. And he must be dedicated to the values of morphology throughout all of society. The way to achieve this is through the rediscovery, in every citizen, of that vocation to beauty and truth which may have been suppressed but never destroyed.

This series of factors has given rise to certain recent contributions to the field of urbanism. These are aimed both at the recovery of formal values and at their quantitative formulation in comparison with that of the values prevailing among other disciplines, especially the social sciences. In *The Image of the City*, one of the most notable of these contributions, Kevin Lynch has written:

A vivid and integrated physical setting, capable of producing a sharp image, plays a social role as well. It can furnish the raw material for the symbols and collective memories of group communication. A striking landscape is the skeleton upon which many primitive races erect their socially important myths. . . . Indeed, a distinctive and legible environment not only offers security but also heightens the potential depth and intensity of human experience. Although life is far from impossible in the visual chaos of the modern city, the same daily action could take on new meaning if carried out in a more vivid setting. Potentially, the city is in itself the powerful symbol of a complex society. If visually well set forth, it can also have strong expressive meaning.

For Lynch the link between the evaluation of the purely formal character of a city, and an evaluation capable of integrating those features into the unified calculations which govern an urbanistic project will be accomplished through a sociological agency, and the physical surroundings shall be evaluated on the basis of the consent of society to certain typical conformations.

It is these group images, exhibiting consensus among significant numbers, that interest city planners who aspire to model an environment that will be used by many people . . . The first order of business will be what may be called the "public images," the common mental pictures carried by large numbers of a city's inhabitants. . . .

This most interesting aspect of the research carried out by Lynch contains in itself a limitation, since there exists the legitimate fear that through any kind of quantification the original ideal may be lost. In this way we should suddenly find ourselves once again being obliged to collaborate with those of other disciplines, while possessing no instruments with which to do so. It is therefore necessary to reconfirm that a constant and qualified contribution on the part of the urban planner, in every phase of the plan, can take place only within the framework of a common discipline, which accepts the condition of a reciprocal respect among the different interests concerned.

The method proposed by Lynch—that of the quantification of morphological values—can serve this end, provided one does not lose sight of its character as an instrument. The ability of the urban architect remains one of aesthetic intuition, to which every "scientific" formulation, in the sense of the natural sciences, seems alien. This means that there should be no weakening in the possibility of the formal choices simply to appeal to wider concepts. The formal choices should not only reabsorb the sense of economic and social choices, but impose themselves as general conceptions of that which must be the state of man, the adjustment of society. Such images may be, peremptorily, the expression of these convictions, beyond their functional results. Yet there is one way, above all, in which the creator of spatial forms can record the process of planning. This is by the offer of new spatial concepts, or new urban architectural elements, which economists, sociologists, and topographists must be made aware of and must evaluate in the light of the means available. The architect is a creator who accepts the values of those who collaborate in the planning, but who does not apostatize from his own role of proposer and producer of solutions. By this means both the urban and architectural ideals discover their precise means of fulfillment.

In its renewal of the arts of topology, architectural composition is presented as an authentically morphological process which constantly enriches the proliferation and constellation of those elements which collaborate in the physical consistency, the physiognomy of the city; a process which unceasingly renews the economic picture, benevolently subverting the rigid values of other arts by offering them new objects for study.

To the pedagogue who tends to assert, on the basis of his own objective experiences, the "best" solution for the school, the architect offers, as only he is able to do, a new organizational solution. The process of advising, therefore, finds new strength on new foundations; neither does it ever prove enclosed within the impassable frontiers of perfectionism.

The new architectural objects evoked by the urban planner, in adherence with the over-all planning process, can therefore be totally new and unite both the micro- and macro-urban ideals. The poverty of ideas in the usual normative instruments, such as the creation of zones, or the barriers of height, etc., can have, as their logical result, a coincidence with their poverty in practice. Accordingly, the "objective" terrain of "proved and indubitable facts" that permit quantitative and freely exchanged evaluations among the various disciplines, must be abandoned not only in response to the exigencies of formality, but because new facts are proved and take their place among the convictions, the likes and the dislikes, of the citizens; and even here the social sciences can offer their indispensable evaluation.

The activity of the architect, who organizes and conforms spatial solutions, is in this way reduced to its unified essentials. The dimensional steps attained through the means of "city buildings" such as those envisaged by Tange and Le Corbusier, lose their discriminatory character. The observation periods for a city and a building fuse one with the other; there no longer exists any solution of continuity so profound that "compact time" does not impair and conclude by revealing itself a fragment of that total time, in which only forms can acquire genuine meaning.

It is clear then that a building cannot be isolated from the environment which surrounds it; and this does not merely include the landscape which visually embraces the place where the building is erected; but also that unity of images born of the most diverse associations, all of which are legitimate by reason of the serrated logic of sensation. The most ordinary and ill-defined house in London, Milan, or Tokyo exists and has its meaning by virtue of a complex superimposition of architectural, atmospheric, and indigenous characteristics which we must not and cannot disassociate from it. Environments existing only in the imagination, but not for this reason less real, and which take form around all architecture that we observe, can occasionally provide the effective city in which that particular architecture can develop. Without loss in significance of continuity and social interrelations, we nonetheless today witness the development of fast-held links stretching over miles and over centuries: and this is not a case of superimposition or subtleties, but of indestructible component parts of that specific image that culture can enrich but not create.

No specific culture but rather a keen sensibility, the individual's awareness of his own participation, is required to understand that in the image of the *Campidoglio* or of the *Piazza del Popolo* there is an interplay of the complex, synthetic image of all Rome. It is precisely because of this that the reproduced image is fatally inadequate. More damaging even than the specific inadequacy of the intermediary employed (drawing, photograph, model, reconstruction) is the absence of the references through which that image lives. Thus it is that the building transported and rebuilt elsewhere—even if the selfsame bricks are one by one reset —or the building whose environs are razed and then replaced by new, suffers intrinsic change. Violence done to one component part of the image of each such building is violence done to the whole image, to its every part, physically intact though it may remain. And it is of extreme importance that these considerations, fortunately commonplace and obvious (even if too often overlooked) should serve to demonstrate the impossibility of discriminating between urban and architectural image, an impossibility which is, however, not so commonplace or obvious. The aforesaid considerations in fact help to make clear the manner in which each single piece of architecture lives and is true in its relation to the city (or to the ideal community of works to which it is bound by associations of images), with the result that the city is not appreciable as form except in its concretization into actual streets, into single works of architecture, into details.

G. B. Piranesi. *Piazza del Popolo*, Rome, 1750.

G. Valadier. *Project for Piazza del Popolo*, Rome. Late eighteenth century.

G. Brustolo. *Election of the Doge in the Piazza San Marco*, Venice, 1763.

The true plan, the plan giving a city its identity and countenance, is that which in some way or other involves the quality of the single constructional works. In at least the vast majority of cases this is a theoretical aim, but it does not therefore alter the fact that the town planner should look for those instruments that will allow him to approach it ever more nearly.

The nature of such instruments can certainly lead to surprises. In his description of New York, in *When the Cathedrals Were White,* Le Corbusier describes the flux between streets and avenues with their plethora of numbers and left and right turn-offs, and conludes:

It will be felt that I delay over an anatomical detail of the city and that I attach a great deal of importance to it. But it is not at all a question of an anatomical detail, but rather the essential biological structure of the city. A question of fundamental principle.

For Le Corbusier the orthogonal pattern becomes a decisive fact and, in the interests of the architectonic quality of each building, considerably more meaningful than the formal intentionality of the single constructions.

What Le Corbusier denounces is the inadequacy of a particular point of view to concentrate on the single building and its decorative details in such a way that the great urban realities, through the intrinsic force of their rationality, might have the capacity to determine the quality and style of each work of architecture within them. It is important that the over-all pattern, which is modifiable by the authors of the plan, generate not only macro-urban images, where the yardstick lies in the dimension of the skyline, but also micro-urban images, in scale with the dimensions of the buildings. This legacy of riches of our architectonic culture should not be misused. But when the sole instrument for topographical delineation has shown itself insufficient to guarantee beyond a certain point the quality of the total image, then we are in duty bound to seek other instruments which will add to its effectiveness. The instrument of sociological mediation is undoubtedly the most stimulating way of asserting a functional content of the formal value, to the point where only the formally successful image proves to be also the fully functional. In this case, of course, the image is no longer the inevitable correlative of correct planning but is an ingredient of it, with all its degrees of freedom. Thus there remains a danger—that of confusing enjoyment

of the image with its total value, which would lead to a utilitarian, or hedonistic, conception of the art in question.

Indeed the enjoyment shown by society in respect to various formal solutions is in fact characterized by a pronounced unreliability of taste. Even if the responsibility for this is not at all, in this writer's opinion, attributable to the teaching of the history of art, it is certainly true, as Walter Gropius wrote, that at the present time "there is no natural, fervid response to the works of modern artists attempting to solve contemporary problems in contemporary ways." We would add that this retarded state of public education in artistic experimentation is today perhaps simply accentuated, since it really proves to be a constant characteristic of the process of spiritual improvement in man that innovating forces form together in spearheads, in limited but penetrating projections. In architecture, and especially town-planning, this means that we should be on our guard against legitimizing only the pleasing, successful solutions. The city that Le Corbusier proposed to the mayor of Algiers caused him the risk of arrest; and it seems quite possible that at least at that time the mayor was truly representative of the wishes of the majority of the citizenry. I like to think that a similar solution, even if then put into effect wholly against majority wishes, could today be the pride of a community, could be an inseparable part of the idea—the image—that each citizen forms of his own town.

In this we find again the same kind of caution that we earlier felt obliged to recommend with regard to the judgments of the social sciences in the field of town-planning. The difficulty is identical, and from it there comes a reconfirmation of the impossibility of tying down future plans to those evaluations which, by their very nature, hark back to already experimented solutions, that is to say, to solutions belonging to the past.

The most important task facing the architect today is that of applying himself to an authentic, morphological renewal, in the sense that the functional invention is realized and occurs in the formal invention, in the image; and of bringing about such renewal by accepting the dialogue with the disciplines that are complementary to architecture and town-planning, without losing his own autonomy and his own special brand of inventive capacity. We have stated the difficulty there would seem to be in such a task, threatened as it is by the apparent contradiction between exchange and freedom.

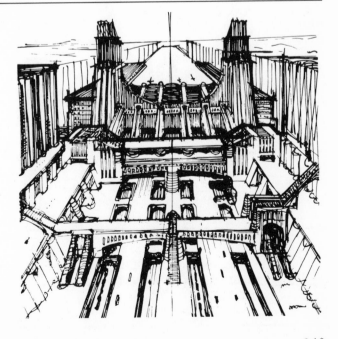

Ludwig Meidner. *A City in the Moonlight*, 1912.

Paul Klee, *The Flowing City*, Bern, 1927.

Antonio Sant'Elia. Station for commuting and landing strip, preliminary study for the "Futurist City," 1914.

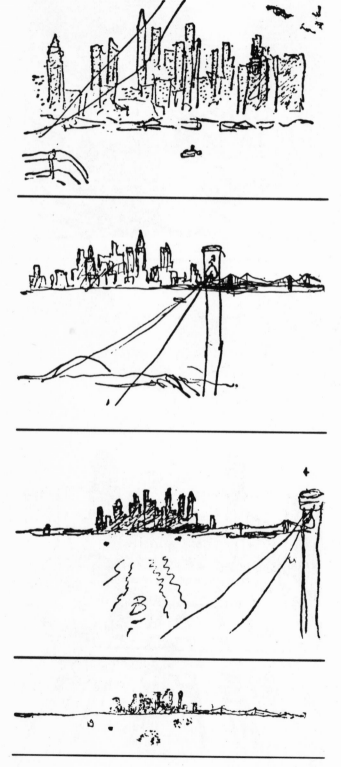

But at the same time we have attempted to show that such a contradiction exists only when the two terms are distorted into "dependence" and "arbitrary will."

There is indeed antinomy between dependence of the spatial project on other disciplines and yielding to their evaluations *ex post facto,* and "arbitrary will." This is so over and above precise economic and sociological verification, and is unavoidable, but resemblances also exist. At a time when the most varied disciplines assert a derivation from architecture, the task of which is to "construct," to "structure," that is, to join and unite the parts, it would be paradoxical for architecture itself to lose its structural modality and to reduce itself to the physical embodiment of heterodox models or to stylistic disgressions.

Defeat of the antinomy can take place in the area of interdisciplinary exchange and of disciplinary autonomy. This, however, does not mean that the inherent antinomy can be overcome easily or taken for granted. As with every dialectical process, it will take place through successive syntheses which historically-arrived-at conditions will never allow to be considered final. The dynamism that we feel should be demanded of and produced in architecture has its source in this revolutionary and necessarily ascending process.

Thus, today, sociological mediation, as brilliantly fostered by Lynch, and on the other hand the creative, dynamic attitudes of personalities such as Le Corbusier, Aalto, Kahn, and Tange, appear to represent the poles between which resolution of the antinomy in question is both necessary and possible. Significantly the common background of these experiences firmly supports the hypothesis of progress, and revision of existing social structures.

Lynch's strict profession of faith in democratic tenets, and the Utopianism of the other masters we have mentioned, confirm in us the conviction that it is the complicity and imaginative gifts of the citizenry that have to be brought to bear. No renewal of the city is possible without a renewal also of its way of life, and the latter is possible only by welcoming its most generous aspirations. Although it may be an illusion to think that society can be modified by a town plan or a work of architecture, it is an outright danger to renounce all effort to plan for the future. It is therefore a question of the architect reconciling with the whole man. His task does not end with architecture but goes farther, through a continuity of professional and extra-professional, public, and private attitudes. Only thus is it possible to plan for the future both as architect and as citizen in equal measure; and, in particular, it is thus possible to plan for future architecture and city without being assailed by the doubts and remorse of empty words and romancing.

These observations take on relevance when we consider the significant and valid role of the image in architecture. Indeed the pregnant task of the architect is to imagine and construct the physical forms in which every social change and progress will take place.

In the Middle Ages and also in the period of Renaissance Platonism, God, or in any case a supernatural authority, was the point of departure for the prototypes from which all possible images were born. Baroque society aimed to supply new references for the artistic image. But while it dislodged the prototype from the empyreal realm and set it in the temporal, the Baroque image still enjoyed the total remoteness of absolute authority. The monarchic ideal, whether ecclesiastic or lay, transmuted the conventionality of the model into a provisional absolute. Baroque art, though infinitely rich in images and sentiments, had as its aim explicit propaganda for power: the gardens of Versailles brought their task and meaning to a climax in a brilliant allegory of regal omnipotence.

The Baroque prototype was less accessible than that of the Middle Ages, even if set in the "existent," inasmuch as the culture through which it could be reached and appreciated was the jealously guarded heritage of an elite.

Today our wish is that the "naked existent" possess an ideal significance, within the grasp of all and shared on as wide a scale as possible. As written in *Casabella*, with reference to matters concerning the plan of the metropolitan area of Milan, but in words that I believe can be extended to every city and every country: "It is my wish that today the image should reflect the consensus of free democratic men, who have no need of transcendental sustenance but who have not renounced imagination; I wish to see a Milan more free from Medieval prototypes and more concrete than Baroque allegories; a city that can be touched, breathed, measured, and not merely comforted by statistics and instrumentalism, but expressing the faith of the total man, who is rational, sensitive and imaginative."

Saul Steinberg. *Galleria in Milan,* from *The Passport,* 1954.

(*Opposite page*) Le Corbusier. *Au revoir, New York!,* from *When the Cathedrals Were White,* 1936.

P. A. MICHELIS

FORM IN ARCHITECTURE: IMITATION AND ABSTRACTION

Painting and sculpture—as the eminently imitative arts they are, or at least were, until quite recently —had a dual problem to contend with in presenting a form: that of imitating the model correctly and convincingly, and lending it a characteristic attitude that would at the same time be artistically interesting. That is to say, they had to solve a problem of both representation and presentation of an object. The latter is undoubtedly the more difficult if the notion of presentation is to be extended beyond the model's characteristic attitude (which is usually unnatural) to the idea it suggests, so that it may become a symbolic form.

Today, with imitation almost completely eliminated, with subject and idea banished from the work, we have reached a point at which these arts no longer seem to represent anything, but merely to present things—and things for the most part little or not at all related to natural models. The object of present-day painting and sculpture being the work itself, their presentations may not only be utterly unnatural and unexpected, but may also be completely abstract patterns. Painting and sculpture have thus drawn closer to architecture and music, which have ever been free of the need to imitate and represent natural objects, and have from their very inception been "abstract" arts.

True, architecture did not in the past wholly reject imitation: the Egyptian column, the Corinthian capital, and a host of decorative motifs, testify, in the language of its morphology, that "in the beginning was the plant." Indeed, architecture has presented even anthropomorphous supports. Nonetheless, at bottom, architecture is an abstract art which has always created original forms, deriving from static laws, laws indispensable to a structure which must—whether with stone, wood, or any other material—cover space to serve man's needs. If architecture cast a glance at the world outside itself, it did so, not in order to represent the plants and human bodies it imitated for their own sake, but in order to give to each constructive element an expression symbolic of the work it performs. Architecture has not, therefore, merely imitated natural objects: it has raised them to tectonic symbols.

Why did architecture choose mainly the plant and the human body as the symbolic medium of its morphology? Obviously, the principle of the metaphor led it there: a phytomorphic column flowers and rises like a plant, or as if it were a plant; an anthropomorphic column stands upright like a man, or as if it were a man. But how should a Caryatid, carrying the burdens of an entablature, stand? Or a phytomorphic column carrying an architrave? The answer to the problem of the attitude or "poise" of these architectural members will also solve the problem of how any member—any vault, or beam, or caisson, which has no counterpart in nature, but which stems from purely structural needs—should be presented. For if such members are to suggest a metaphor, they must be so presented as to display their ability to excel their technical function, and so to acquire a higher significance. Only then can they become symbolic tectonic forms.

The fact that the Egyptians painted the sunken panels of their ceilings blue and interspersed them with stars and flying vultures clearly shows their intention of making the flat ceiling symbolize the sky. How would this metaphor have been conveyed without the stars and vultures? To us any ceiling in some way represents an artificial sky, provided its beams are not too obviously massive and it does not appear to rest too clumsily on its supports. Yet even a Byzantine dome, despite its spheric shape, will fail to symbolize the sky if it rests heavily and clumsily on the arches that carry it. The problem of attitude, therefore, concerns the coordination of the members, as well as the form of the whole edifice.

To say of a building that its walls rise perpendicularly, that its columns stand upright and carry horizontal beams, arches, or domes that bridge the voids; or that they form a flat or a domed roof; or that its façade is a succession of masses and voids divided off by cornices, is to give but one aspect of the picture it presents: its schematic geometrical design. A building's very façade must display an attitude, a characteristic poise, as if to proclaim by its style what is being enacted behind it, very much like a face revealing a person's character. A cogent illustration of this is provided by the Parthenon, in which the columns are not absolutely vertical but of pyramidal inclination; the stylobate and architrave are curved; there is a total absence of straight lines, whether vertical or horizontal; also the rhythmic colonnade grows denser at the extremities, so that masses and voids, cornices and friezes tend to suggest a purpose beyond the mere construction. Again, the façades of Baroque buildings express their dynamism by inward and outward curvatures. Every architectural work, inasmuch as it has style, has its own artistic poise.

The artistic "poise" or attitude of the Parthenon, for instance, springs from the Classical Greek conception of form, with its triadic articulation of base, trunk, and crown, in an art which was anthropocentric. The Parthenon's forms, though by their poise they counteract the geometric scheme induced by their system of construction, nonetheless preserve this scheme faithfully and do not betray it. They merely transfigure, or spiritualize it, as happens indeed with the works of any art style worthy the name—Byzantine, Gothic, Renaissance, contemporary. Briefly, there are two aspects to a structure's attitude: the technical and the artistic.

Technically, the forms must follow the presiding system of construction. Thus, in Classical architecture which employs the system of lintel on columns and builds loose constructions without mortar that balance by their own weight, the columns must on principle be vertical, the beams horizontal, and their dimensions such as to stand up structurally to the function they perform. However, the column's cross section (in ancient times arrived at empirically, and today based on our scientific knowledge of the strength of materials) is a purely quantitative matter and is not sufficient to give the column form. The question of its profile must still be determined. The right proportions of its form (today as always) is a purely artistic consideration, in other words a qualitative matter. The architect may, without altering the statically necessary area of the cross section, so regulate its proportions and its form, that the architectural member becomes elegant, or powerful, or graceful, as the case may be; it appears not as tortured, but as having triumphed over its static task, without yet ceasing to perform it. The whole edifice will then proclaim that it not only stands according to the laws of gravity and of statics, but also, that having properly exploited those laws, it has passed beyond its functional scope to express the triumph of its spirit over matter. Thus presented, it will leave the spectator's mind free to grasp the metaphor and see the column as a flowering plant; the Ionic volutes as an elastic spring support; the temple as the dwelling place of the gods; the Byzantine dome as the sky's vault; and the interior of the cathedral as a place in which the omnipresent spirit of the One and only God "hovers and resides."

But what principle guides the choice of the profile of each member—specifically, let us say, in the unnatural inclination of the Doric column? Or, again generally, in the peculiar coordination and attitude of the whole Doric temple, which at a first glance seems to be contradicting its own statically rational coordination and attitude? Perhaps the example of the Erechtheum Caryatid, which is both statue and architectural member, will help us to determine the question (Fig. 1).

The Caryatid carries the entablature and must not succumb to its burden. Its cross section must naturally be adequate to withstand the weight. From the artistic point of view its attitude must show that the carrying figure bears its load comfortably, so that it both accomplishes its technical function and transcends it to become a symbol. Now what do the Caryatids symbolize? Vitruvius believed that they are performing a servile duty because, according to the myth he tells, they were enslaved maidens who are thus symbolically punished to eternity by being made to support the entablature. The myth, however, only misleads the spectator (as does the subject of a painting), for it does not allow him to contemplate the forms impartially and realize that artistically the Caryatids symbolize the very reverse of what Vitruvius relates. They symbolize that the carrying members of Classical architecture act like living organisms, able to rise and move, and thus achieve the conquest of spirit over the weight of matter. The work they perform is not, therefore, of a servile nature, but a free duty discharged seemingly on their own initiative. The Caryatids, like the Canephori, perform a sacred task, upholding the entablature of the temple's porch as an offering to the gods. At least that is how they appear, and only when one has contemplated them in that spirit, may one refer to Vitruvius' myth and realize that these maidens, even had they once been slaves, are now liberated because dedicated to the service of the divinities. The myth then acquires a sublime content and becomes an artistic allegory.

By what attitude or poise do the Caryatids succeed in giving this impression? Their bodies seem to rest on one foot. The other foot, although it touches the ground, seems to be only momentarily resting there, because the knee above it is bent. We thus feel, that had their bodies rested on both feet, they could have supported even greater burdens. Consequently, the maidens are not making their utmost effort and are not being tortured. Moreover, the bent knee implies potential movement: they seem about to take the next step, but the imaginary line from outthrust knee to bust throws the body slightly backward, as if suddenly arrested in its forward movement. The whole figure thus appears to have only just stopped in its progress. With the knee outthrust toward the axis of symmetry of the porch, the supporting foot is brought to the edge and, together with the folds of the dress, creates a sense of stability at the dangerous point. At the same time, viewed from the side, the figures seem able to step rhythmically together if once they start. In order not to appear to crush the female figures, the entablature is lighter than usual, with a series of indentations in place of the frieze. It is carried by the heads of the maidens on an intervening ornamental calathus, a sort of echinus. They might indeed be Athena's Canephori carrying baskets of flowers on their heads. Their outthrust knees, moreover, make

Fig. 1. Caryatids of the Erechtheum, Acropolis, Athens.

their bodies appear wider below and narrower above; that is to say, they acquire diminution and entasis. The curve of the body, which raises its center of gravity, suggests readiness to rise. The attitude of the Caryatids, then, presents the "fertile moment" of their action. It implies that, poised as they are, they are ready to raise the entablature, and thus like living human beings, they are performing their work by their own volition and overcoming the inertia of matter and gravity by the force of spirit. The Caryatids can thus stand there to eternity.

The merit of the attitude of the Erechtheum Caryatids becomes at once apparent when compared with the many Renaissance, Baroque, or Neoclassic Caryatids, which are presented supporting the entablature either with their hands, head bent as though in shame, or on their shoulders, like Telamones. They thus give the impression of groaning under their burden and of being incapable of raising their load or of rising freely.

The principle of the fertile moment again explains the form of the Doric column and its position in the temple as a whole (Fig. 2). The column's diminution and entasis help to make it appear as if stretching upwards in overcoming the burden it supports, without ceasing to act as it takes over the load in its abacus and echinus, whose curve, in turn, suggests a corresponding entasis and upward straining. But the column is not alone; it belongs to a whole. And in this context, its inclination toward the sekos and toward the axis of symmetry of the sides ranks it as a participating member which contributes to the pyramidal tapering and consequent upward sweep of the whole. Again, the colonnade, by becoming denser at the corners, reinforces the temple at these points so that it resists the thrusts of the gable roof. And again, with the curvatures of the stylobate and of the architrave showing that they refuse to succumb to bending, the whole temple strains upwards raising its center of gravity, as does each column by its own entasis. The part is thus explained by the form of the whole and vice versa; the temple appears at the fertile moment of its action, that is to say, at the moment at which it overcomes gravity and stands free by its own forces, proclaiming the victory of spirit over matter. Its form seems to be taking shape all the time, for though petrified in eternity, it is yet continuously in action.

The so-called optical corrections of the temple also contribute to this effect. Vitruvius misguidedly thought them to be inverse illusions which aimed at restoring the temple's geometrical rectilinearity. In fact, they are refinements of form, the artistic devices of an architecture which is repulsed by rigid geometrical formality and seeks to give its work the pulsation of life.

Fig. 2. Parthenon, Acropolis, Athens. Photo Magnum.

The fertile moment has ever been a principle of architectural morphology, although it has not always found so energetic and delicate an expression. For instance, the Egyptian column as compared with the Greek column, would not seem to be an expression of the fertile moment, but merely the passive imitation of a plant. But because diminution and entasis are inherent qualities in the plant, the column possesses them, too, although in this case the diminution and entasis may fail to correspond as they should with the strictly tectonic function of the column. The Egyptian architect did not see the column as a purely tectonic element, as an abstract technical form. He saw it rather as an imitation of an actual natural model, by which to give a structural member a form and an attitude free of the servility of pure load-bearing. The bell-like capital of the Egyptian column has a small abacus, so that the calyxes on the capital appear to be a free ending under the architrave (Fig. 3). The column thus seems to be growing from the earth and to flower high up on its stalk without supporting anything. The roof appears only just to touch it, seeming almost suspended over the massive columns. The volume of the columns is in itself sufficient to suggest their endurance, while they are redeemed from their massiveness by their phytomorphic figuration, their coloring, and the fertile moment of their action through which they appear as vast artificial plants in bloom.

The formation of an architectural member is, therefore, morphologically guided by two poles of contemplation: imitation and abstraction. Imitation attempts to refer the static function of an architectural member to some natural model with a kindred function. It thus introduces a metaphor while borrowing the forms themselves from outside. Abstraction attempts to derive the morphology of the architectural members from their structural function, from within, and to express the forces at work within the members. The metaphorical reference to the natural indeterminate forms is only subtly suggested, as in the fluting of the Doric column or the ribbing of the Gothic vault. Where, however, architecture refuses every imitation or metaphor, as happens in contemporary "functional architecture," all that remains to determine its form is its structural function. Hence, the motto of contemporary architecture: "form follows function." But even in this extreme case, there is still—after the cross section has been determined by the science of statics—the artistic problem of the form's proportions and attitude. The problem chiefly involves the principle of the fertile moment: the moment at which the architectural form, by natural static, shall display its dynamism. That is to say, it shall display the movement of the forces operative within those forms by means of a characteristic attitude of their action, leaving the spectator's imagination free to introduce the suggested metaphor.

Now, how can an abstract tectonic form make the movement of the forces at work within it

Fig. 3. Hypostyle Hall, Ramesseum, Thebes. Photo G. E. Kidder Smith.

perceptible to the spectator? How is it that, even in the Greek column which is not purely phyto-morphic, we are aware of its diminution and entasis as the expression of the inner active forces? German aestheticians have called Greek architecture "muscular," because its members stretch and react, as do the muscles of the human body; and because our experience of how the muscles curve makes us aware of what the curves mean in architectural members. Another explanation is that of the spectator's symbolic empathy (*Einfühlung*), which maintains that we look at the forms as if they were acting like ourselves. Theodor Lipps, basing himself on this theory, evolved his "aesthetic mechanics" which perceives action and movement in every line, even in those of a geometrical diagram. Thus, even the proportions of a form begin to acquire a special significance. The more height predominates over width, the greater the upward straining implied; predominance of width, on the other hand, expresses inertia and serenity. There is certainly some truth in all these theories, despite their often undue preoccupation with lines and words which have little reference either to the functional expediency of a form—which the spectator, even if vaguely, divines—or to man's inherent "sense of statics"—which informs him, by intuition, how bearing and load is realized in order to erect an edifice so that it can react to gravitation and to the forces of pressure, bending, and traction.

Of course, it is not sufficient for an edifice merely to stand; it must also show that it stands firmly and comfortably and has overcome its technical effort. It is precisely to these effects that the refinements of Classical Greek architecture contributed. From the point of view of statics, they are meaningless, but artistically they are devices of the greatest importance. Far from conflicting with the statical requirements, however, they are perfectly in keeping with them: upward tapering subtracts from the column's mass precisely where this is statically superfluous; entasis at no point allows the column to exceed the diameter of its base, so that above all, the columns seem firmly seated; the inclination of the columns does not weaken their stability and by becoming denser at the corners the columns seem at the same time to resist the thrusts. A refined science of statics may well arrive at conclusions and the technical form approximate the artistic. This is precisely what Pier Luigi Nervi has recently claimed.

In the statical study of a building, the cross section of an element is not made bigger than necessary. It is kept within the margin of strength that will prevent the material's fatigue and ensure the safety of the structure. The "coefficient of safety" as regards the material affects to a large extent the expression: the bigger this factor the more bulky the structure. However, the progress of the science of statics and of our knowledge of materials has allowed the reduction of the coefficient of safety and the diminution of the cross section. So also has the discovery of more resistant materials, like prestressed concrete. It follows then that statics aim at the highest results with the minimum waste of material.

Architecture, however, which must also aim at aesthetically perfect results, is not always guided by this principle alone. The Doric column, for instance, could have been made more slender if the drums had rested upon their whole surface and not only on a peripheral crown a few centimeters wide. Yet, it is this very waste of material that gives the Doric temple its severity of style. Nor, strictly speaking, is this waste, since in a statically loose structure like the Doric temple the increase of weight by means of mass lends stability.

Let us now turn to the form of the structural element. Here the science of statics seeks the best form for the function of the particular element. For the columns the cylindrical form is preferred as being the safest; its diameter and height are calculated to exclude any risk of flection or overturning. If we consider here how the drums of the Doric column rest on their base, we shall see that the column's inclination approaches the danger point without reaching it.

Naturally the attitude and form of each member to a great extent determine the over-all system of construction. In Greek architecture, the elements balance by their own weight; they are tortured with pressure and bending; and owing to the post and lintel system of construction all the forces are directed vertically. In Roman, Byzantine, and Gothic architecture, in which the stones adhere with mortar, the elements are again tortured with pressure and bending; but with the system of vaults, domes, and flying buttresses, the forces are directed diagonally as well as vertically. Only in contemporary architecture of reinforced concrete are the structures all of a piece, with rigidly cohering elements, so that in being tortured with pressure, bending, and traction, the forces run vertically, diagonally, and horizontally.

In the reinforced concrete construction, it is easy to see how the statical calculations give a form proportions that correspond to its function. The cross section of an arch, for instance, widens at the base if it is a cantilever arch; it diminishes at the base if the arch is two-hinged; and it diminishes both at the base and in the middle if the arch is three-hinged. But such formation does not suffice to create the aesthetic form of the arch. The limits set by the coefficient of safety—which the cross section cannot exceed—always allow for the play of a relatively lighter or heavier form. If such play becomes excessive, it both endangers the structure and makes it appear precarious. In other words, the form of a member falls within the general economy of the whole; an economy which, over and above the statical balance, is concerned also with the expression in a certain style. Thus we find that the same technical means and the same system of construction produced the archaic Doric order, the lighter Classical Doric, as well as the Ionic order which is essentially graceful.

Hence it follows that there is not only one true form, as Nervi would seem to claim, nor can the science of statics alone determine an architectural form, unless at the same time it determine what this form will express, whether, let us say, the slender grace of the Ionic proportions, or the grandeur of the Doric. The architect, like the musician, must tune his work to a scale and be possessed by an intention which seeks expression. Beyond the economy of statics, composition presides over and directs the former to a creative purpose. The dialectics of the various forms in a work of architecture, like the various notes in music, are directed to the dialectics of a melody. Indeed, each architectural form serves a purpose, a practical need, while simultaneously it joins the others in singing the melody of the work.

In the Doric temple neither column, nor architrave, nor stylobate stands alone; all three collaborate. They set up a dialogue among them assisting one another not only to stand upright, but also to make their action perceptible to the spectator. A single column is not the same as one standing in the rhythmic row along the sides of the temple, where it also carries the entablature. When it stands singly, it is not a symbol of support, although by its mere vertical balance it may be a symbol of victory. Furthermore, in a work of architecture the dialectics of the members become complex because of the suggestions of the morphological details, the moldings, the lighting, the color, so that these alone may suffice to modify the real proportions and lend apparent weight to what is slight, or vice versa. An Ionic column with bulky moldings at the base, for instance, will lose its grace.

This complex dialectical economy always operates between some definite relations of the supporting and the supported members. In the Classical orders, supporting and supported members are harmoniously balanced, without the one exceeding the other. In the Byzantine style, on the other hand, the supported members appear to predominate over the supports, as though the church began at the vaults and the dome, and the columns carried loads greater than their strength. This contrast is redeemed, however, by the elevated arches and the smooth vault surfaces, which are two-dimensional and seemingly dematerialized. In the Gothic style, this relationship is reversed and it is the supports which are given predominance. The ribbed piers soar upwards to resolve themselves into the ribbings of the cross vault. A carrying skeleton is thus created in which the forces are grouped and the walls become noncarrying screens, replaced for the most part by stained glass. Thus the Gothic is an analytical articulation, in contrast to the synthetic articulation of Byzantine architecture where the skeleton is obliterated and mass predominates.

In neither Classical nor Byzantine architecture is the principle of the fertile moment abandoned. In the Byzantine, in which mass predominates, the elevated arches and dematerialized shells of the domes counter the predominance of the carried members over the carrying. In the Gothic cathedral in which the skeleton predominates, the disposition of the flying buttresses around the exterior of the cathedral leaves the tall piers in the interior apparently without buttressing, thus creating the impression of precarious balance restored at the last minute, as that of a dancer momentarily poised on one foot. Auguste Choisy remarks that the amazement thus caused in the spectator is not a pleasing reaction. Yet the aesthetic appeal of the Gothic structure lies mainly in this very feat, in the fertile moment presenting the daring action which jeopardizes yet succeeds in retaining the structural balance. Certainly amazement is not a genuine artistic sensation, particularly when it derives from the balance of an architectural work, but the dynamic conception of balance in the Medieval styles, which succeeded the static conception of the Classical orders, brought a certain intensity to the fertile moment.

When balance sometimes reaches the point of a dangerous acrobatic feat and the display of the technical achievement becomes an end in itself, the fertile moment produces not merely amazement, but also anxiety, as when we are watching a risky acrobatic performance with bated breath. Contemporary architecture with its vast technical possibilities, is full of examples of such technical achievements displayed in acrobatics. Enormous cantilevers, cubes on posts floating in space, and other improbable structures which are often bereft of both practical value and elegance make little appeal to the spectator. However, there is a justification for the present predilection of architecture for singularity. This is the first time in the history of architecture that monolithic, continuous structures, with rigidly cohering elements constituting—technically at least—a homogeneous entity, have come into being.

The most important expression of this entity is found in the delicate, self-supporting shell structures, like the vast shell of the CNIT building in Paris (Fig. 4). This rests at three points on the ground, from which three fans spring to meet at their peak, and so together form a single dome. Supporting and supported members merge indistinguishably. The scale of the work is provided only by the edges of the intersecting vaults which form the surface of each fan and by the glass screens and fore-structures. The curve of the dome, however, is so balanced as to appear to spring from the earth rising to bridge the gap. Its attitude reveals the fertile moment of its action. A vast exotic foliage appears to cover the space.

In these contemporary forms, the attitude of the fertile moment is again of the highest significance, and now for the special reason that with the inherent continuity of the elements and the resultant inner unity of the structure, the architect almost ceases to seek the expression of their unity by external artistic means. All previous architectural forms tended to suggest by their dialectics that unity is restored in the variety of their members, at least externally. In the Doric temple, for instance, the architrave is obviously a separate element which rests on the columns by its weight and the column itself consists of superposed drums. Despite the effort to conceal the joints of these drums and to give the impression that the column is monolithic, technically each drum is just as separate an element as the column and the architrave. Only artistically do they form a unit. Classical architecture, indeed, exploits constructional divisibility even in the morphology of its members, so as to emphasize the autonomy of each. That is why intermediate, transitional elements such as various moldings separate the column from the architrave, the abacus from the echinus, or the architrave from the frieze. This tendency to differentiate in the usual triadic Classical morphology of base, trunk, and crown, weakens in the medieval styles like the Byzantine and the Gothic, which resort to more continuous forms, as though of indivisible, unbroken construction. The ribbings of the Gothic piers, particularly in the later period, spring from the ground and continue without interruption to the cross vaults. The Byzantine vaults, free of ribbing, appear like the continuous surface of a shell. Hence, medieval morphology is closer to the modern architecture, which has, at least technically, realized the dream of producing monolithic continuous structures. Now, what are the artistic consequences of this technical achievement?

We are passing from the "aesthetics of differentiation" to the "aesthetics of integration." The form ceases to be an assemblage of parts which achieve balance either by gravity or by being jointed, and becomes a nondivisible entity. From the morphological point of view, the language of architecture no longer forms words with the letters of the alphabet, but presents them by symbols, as the ancient Egyptian script. Each symbol is a word, each word a symbol. In these contemporary structures the fertile moment no longer refers to the association of support and burden, but to their form as a continuous, nondeformable whole. Indeed, "resistance through form" is the motto of contemporary statics, as applied to its pioneering shell-like structures. For clearly, in such works the form contributes to the stability of the massive, continuous structure and so long as the form is preserved, continues nondeformable, the solidity of the whole structure is also preserved.

Today we have a development unprecedented in the annals of architecture: with the use of reinforced concrete a form may be erected upside down. A cylindrical shell, for example, may be suspended in reverse, or a cone of great dimensions placed with its point facing down. An instance of the latter is offered by Oscar Niemeyer in Brasilia (Fig. 5). Or still a cylinder may be placed horizontally, as a tube in aqueducts or bridges.

This does not mean that we may reverse any and every concrete construction, but it does mean that it would be possible to do so, if we provided for the necessity statically. It also means that to the spectator's imagination, the architectural form is, to a certain extent, liberated from the laws of gravity. He can thus contemplate it in and for itself, as a closed entity, nondeformable as a sphere or a box, which retain their shape whichever way we look at them. In Classical architecture, such reversals were technically impossible, since the structure achieved balance by its own weight, and rose pyramidally, tapering at the top to show that it becomes progressively lighter and so overcomes gravity. The morphology conformed with this. An inverted Doric column is no less unthinkable than an inverted Doric temple. True, the Mycenaean column tapered below and spread above, but this was probably because it developed from wooden constructions in which the columns were linked above with an architrave, as are table legs which may also be reversed without being deformed. The Egyptian column, however, which cannot even remotely be associated with wooden links, displays upon its bell-shaped capital a small abacus which gives it a free termination, so that it appears to be flowering unimpeded. Here, there can be no thought of reversing the form, or of resistance through form. Only the level floating ceiling resembles an inverse image of the floor, so that the stereometric enclosure of space may seem like a reversible box whose sides mirror one another respectively.

Fig. 4. CNIT Building, Paris. Architects: Camelot, de Mailly, Zehrfuss. Engineers: Balency and Schuhl, Boussiron, Coignet.

Fig. 5. Congress Building, Brasilia. Architect: Oscar Niemeyer. Photo Jean Biaugeaud.

The vision of a building upside down is realized only when we see its reflection in water, as in the case of this façade in the Alhambra shown here (Fig. 6). This picture appeals to us, despite its vertical symmetry, which is always intolerable and especially so in architecture. For us, the axis of symmetry is the erect human figure, and gravity is exercised vertically so that the upper parts must appear lighter, or else obviously heavier. In this latter instance, its balance will appear precarious, but interesting. The horizontal axis is the axis of immobility and dissection. If the reflection of the façade appeals to us despite its vertical symmetry to the real one, it is, firstly, because we see it as an imaginary reflection, a two-dimensional image, while the actual façade is in space and is three-dimensional; secondly, because the reflection allows us to abstract the actual form of the façade and contemplate it in and for itself, free from any sense of statics or equilibrium. Painters often resort to the device of looking at their work in a mirror, sometimes even upside down, in order to appreciate the value of the forms and the colors as such, divorced from other association. It is well known how important Kandinsky's chance view of a painting hanging upside down proved to the development of abstractionism in painting. Thus the reflection of the façade pleases us because its inverse form rids us momentarily of our sense of statics and gravity. Our memory can then retain the form of the façade, detached from its attitude in space, just as it retains the form, say, of a glass or gun, which we had revolved in our hand. All these enchantments of the reflected form overcome the disturbance of the vertical symmetry.

Fig. 6. Court of the Myrtles, Alhambra Palace, Granada.

Indeed, the release from our "sense of statics" and the consequent independence of form from gravity, are the reasons for our pleasure in observing buildings from a bird's-eye view, or from very near, or in seeing them aslant, as often reproduced in advertisements (Fig. 8). Hence, too, the appeal of leaning towers, like those of Pisa or Bologna (Fig. 7). Of course, we always anticipate the return of these buildings to their original positions, or our imagination subconsciously restores them there, for otherwise we should be overcome with vertigo, as though we had lost our balance. Dizziness, provided it is only vicarious, pleases us because it constitutes a sort of liberation. Nor is it only slantwise perspective views of a building that undermine its statical balance. This is no less obliterated by the slanting shadows of the building itself which, like black specters, extend its mass into mysterious depths. Indeed, the appeal of shadows derives less from their display of a form's plasticity than from their mysterious projection of the form. That is why dynamic Baroque art used chiaroscuro to the utmost. Conversely, the charm of contemporary indirect lighting of interiors and, more particularly, the floodlighting of buildings, is based on the principle of elimination of shadows. Floodlighting projects buildings against the black background of the sky, like phantasmagoric apparitions.

Fig. 7. Towers, Bologna. Photo Aurosmalto.

Fig. 8. Pirelli Building, Milan. Architects: Ponti, Fornaroli, Rosselli and Valtolina, Dell'Orto. Photo Fotogramma.

8

There is, of course, a certain type of façade which may easily be reversed in imagination, without losing its architectural importance. This is the cubic façade, which has neither windows nor door to relate it to man, or which is wholly disguised by a rhythmic network of glass, or by grilles, as in buildings designed by Edward Stone (Fig. 9). The independence of these apertures from the purpose they serve is what older buildings sought to achieve by the rhythmic alignment of windows. This is also what many modern buildings seek by the superimposition of horizontal window strips, as if the façade had equivalent slits, so that optically its reversal would make no difference. An even more marked effort toward independence is the contemporary tendency to create complex façade rhythms— jazz rhythms, as they have been called—with grilles, parapets, and windows, as in the case of Chandigarh. Thus, the rhythmic monotony of the slits is avoided, and a confusion of functions introduced, so that it is impossible to differentiate between window and parapet, between what lies above and what below, what to the left and what to the right. So complete an escape from the sense of statics leads to its oblivion.

Fig. 9. Dormitory Building, University of South Carolina, Columbia, South Carolina. Architect: Edward Stone.

Differentiation between upper and lower parts has always been of great importance in architecture, particularly in the Classical styles, but differentiation between right and left is less essential except in asymmetrical buildings. Symmetrical buildings—and they constitute the large majority—display no difference between right and left. Think of the symmetrical pattern on either side of a folded sheet of paper which has been formed by a splash of ink along the crease of the fold; or again of a pair of gloves placed exactly palm to palm. In both cases, the one is, as it were, the inverted image of the other in space. In other words, horizontal symmetry is not the rhythmic repetition of a pattern about a vertical axis, unfolding in time and in succession, except as the inverted reflection of another pattern in space, which can be superimposed on it. There is neither rhythmic repetition nor progression in horizontal symmetry. There is rather a constant return to the axis. Unlike a rhythmic succession in music, in which we go from beginning to end, here we are led from a beginning or an end to the middle, or from the middle to the two opposite ends; for here there is no beginning and no end. Horizontal symmetry may, therefore, be said to be virtually "static" in space, and inert in time.

In architecture a horizontal symmetrical pattern conflicts with rhythmic unfolding; the static arrangement of symmetrical images in space counteracts their dynamic succession in time. That is why a row of columns, or windows, which constitute a rhythmic succession of elements in space and at the same time present symmetrical reflections of one another, is of special value in architecture. For then, in addition to symmetry, succession is suggested by partially symmetrical patterns, in which there is—even if only faintly discernible—a beginning and an end, as there is in the unfolding of a musical composition.

The inertia of horizontal symmetry in architectural elements, however, is opposed by the dynamic vertical juxtaposition of elements, from which symmetry is excluded, because prevented by gravity. But here, too, the dividing of a façade into base, trunk, and crown, while on the one hand it stresses the static nature of the work in marking the accumulation of weight downwards, on the other it suspends the direction of gravity by the syncopes it creates. Furthermore, the intermediary moldings, the friezes, and a number of other rhythmic and harmonious relations lull the spectator's sense of statics. In modern architecture the suspension of gravity is achieved by abstraction: either by creating dematerialized forms without differentiation or projections, or by means of abstract designs, in which confusion prevails. Hence, a building resting on posts often appears to be floating in space, as though it had lost its weight. This is especially true if the building is of glass. In any case the tendency to become oblivious to our sense of statics is not unnatural, since architecture begins to exist as a spectacle only from the moment it achieves perfect balance statically, so that it can fill us with serenity and calm, like the view of a mountain resting immovably on the earth. It is no chance event, then, that most spectators and aestheticians explain architecture by referring only to the harmonious relations of its form, leaving their sense of statics dormant. Or if they do rouse it, it is only to lull it again in the enjoyment of the artistic achievement of the fertile moment. The Classical style does this; the contemporary styles fluctuate between the two extremes of acrobatics and abstraction.

When, as happens in contemporary architecture, the suggestion of gravity is attenuated in the vertical direction because the façade becomes an abstract form, a pattern unrelated to man, the sense of statics is also attenuated. Architectural form in itself then becomes the object of this art, as the painting itself becomes the object of abstract painting. The work is thus "dehumanized."

Indeed, architecture, like every art, begins to exist with abstraction: it abstracts man from the earth and puts him on an artificial, geometrically horizontal plane; architecture, in order to make its own abstract world, creates artificial interiors, in which man feels removed from his natural environment. All structural elements—walls, floors, columns, ceilings, arches, and domes—are no more than artificial forms, products of intellectual abstraction, no matter whether they sometimes evoke a natural form, as a dome, for instance, evokes the vault of the sky. As soon as this artificial world is created, however, a contrary phase sets in: the approach to the natural, whether by the imitation of forms, or by interpenetration of interior and exterior space, or by the diffusion of light, or by colors. The dialectics of artificial and natural world never cease, and indeed never must, for then art would lose its enchantment. Indeed they do not cease even today when architecture has reached the maximum of abstraction and refuses every imitation. Rather, in contemporary architecture the value of form, space, and light in themselves is vindicated.

"Everything in this world is nonsense; the whole of life is a plethora of ludicrous absurdities, one more fanciful than another. The crown is nothing, the ring is nothing, too. Each would mean nothing but nonsense and empty foolishness except to the eyes which behold the symbolism behind them. Yet they, because of their meaning, dominate the world. Only one form of metal there is, which is a meaning in itself—the sword," wrote E. Temple Thurston in *The City of Beautiful Nonsense*.

What is unique in human behavior? The answer is unequivocal and generally accepted. The monopoly of man, made possible by the evolution of his forebrain that profoundly distinguishes him from other beings, is the creation of a universe of symbols in thought and language.

Man's unique position is based on the dominance of symbols in his life. Except in the immediate satisfaction of biological needs, man lives in a world not of things but of symbols. A coin is a symbol for a certain amount of work done, or for food and other utilities available; a document is a symbol of *res gestae;* a word or concept is a symbol of a thing or relationship; a book is a fantastic pile of accumulated symbols; and so forth *ad infinitum*.

Symbols can be defined as signs that are freely created, represent some content, and are transmitted by tradition. It appears that the characteristics indicated are necessary and sufficient to distinguish symbolism, and language in particular, from subhuman forms of behavior.

By "freely created" I mean that there is no biologically enforced connection between the sign and the thing denoted. In conditioned reaction, the connection between the signal and the thing signaled is imposed from outside. It may be a natural connection, as when a child or kitten seeing a flame moves to avoid the fire, because the child or the kitten has previously been burned. Or the connection may be arbitrary and imposed by the experimenter, as in the case of the Pavlovian dog that learned to secrete saliva when a bell was rung because this was followed by a meal during the conditioning period. In contradistinction, there is no biological connection between the words *father, pater, père, otec* (or whatever the word may be in any language) and the person so designated. This does not imply that the choice of symbols is completely arbitrary; modern psychology is engaged in seeking out its principles.

Furthermore, a symbol connotes or represents a certain content and thus is different from language as expression or as command found also among animals. A bird's song expresses and communicates to its mate a certain physiological and, we may be sure, psychological state, but it does not denote a thing. The barking of a dog warns of some danger, but it does not indicate whether the source is an intruding burglar or the neighbor's cat.

Finally, symbolism and language are defined as being transmitted by learning and tradition. For example, the language of the bees, admirably described by Karl von Frisch, is representative. By means of intricate dances, the workers communicate to their colleagues the direction and distance of the place where food may be found. But this language is innate and instinctive. We can teach a dog all sorts of tricks, but we have never heard that a particularly clever dog has taught its puppies to do them.

There is little doubt that the origins of symbolism are closely related to magic practice and thought. For primitive man, an image, be it material or acoustical, *is* the original and gives him control and dominance over it. This is the essence of sympathetic magic. Think of a very primitive and common form of magic. A puppet made from clay *is* the enemy, and the enemy can be killed if a needle is thrust into the image. When the Paleolithic hunters painted those grandiose frescoes of deer and mammoth on the walls of caves in France and Spain, we may be sure that it was not just *l'art pour l'art;* but rather a powerful charm for successful hunting.

The same applies to an acoustical or onomatopoetic image. Man takes possession of the world in symbolic images by naming things. For this reason, Adam's first work in Paradise was to give names to animals, plants, and things. Naming a thing gives power over it. In contradistinction, Yahweh's name is unspeakable. For if His name should be uttered, He would be submitted to the will of him who knows it. The sorcerer evokes the demons of hell by calling their names.

Hence, the assumption that the origin of human language was in verbal magic does not seem to be far-fetched. A sound uttered may give some onomatopoetic image of an animal or person or may be connected with some biological function. For example, the word for *mother* begins in nearly all languages, irrespective of their structure, with an *m* (after Clyde Kluckhohn), apparently a sound connected with the smacking by the baby at the mother's breast. Thus a sound may become an image of a thing. Consequently, the sound will be identified with the original just as the clay image is identified with the enemy, and then uttering the sound will govern the thing designated. Thus, language may be born of magic, a process certainly infinitesimally slow in its beginnings, but man has had many hundred thousands of years at his disposal to come from an anthropoid to Pithecanthropus, Sinanthropus, and Homo sapiens.

Whatever the origin of symbolism, its consequences are enormous. The first consequence is obvious. Phylogenetic evolution, based on hereditary changes, is supplanted by history, based on the tradition of symbols. In the biological sphere, progress is possible only within an evolutionary time-scale. For example, the societies of ants have remained unchanged for the past fifty million years. In contrast, human history has a time-scale of generations, comprising almost all high cultures in a span of five thousand years, and it may even be thought that cultural time has a logarithmic rather than an arithmetic scale, with changes taking place at an ever increasing pace.

The second consequence is that corporeal trial and error as found in subhuman nature is replaced by reasoning—by trial and error in conceptual symbols. An animal placed into a maze, faced with a complicated lock or confronted with some other problem, runs around until it finds the way out. It tries until the mechanism opening the door or the solution of the problem is discovered by chance. Then the way leading to success is gradually fixed. Man in a corresponding situation sits down and thinks; that is, he experiments not with the things themselves but with the symbolic images of things. He scans different possibilities, discounts those that seem ineffective without laboring to try them materially, and accepts the apparently successful solution as the basis for overt behavior.

A third and more profound consequence of symbolism is that it makes true purposiveness possible. Purposiveness in a metaphorical sense—that is, regulation of function in the way of maintenance, establishment, and re-establishment of organic order—is a general characteristic of life. It is based on such principles as equifinality of the steady state of the organism, homeostatic feedback mechanisms, learning by trial and error and conditioned reflex, selection in evolution, and so forth. But even in the most amazing phenomena of regulation and instinct we have no justification for or definite reasons against the assumption that these actions are carried through with foresight of the goal. This true or Aristotelian purposiveness is unique to human behavior and is based on the fact that the future goal is anticipated in thought and determines actual behavior.

When man passed the stage of barbarism, he had to realize that verbal magic was impotent. Thrusting needles into the enemy's image did not as a rule kill him. Similarly, a name is just a label attached to a thing and not the thing itself. It is true enough that relics of primeval verbal magic are still with us, much more than is desirable. In speaking of a "nation," "state," or "party," we behave as if those names were things, whereas actually they denote personificative fictions, hypostatizing groups with their egoistic interests, little intelligence, and exaggerated passions for mythical entities.

If verbal magic was deceptive, another sort of symbolic magic was discovered that was extremely powerful. We may call it the magic of the algorithm.

An algorithm is a system of symbols connected according to pre-established rules. Take the simplest example, that of the decimal notation, the name of whose propagator, Al-Khowarizmi, is immortalized in the word algorithm. In Roman numbers even a trivial multiplication, such as LXXVI × XCIII, is quite a formidable operation. However, the simple trick that the last digit of a number in Arabic notation means units, the second tens, and so on, and that corresponding figures are written in columns, makes the operation child's play. Thus an algorithm means a machine of thinking, performing operations by suitable connections of symbols, and giving results difficult to attain or unattainable otherwise. Or, conversely, calculating and thinking machines, mechanical or electronic, are only the materialization of algorithms. Algorithmic magic is commonly known as science and scientific technology.

So long as symbols stand alone they are unproductive and do not convey more information than that contained in the individual symbols. Thus in the flag language used by seafarers each flag symbolizes a certain fact or command, but an array of flags is just the sum of the individual meanings.

This is profoundly altered if symbols are combined according to established rules of the game, if they are elements in an algorithm or, as we may say, if a language has not only a "vocabulary" but also a "grammar." Then the system of symbols becomes productive and fertile. With a suitable choice of terms and of rules presupposed, we can handle the symbols as if they were the things they represent. If the symbols, as well as the grammar, are well chosen, the result of the mental operation of symbols will correspond to that of the real course of events. The consequences of the images will be the images of the consequences, to use Heinrich Hertz's expression.

In this way a true magic is possible with systems of symbols. We can predict facts and relationships still unknown, can control still unrealized combinations of natural forces, and so on.

Science, to a large extent, consists in the invention, elaboration, and application of suitable algorithms. Trivially the algorithm of physics is mathematics in the ordinary sense. But the language of, say, chemical formulas or of genetics also represents algorithms suitable for the particular realm. The same is true even if the system is remote from what is ordinarily called mathematics, as is the Linnean system of classification. With its binary nomenclature, this classification of organisms into species, genera, families, classes, and so forth, is also an algorithm symbolically representing certain aspects of reality—the manifoldness of, and relationships between animal and plant forms, allowing to a certain extent for scientific prediction.

The universe of symbols, although created by man, wins a life of its own, as it were. The development of the Roman law, of the British Empire, of atomic theory from Democritus to Heisenberg, or of music from Palestrina to Wagner, is certainly borne by a number of human individuals. But it shows an immanent logic that widely transcends the petty personalities, the human and all-too-human creators.

This autonomous life of the symbolic world has a most important positive aspect. The symbolic universe becomes, so to speak, more clever than man, its creator. Thus the symbolic system of language, and particularly of the artificial languages called mathematics and science, develops into a colossal thinking machine. An operational command, a hypothesis with the necessary specifications, is fed in; the machine starts to run and eventually by virtue of pre-established rules of the connection of symbols, a solution drops out which was unforeseeable in the individual mind with its limited capacity. This is the general characteristic of scientific reasoning, be it a simple arithmetic operation or the solution of a differential equation, the prediction of still undiscovered planets and chemical elements, or the construction of some masterpiece of modern technology.

Besides these triumphs of symbolism, there are, however, its pitfalls. The conceptual anticipation of future events that allows for true purposiveness is at the same time the origin of anxiety in regard to the future and fear of death, which is unknown to brutes. The invention of the symbolic world is the Fall of Man. The notions of sin and evil arise with the invention of symbolic labels attached to certain forms of behavior. War also is a human invention. It is not a biological phenomenon, the continuation of the omnipresent biological struggle for existence. Even if nature were "red in tooth and claw," which it is only to a limited extent, organized intraspecific warfare would still be unknown in the subhuman world. Apart from the rather rational strifes of savages who go out and kill enemies in order to eat them, war is caused by head-hunting, illusions of grandeur, ideologies, economic reasons based upon symbol-charged values, religion—all of them only superficially different kinds of verbal magic.

If there is a clash between the symbolic world built up as moral values and social conventions on the one hand, and basic biological drives on the other, then, with respect to the individual, the situation of neurosis arises. Somewhat extending the narrower definition of Freud, it seems that a neurotic situation results from the conflict of a symbolic universe with biological drives, or of opposing symbolic worlds. As a social force, the universe of symbols, which is unique in man, creates the sanguinary course of history. Thus man has to pay for the uniqueness that distinguishes him from other beings. The tree of knowledge is the tree of death.

The basic symptom of present society seems to be the uprise of the masses or the proletariat, as depicted so vividly by authors like Ortega y Gasset and Toynbee. For the present discussion let us forget about the demographic aspects, the increasing overpopulation of our planet, and the Malthusian threat, and concentrate on the behavioral aspect. I believe that a precise answer to the problem can be given in biological terms.

I am inclined to define the "revolt of the masses" as a return to the conditioned reflex. The unique characteristic of human behavior is the ability to make decisions at a symbolic level. This, of course, does not mean that conditioned behavior is negligible. Any human achievement, from toilet-training to speech, driving a car, or learning calculus and theoretical physics, is based on conditioning. However, the dignity of man rests on rational behavior—that is, behavior directed by symbolic anticipation of a goal. In modern man, however, this *vis a fronte*, to use Aristotle's term, consisting of goals the individual or the society sets itself, is largely replaced by the primitive *vis a tergo* of conditioned reaction.

The modern methods of propaganda, from the advertisement of a tooth paste to that of political programs and systems, do not appeal to rationality in man but rather force upon him certain ways of behavior, by means of a continuous repetition of stimuli coupled with emotional rewards or punishments. This method is essentially the same as that applied to Pavlovian dogs when they were drilled to respond to a meaningless stimulus with reactions prescribed by the experimenter. Not that this method is new in human history. What is new, however, is that it is applied scientifically and consistently and so has an unprecedented power. The modern media of mass communication, newspapers, radio, television, and so on, are able to establish this psychological constraint almost without interruption in time, reaching all individuals in space with maximum efficiency. If a slogan, however insipid, is repeated a sufficient number of times and is emotionally coupled with the promise of a reward or the menace of punishment, it is nearly unavoidable that the human animal establishes the conditioned reaction as desired. Furthermore, to apply this method successfully, the conditioning process must be adjusted to the greatest common denominator; that is, the appeal has to be made to the lowest intelligence level. The result is mass-man—abolishment of individual discrimination and decision, and its replacement by universal conditioned reactions.

Obviously there is no easy solution to the problem, and it is wise not to join the quacks who have found the wonder drug to cure the ills and entanglements of humanity. However, precisely because of the predominance today of psychological techniques, realization of the motive forces of human behavior becomes the more important and urgent. Besides the menace of physical technology, the dangers of psychological technology are often overlooked. Perhaps even more dangerous than the material existence of the bombs are the psychological forces that may lead to the dropping of them. As we try to put atomic energy to peaceful use, it may even be more urgent to put to intelligent use the psychological mechanisms revealed by behavioral science.

BIOGRAPHICAL NOTES ON THE AUTHORS

Rudolf Arnheim — Psychologist. Born Berlin. Studied at Berlin University: dissertation on the psychology of visual expression. 1933–38: Associate Editor of Publications, International Institute for Educational Film, League of Nations, Rome. In 1940 emigrated to the United States. 1941–42: Fellow, Guggenheim Foundation. Since 1943: teaching psychology and psychology of art, Sarah Lawrence College, Bronxville, N.Y.; Graduate Faculty, New School for Social Research, N.Y. 1959–60: Fulbright Lecturer, Ochanomizu University, Tokyo. Author: *Art and Visual Perception* (1954); *Film as Art* (1957); *Picasso's Guernica: The Genesis of a Painting* (1962); *Toward a Psychology of Art* (1966).

Saul Bass — Designer. Born New York, 1923. Since 1946 established on the West Coast of the United States. During this period he has received international recognition in the fields of graphic, industrial, film, and exhibition design. His best known works are for the motion film industry, including: epilogue for *Around the World in Eighty Days;* prologues for *Walk on the Wild Side* and *Mad, Mad, Mad, Mad World;* and designs for *The Man with the Golden Arm, Exodus,* and *The Cardinal.*

Ludwig von Bertalanffy — Biologist. Born Austria, 1901. 1934–48: Professor, University of Vienna. 1949–54: Professor and Director of Biological Research, University of Ottawa. 1955–58: Director, Biological Research, Mount Sinai Hospital, Los Angeles. 1958–59: Sloan Visiting Professor, Menninger Foundation. Presently Professor of Theoretical Biology, University of Alberta. Distinguished pioneer in the field of theoretical biology and active member and officer of many international scientific societies. His innumerable publications include: *Modern Theories of Development* (1933); *Theoretische Biologie* (1942); *Problems of Life* (1952). He was also the editor of the twelve volume *Handbuch der Biologie* (1942 ff.).

John E. Burchard — Educator and architectural historian. Born 1898. 1928–38: research vice president with Bemis Industries, Boston. 1938–48: Professor and Director of Bemis Foundation, M.I.T. From 1948, Dean of School of Humanities and Social Sciences, M.I.T., now emeritus. Among his publications: *Fundamental Principles of ARP* (1943); *Q.E.D. a History of M.I.T. during World War II* (1948); co-author, *The Evolving House* and *Architecture of America.* To be published this year: *The Voice of the Phoenix: Postwar Architecture in Germany.*

Edmund Carpenter — Anthropologist. Studied at University of Pennsylvania. Has carried on fieldwork in the Arctic, Micronesia, Siberia, Borneo, and Outer Mongolia. Author: *Eskimo; Anerca; Explorations in Communications.* Film-maker: *Yonder Comes Day; Eskimo Art.* Presently Chairman, Department of Anthropology, San Fernando Valley State College, Northridge, California.

Henry Dreyfuss — Industrial designer. Born New York, 1904. Opened industrial design office in New York, 1929. Now maintains offices in New York and California, serving clients in many different fields. Frequent lecturer on industrial design, he is author of *Designing for People* (1955) and *The Measure of Man* (1960).

Heinz Von Foerster	Biophysicist. Born Vienna, 1911. 1935–45: Director, Microwave and Plasma Research Laboratory G.E.M.A., Berlin. 1946–48: Director, Research Laboratory, E. Schrack A.G., Vienna. 1949 to University of Illinois, where he is Professor of Electrical Engineering in the College of Engineering and Professor of Biophysics in the College of Liberal Arts and Sciences. Since 1958, Director, Biological Computer Laboratory. 1949–55: Secretary, Josiah Macy Jr. Foundation, Conference Program, Cybernetics. Author of some fifty articles in the fields of electrical engineering, cybernetics, and biophysics.
Lawrence K. Frank	Psychologist. For many years a foundation executive concerned with studies of human development, mental health, marriage, and family life. Has taught as visiting professor at M.I.T. and Brandeis University. Contributor to many professional journals and author of the following books: *Society as the Patient; Projective Methods; Nature and Human Nature; The Conduct of Sex;* co-author with Mary H. Frank, *How to Help Your Child at School* and *Your Adolescent at Home and at School.*
James J. Gibson	Psychologist. Spent war years as Air Force psychologist working on problems of depth perception in aircraft landings and on the use of pictures and films. Since 1948 Professor of Psychology, Cornell University. Author: *The Perception of the Visual World* (1950). Now writing a general treatment of the use of the senses for perception. Experimental research on visual perception and on the knowledge obtainable from pictures has convinced him that the classical conceptions of seeing and perceiving are inadequate and that a new approach is required.
S. Giedion	Historian. Born 1894. Studied in Zurich, Berlin, and in Munich with Heinrich Wölfflin. In 1938 gave the Charles Eliot Norton Lectures at Harvard University, resulting in his important book *Space, Time and Architecture.* Another book of fundamental importance, *Mechanization Takes Command,* was published in 1948. In 1957 he gave A. W. Mellon Lectures in Fine Arts, since published as *The Eternal Present* in two volumes: *Beginnings of Art* (1962) and *Beginnings of Architecture* (1964). In 1961 he delivered the first Gropius Lecture at Harvard, where he teaches during part of each year.
J. P. Hodin	Art historian and critic. Born 1905. Studied at Charles University, Prague; University of London; Art Academies Dresden and Berlin. Active member of many art and aesthetic societies, as well as editor of various periodicals in the field. A prolific writer, his publications include: *Sven Erikson* (1940); *Ernst Josephson* (1942); *Edvard Munch* (1948); *Isaac Grünewald* (1949); *Art and Criticism* (1944); *J. A. Comenius and Our Time* (1944); *The Dilemma of Being Modern* (1956); *Henry Moore* (1956); *Ben Nicholson* (1957); *Barbara Hepworth* (1961); *Lynn Chadwick* (1961); *Alan Reynolds* (1962); *Bekenntnis zu Kokoschka* (1963); *Edvard Munch, Der Genius der Nordens* (1963); *Emilio Greco* (in preparation).

Gyorgy Kepes	Painter and designer. Born Selyp, Hungary, 1906. 1930–36: worked in Berlin and London on film, stage, and exhibition design. In 1937 came to the United States to head the Light and Color Department, Institute of Design, Chicago. Since 1946 Professor of Visual Design, M.I.T. Author: *Language of Vision; The New Landscape in Art and Science*. Editor of *The Visual Arts Today*. Most active as painter. His works are in the permanent collections of many museums, including: Albright-Knox Art Gallery, Buffalo; Museum of Fine Arts, Boston; Museum of Fine Arts, Houston; Museum of Modern Art, New York; Museum of Art, San Francisco; Whitney Museum of American Art, New York.
Abraham H. Maslow	Psychologist. Born New York, 1908. Since 1951 Professor of Psychology, Brandeis University. Active member and fellow of innumerable psychological organizations, as well as author of many books and articles in the field. Major publications: with B. Mittelman, *Principles of Abnormal Psychology* (1951); *Motivation and Personality* (1956); editor, *New Knowledge in Human Values* (1959); *Toward a Psychology of Being* (1962); *Religions, Values, and Peak Experiences* (1964).
P. A. Michelis	Art historian and aesthetician. Professor of the Theory of Architecture, National Technical University, Athens. President, Hellenic Society for Aesthetics; Editor, *Annales d'Esthétiques;* General Secretary, International Committee of Aesthetic Studies, Paris. Organized IVth International Congress of Aesthetics, Athens, 1960. Major publications: *Architecture as an Art* (in Greek); *An Aesthetic Approach to Byzantine Art* (1955); *Esthétique de l'Architecture du Béton Armé* (1963); *L'Esthétique d'Hagia Sophia* (1963).
Rudolf Modley	Born Vienna, 1906. Early collaborator of Otto Neurath, the "father" of the isotype system of pictorial symbol. 1930–34: Curator of Social Sciences, Chicago Museum of Science and Industry. 1934 established Pictorial Statistics, Inc., and Pictograph Corporation which he headed until 1945. Since then he has headed a project on Graphic Symbols for the Fund for the Advancement of Education of the Ford Foundation. Co-chairman with Margaret Mead of Glyphs, Inc., an organization for the development of universal graphic symbols. Among his publications: *How to use Pictorial Statistics* (1937); *The Challenge of Symbology* (1959); *Graphic Symbols* (1964).
Charles Morris	Professor of philosophy, University of Florida. Author of *Signs, Language and Behavior; Paths of Life;* and *Varieties of Human Value*. His most recent book, *Signification and Significance: A Study of the Relations of Signs and Values* (1964) deals further with the topic of the article in the present volume. A book of philosophical poetry, under the title *Festival,* has been published in 1966.
Robert Osborn	Artist and illustrator. Born Oshkosh, Wisconsin, 1904. Since 1947 has illustrated over thirty books and executed drawings for various periodicals in the United States and Europe. He has also illustrated some sixty *Sense Books* for the U.S. Navy and U.S. Army and produced and published 7,000 "Dilbert" posters for U.S. Naval Aviation. Among the many books which he has both written and illustrated are: *How to Shoot Ducks* (1939); *War Is No Damn Good* (1946); *Osborn on Leisure* (1957); *The Vulgarians* (1961); and *Dying to Smoke* (1964).

Ad Reinhardt	Painter. Born Buffalo, New York, 1913. Member of American Abstract Artist since 1937. First one-man show, New York, 1943. Since then has had innumerable one-man shows both in the United States and abroad, and has participated in major group exhibitions. Works in many public collections, including: Museum of Modern Art and Whitney Museum of American Art, New York; Toledo Museum of Art, Ohio; Museum of Art, San Francisco; Art Museum, Philadelphia; and Albright-Knox Gallery, Buffalo.
Paul Riesman	Anthropologist. Born 1938, near Buffalo, New York. B.A. from Harvard University in 1960, with honors thesis on the Eskimo. 1962–64: Instructor in Anthropology at San Fernando Valley State College, California. At present studying at the University of Paris and the Ecole Pratique des Hautes Etudes. Plans extended field trip to Nigeria or the Cameroun to study the Fulani.
Ernesto N. Rogers	Urban designer, industrial designer. Born Trieste 1909. Professor of Architecture at Polytechnic of Milan. Former editor of *Domus* and *Casabella-Continuità*. Author: *Stile; Il Piano Regolatore della Valle D'Aosta; Auguste Perret; Esperienza dell'Architettura; Utopia della Realtà*. In private practice with Lodovico B. Belgiojoso and Enrico Peressutti (Studio Architetti BBPR). Works include city planning, houses, factories, pavilions.
Werner Schmalenbach	Art historian and museum director. Born Göttingen, 1920. Studied at University of Basel. 1939–45: organized important film exhibitions and wrote extensively on the film. 1945–55: organizer of numerous exhibitions at Gewerbemuseum, Basel. 1955–62: Director of Kestner-Gesellschaft, Hanover. Since 1962, Director of newly founded Kunstsammlung Nordheim-Westfalen in Düsseldorf. Author of many books and articles on the film, and on primitive and modern art.
Frank Sciadini	Psychologist. Assistant professor in logic and the humanities, University College, University of Florida. Main field of interest: experimental aesthetics.

Designed by the arts staff, George Braziller, Inc.
Printed in offset by Connecticut Printers, Inc., Hartford, Conn.